Gatewood

Gatewood

KENTUCKY'S UNCOMMON MAN

Matthew Strandmark

UNIVERSITY PRESS OF KENTUCKY

Scholarly publisher for the Commonwealth, serving Bellarmine University, Berea College, Centre College of Kentucky, Eastern Kentucky University, The Filson Historical Society, Georgetown College, Kentucky Historical Society, Kentucky State University, Morehead State University, Murray State University, Northern Kentucky University, Spalding University, Transylvania University, University of Kentucky, University of Louisville, University of Pikeville, and Western Kentucky University.

Editorial and Sales Offices: The University Press of Kentucky
663 South Limestone Street, Lexington, Kentucky 40508-4008
www.kentuckypress.com

All images courtesy of the University of Kentucky Special Collections Research Center.

Cataloging-in-Publication data is available from the Library of Congress.

ISBN 978-0-8131-9841-5 (hardcover : alk. paper)
ISBN 978-0-8131-9920-7 (pbk.: alk. paper)
ISBN 978-0-8131-9844-6 (epub)
ISBN 978-0-8131-9843-9 (pdf)

This book is printed on acid-free paper meeting the requirements of the American National Standard for Permanence in Paper for Printed Library Materials.
♾
Manufactured in the United States of America

Member of the Association of University Presses

To Gatewood's most lasting legacy: his daughters.

To the memory of Summer, her family and loved ones, and to Abby and Molly, who share Gatewood's love, dedication, and passion for justice.

Contents

Prologue

Thirty miles south of Paducah, Kentucky, is Fancy Farm, an unincorporated village of less than 500. A community picnic and fair began outside of Fancy Farm's St. Jerome Catholic Church in 1881. In 1931, political candidates for statewide offices in Kentucky began attending and making speeches to the gathering, which had begun to attract people from throughout the region. The oratorical tradition grew over the years, making "Fancy Farm" the most important political event in the beginning of Kentucky's campaign season.

The first Saturday of every August, more than 15,000 Kentuckians descend on the tiny village. Fancy Farm represents Kentucky's most authentic attempt at keeping alive the southern political tradition of jeering, insulting, booing, and cheering candidates as they vie for votes and support. Spectators crowd under the one main shelter at Fancy Farm, an un-walled pole barn with a bunting-festooned stage at one end. Supporters of one party usually sit together on either side, the left and right split providing an easy means of separating seating and ideology. The ceiling fans that line the roof of the shelter are woefully outmatched by the sweltering August heat and humidity of western Kentucky. The candidates try to sweat as little as possible and then try to hide the perspiration they cannot stop. One sees campaign signs at Fancy Farm, but the most important pieces of campaigning material are the paper fans the candidates hand out to the spectators. You cannot watch a Fancy Farm speech without seeing hundreds of fans bobbing throughout the sweltering crowd.

Stump speeches at Fancy Farm always hit the high notes of the candidates' platforms as they inevitably criticize their opponents. They always have prepared a few zingers to score points with the crowd. It is a proud tradition, and anticipation for Fancy Farm builds well in advance of the late summer event. It is an event that officially kicks off election season in Kentucky, as more ads hit the airwaves, and as political signs dominate every major intersection, suburban neighborhood lawn, and billboard across the commonwealth.

On August 6, 2011, Fancy Farm began like all those that came before. Candidates gave speeches through their sweat, the crowd fanned and jeered, the smell of roast pork, mutton, and fried chicken wafted across the grounds. After the major party candidates for governor made their pitches, the Fancy Farm emcee walked to the microphone and introduced Gatewood Galbraith.

Galbraith sauntered to the podium wearing slacks and a light blue dress shirt with collar unbuttoned and sleeves rolled up his forearms. His reading glasses rested far down his nose, attached to a strap strung around his neck. He also wore his signature hat: a tan fedora, strapped in dark brown, pushed back on his head. Some politicians are just not built for Fancy Farm. They cannot pull off the look, the nonchalance needed for public jibing and fanfare. Louis Gatewood Galbraith seemed born for Fancy Farm as he began his talk.

"First of all, I'm going to go away from my regular speech for a second and tell you, Governor Beshear, that was the worst darn speech I ever heard anybody give." The Republican opponents of incumbent governor Steve Beshear cheered enthusiastically in response. Gatewood continued in his Kentucky-accented staccato, speaking rapidly but pausing often for dramatic effect. After a few more lines attacking Beshear's lack of patriotism and support for the military, Galbraith rebuffed a heckler and then broke into his stump speech. He knew it by heart. It had not changed in fifty years.

"People say, you know, Galbraith, you're a perennial candidate. And I say, Kentucky's got perennial problems!"

He was right. In 2011 Kentucky remained stuck in the doldrums of the Great Recession. Kentucky's 9.4 percent unemployment rate hovered a shade above the nation's. Facing a shrinking tax base and recurring problems, the commonwealth had recently reduced spending on public K–12 education, state universities, and infrastructure. Kentucky was also shorting public pension obligations to the tune of $3.8 billion over a thirteen-year period. Already crippled by failing public health systems and years of poverty, Kentucky voters were more pessimistic than normal. In the 2011 Gallup Community Well-Being Index survey, Kentuckians ranked themselves forty-ninth out of fifty states in overall well-being. This included forty-ninth in physical health, healthy behavior, and life evaluation. For emotional health, Kentucky respondents placed themselves dead last in the country.[1]

As candidates make their stump speeches, they are heckled and cheered, often at the same time. It is normal for chants to erupt in the middle of speeches and for politicians to turn the tables and insult their opponents in the crowd. Fancy Farm is far more about theatrics than about expressing policy positions. The majority of onlookers are already convinced of who they are voting for in November. They come from across the commonwealth to sit in the oppressive heat for this unique entertainment. They anxiously await the off-the-cuff one-liners and quips that the politicians have been workshopping for months with their campaign advisors. The pols, for their part, have rehearsed how to deliver the stinging lines in ways that make them look natural, clever, and easygoing. Some are better at this than others. Some are not good at it at all. Gatewood Galbraith was always comfortable speaking in front of a raucous crowd, serene in the midst of engineered chaos.

"If the people who had beaten me the first time had solved the problems, I wouldn't-a had to run again! But they didn't. And they haven't. And they can't! Because neither party can produce a candidate that can disengage from the partisanship long enough to work with the other side to actually get the job done!" Galbraith's Kentucky accent flared as his speech sped up, emphasizing the last words in every sentence with his deep baritone. "The leadership of both parties have their horns locked up like two white-tailed buck fightin' over territory while our business lies dead in the *dust*!" These kinds of oratorical flourishes were difficult to pull off for the staid career politicians at Fancy Farm. But not for Gatewood. He was simply being himself, no rehearsal required.

Galbraith had made similar speeches countless times. Decrying partisanship, advocating for common sense reforms, prioritizing the lives and livelihoods of Kentucky's farmers, and families, and young people. After all, it was his ninth and final time running for public office, and his fifth official run for the governorship. But putting aside the hostile environment, the jeering, and even some applause, one deciphers a far deeper message in this speech. Gatewood was disgusted, fed up with a political system he had strained against his entire adult life. He remained angry that the people in his state, whom he cared about on an actual, individual level, were suffering. People like him. People who were his neighbors, clients, and family. He was at the end of his rope.

He reviewed the highlights of his independent platform: the end of corruption in Frankfort, a voucher to support both vocational and higher education, job creation, environmental protections, tax reform, eliminating special interests, smaller government, gun rights.

"I would tell you this, folks. . . . I've been trying to tell you the truth. Somebody the other day said, I'm gonna endorse ya. I said, why ya gonna endorse me? He said, cuz you never lied to us. I said hell, if I was gonna lie to ya, I'd already been elected governor!"

Gatewood finished his speech to a small smattering of applause, gathered his notes, and sauntered off the Fancy Farm stage for the last time. He died five months later.

Introduction

Even nearing the end of his life, Gatewood Galbraith did not cower from his reputation as a political outsider or as a perennial candidate. His best statewide political campaign showing was when he secured 15 percent of the vote as the Reform Party candidate for governor in 1999. Even while losing nine elections, most of them in the primary stage, he became a cultural symbol of Kentucky politics and the proud individualism of Kentuckians. He was best known for his aggressive support of hemp and marijuana legalization in a conservative state, before national opinions had changed and long before the majority of United States citizens had access to legal or medical marijuana. This support, and his adherence to this platform, garnered him some measure of fame. It also overshadowed everything else that Gatewood fought for.

He was a fiscal conservative who fought for marijuana legalization. He was a libertarian who believed strongly in environmental protections. He was a reformer who despised the influence of New Deal politics and its effect on his home state. He advocated for smaller government and lower taxes while supporting new government support programs and industrial regulation. His political beliefs compromised his ability to organize for, fundraise for, and win elections. These conflicts and his unwillingness to concede his beliefs endeared him to many Kentuckians but alienated many others. Political power meant nothing to Gatewood if it resulted in more of the same: the inability to improve the lives of his fellow Kentuckians.

But Gatewood Galbraith was much more than a perennial candidate, or a "stoner" trying to make a name for himself. He was kicked out of high school for misbehavior and failing grades. In one period in the late 1960s, he hitchhiked from coast to coast three different times in forty days. He tried and failed for years to pursue a college education. While a student at the University of Kentucky, he organized protests and demonstrations that led to the local FBI field office opening an investigative file on his activities. He courted famous friends: Woody Harrelson, Jack Herer, Julia "Butterfly" Hill, Ralph Nader, and most prominently Willie Nelson, who was Gatewood's longtime friend and who regularly played fundraising concerts for

Galbraith's political campaigns. As an attorney specializing in criminal law and personal injury, he would often defend clients pro bono, as in the 1997 case of the Reverend Mary Thomas-Spears, the first felony medical marijuana defense case in Kentucky. His efforts resulted in a stay issued by the Kentucky courts and led to further hemp and marijuana reforms. He acted on his beliefs in a 1995 public demonstration by disrupting the Lexington Fourth of July parade in protest of a United Nations–themed float and the laws that criminalized cannabis. He was a cultural mainstay in Lexington and was deeply loved by young citizens, college students, and left-leaning citizen groups. He advocated for criminal justice reform and racial justice and was a staunch advocate for civil rights. He was extremely knowledgeable, regularly spouting obscure statistics, constitutional provisions, and legal precedents without pausing for breath.

Gatewood's political and social advocacy existed alongside his personal struggles. He was honorably discharged from the United States Marine Corps as a result of chronic asthma. He filed for bankruptcy twice, famously noting, "Losing statewide elections doesn't pay worth a damn." He navigated the landscape of divorce and the struggles of familial relationships. He also advocated for many of the issues that one would not associate with progressive reformers, most particularly his strong belief in Second Amendment rights and support of national gun groups. It is in these conflicts and these contrasts that the life and work of Gatewood Galbraith remains so valuable to the history of Kentucky.

I knew little about Gatewood until 2017 when I supervised an exhibition of his archival materials at the University of Kentucky Libraries. Because of my work with the exhibition, I was invited to appear on a local radio show to discuss it. I came prepared and spoke highly of Gatewood's lifelong efforts at social justice and reform, noting that in the areas of hemp and marijuana legalization, he was truly ahead of his time. He advocated for many of the reforms we witness becoming law across the country today. For example, a few short months after Galbraith passed away, Colorado and Washington became the first two states to legalize the recreational use of cannabis. Some 109 million American citizens now have access to fully legalized recreational marijuana. According to the Pew Research Center, 88 percent of Americans now say that marijuana should be legal for medical use; 59 percent say it should be allowed for medical *and* recreational use.[1] In Gatewood's home state of Kentucky, 90 percent of the population support medical marijuana, while nearly 60 percent support legalizing cannabis for any reason.[2]

However, what motivated me to share a fuller measure of Gatewood's fascinating story had little to do with his public and political life, or his support for marijuana legalization. In the short twenty minutes I was on the radio show, the host simultaneously spoke with me and fielded calls from listeners who fondly remembered Gatewood and the person he was. They volunteered that in private he was caring, compassionate, sacrificial, and quite literally willing to give someone the shirt off his back. One caller recalled Gatewood's gentle nature. She worked in a Lexington convenience store where Gatewood visited frequently for his morning coffee and newspaper. She recounted that every morning he would also get change from bigger bills. With these, he would head downtown and distribute them among Lexington's homeless. The host recalled that on Saturday mornings Gatewood would often go through the McDonald's drive-thru, order dozens of breakfast sandwiches, and then drive around town and hand them out to the less fortunate. Gatewood was not a typical blustery politician, scoring points in public or for personal gain. This was his true nature: a smart, caring, flawed man trying to lift others up. These qualities gave birth to his folk hero status in Kentucky.

This biography investigates Gatewood's legacy and his place in Kentucky history by emphasizing the ways in which he influenced the lives of other people. It does rely on local, regional, and national coverage of Gatewood and his life, as well as his own recollections. Gatewood's archive of personal documents, ephemera, and photographs allows a thorough glimpse into his life and work. However, the bulk of this book relies on personal conversations with those who knew Gatewood best: his family, friends, community leaders, political allies and adversaries. It stresses the importance of his private life and relationships in better understanding the public figure so many knew and admired.

This book quotes heavily from oral history interviews held by the Louie B. Nunn Center for Oral History at the University of Kentucky. By the time of publication, most of the interviews will be publicly accessible. Oral histories document the personal memories and recollections of those interviewed. Oral histories can be tricky things. Some of you reading this account might disagree with some of the opinions, characterizations, or explanations offered by interviewees or by myself. Any factual errors are mine, but as far as opinion goes, everyone recalls memories through their own lens and with their own unique understanding. All I ask is that you be mindful of this as you read.

In addition to oral history interviews, the book relies on quotes from Gatewood Galbraith's autobiography, *The Last Free Man in America: Meets the Synthetic Subversion*. Often when you see Gatewood's own words or perspective on the events of his life, it comes from this work. I would encourage you to read the autobiography; it vibrates with Gatewood's passion and life.

Perhaps most importantly, this book clarifies his legacy for a new generation of Kentuckians, and Americans, who have never heard of Gatewood Galbraith but are beneficiaries of his lifelong work. It is past time that more people have the opportunity to know, and better understand, the life and times of Louis Gatewood Galbraith.

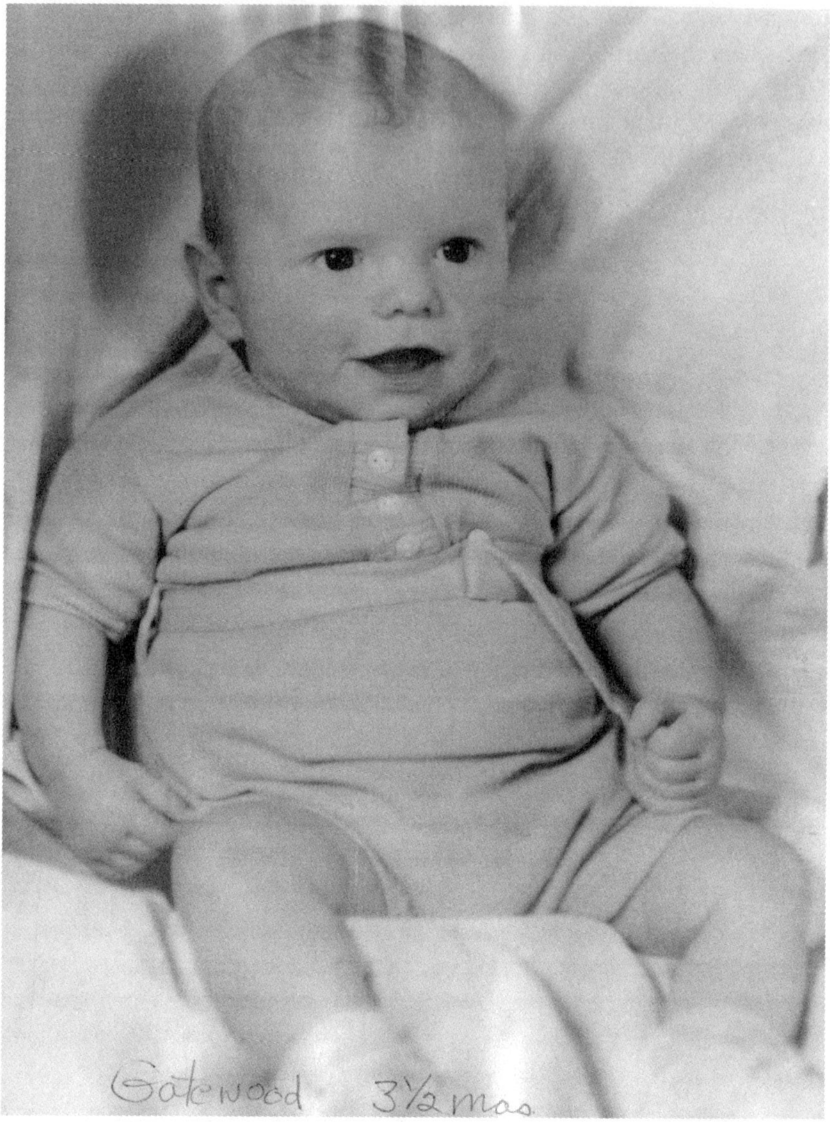

Louis Gatewood Galbraith at three and a half months, May 1947. He was born in 1947, the fourth of seven children, to Dollie and Henry Clay Galbraith in Carlisle, Kentucky.

1

"Wild as a March Hare"

Long before Gatewood went on to fame, renown, and popularity, he was a young boy growing up with six brothers and sisters in the small town of Carlisle, Kentucky. His father, Henry Clay Galbraith, had dropped out of school after the tenth grade and gone to work for the highway department, building roads. A dreamer, entrepreneur, and hard worker, he eventually ran a successful auto garage in Carlisle and began a career selling cars in the town of around 1,500 people. From an extended and traditional Carlisle family, H.C., as he was called, was outgoing, magnetic, and ambitious, all values he would eventually pass on to his son.

While working as a young man, H.C. took an interest in Dollie Gatewood, the daughter of the local soda fountain purveyor. Following a brief stint working for the state government in Frankfort, Dollie's father, Quince, had opened his business on Main Street in Carlisle. Dollie's parents were progressive and committed to the idea of education for their kids. After Dollie helped with the store and graduated from Carlisle High School, her parents sent her to Peabody College in Knoxville, Tennessee, where she completed a teaching degree in 1934.

Returning to town, she pitched in to help her parents at the store. It was the main center of community and entertainment for young people in town, and Dollie had a chance to talk to everyone who came in. One day H.C. sat down to talk with her and was drawn to her wit and frankness. H.C. must have been a good talker, because he got Quince's blessing to marry Dollie. They married in 1937 in Carlisle.

Dollie was a devout Catholic who had grown up in a home committed to the faith. She was smart, witty, well educated, and compassionate, and she found the love of her life in an unlikely package. As part of the deal, Quince made H.C. promise to never interfere with Dollie's Catholic faith. A result of this bargain, the Galbraith children began to arrive. H.C. was now a gasoline truck driver and worked hard for his family as it grew. Louis Gatewood Galbraith was born on January 23, 1947, following Judy, Elizabeth, and Henry Clay Galbraith Jr. By 1955 the family had added Edna, Michael, and Timothy, and the Galbraith kids had the run of their small town. It seems that H.C. took Quince seriously on his promise, as Dollie was actually pregnant eleven times during their marriage, with "seven survivors," as Gatewood put it.

Never going by his first name, Gatewood or just "Gate" quickly established himself as the most rambunctious, mischievous, and energetic of the brood. When his parents had an engagement or wanted to escape their house for a night out, they hired two babysitters: one for the other six kids, and one for Gatewood.[1]

It is difficult to overemphasize the role that Carlisle played in Gatewood's future life. He often likened the town to the Mayberry of Andy Griffith fame, a bucolic, tightly knit community where kids could play outside for hours on end and where everyone knew everyone else. This was sometimes a disadvantage for Gatewood: it was difficult to get away with things.

Henry Clay Galbraith Sr. had made a real name for himself in the small town. He opened his own auto repair garage, and he became the Buick dealer in Carlisle. He engaged in a variety of other small business pursuits, including managing a small farm on the family's property. He and Dollie were community leaders in Carlisle, where Gatewood's mother lived out the charity and compassion central to her faith. Times were good for the Galbraith family.[2]

Henry Clay Jr., or Hank, remembers his little brother tagging along on his adventures, and was often dragged into Gatewood's mischief. One day Hank, Gatewood, and other kids from their neighborhood were playing in an old coal house on their property. The kids had lined the shed with old mattresses and would spend hours playing cards, roughhousing, and having "secret club meetings" in their primitive headquarters. This day, the kids started a match fight and flung lit matches at one another in the coal house. When they were called to dinner, they vacated the premises without cleaning up. Later that night a neighbor banged on Dollie and H.C.'s window. One of the matches had fallen deep in between the mattresses in the coal house and smoldered for hours before starting a blaze that engulfed the kids' erstwhile headquarters. H.C. ran outside to see what was going on, forgetting, or maybe not minding, that he always chose to sleep in the nude. Standing outside next to the old widow who had woken him up, he observed the inferno. She said, "H.C., I expect you better go put your pants on before anybody else gets here." Even though the fire didn't damage any other property, H.C. was livid. After a brief questioning the next morning, Hank and Gatewood confessed to the arson. H.C. promised his sons a good whipping, so Gatewood wore five or six pairs of underwear for the next week until the empty threat subsided.[3]

Gatewood, as he quickly became known, led a mischievous and idyllic childhood in Carlisle, part of a tight-knit community and large extended family.

In his own recollections of life in Carlisle, Gatewood recalled that his parents encouraged his brothers and sisters to work hard and to find some ways to make money. He wrote about picking strawberries and going door to door selling them to neighbors starting when he was eight years old. This taught him grit and entrepreneurship from an early age. While he certainly did participate in these pursuits along with his siblings, his big sister Liz remembers that Gatewood also had an innate talent for getting *out* of work. “If Gatewood could get out of doing that, he would, every time. So he’d go to the strawberry patch and he’d eat all the strawberries, or he’d hide in the field so you couldn’t see him.” This didn’t stop Liz from remembering her rambunctious little brother fondly. “He was funny, he had a great personality, and he was just a one-line comedian, really.” Gatewood was a sweet, intelligent child who was “wild as a March hare.”[4]

These are the kinds of memories that followed Gatewood throughout his life. He always had a special place in his heart for rural communities and for close-knit, simple, and unassuming people. Later in life he fought fiercely for those that he felt were taken advantage of by large corporations or victimized by free trade agreements, urbanization, and government overreach. During his runs for public office, when he spoke about the evils of the "Petrochemical-Pharmaceutical-Military-Industrial-Transnational-Corporate-Fascist-Elite-Bastards" at every stump speech, he was thinking of his childhood in Carlisle, of a time that he ever held up as the highest standard of the American dream.

This picturesque childhood wasn't without challenges. Gatewood, more than any of his siblings, dealt with a variety of health afflictions as a youngster. First, he suffered from an early age with chronic asthma, which forced him into multiple hospitalizations and painful breathing treatments. Gatewood wrote about the anxiety caused by these frequent attacks, never knowing when his lungs might be robbed of air. His asthma would play a major role in his life and even set him on certain paths as an adult. Little was known about effective treatments in the 1950s, so Gatewood was always searching for a cure, even in the most unlikely or controversial places.

Along with his tendency to climb tall trees and jump off of buildings, Gatewood's frequent health issues made him a regular visitor to the local hospital. When he was seven years old, he was loath to get out of bed on Christmas morning. His appendix had ruptured during the night, and he spent a few nights in the hospital recovering from his surgery.[5]

A couple of years later, he was roughhousing at school and fell into the end of the bleachers. Gatewood experienced immense pain but was told to go back to class. He lasted little more than an hour before he felt too sick and headed home. Walking through town on his own, he had to stop frequently due to the pain. When he made it home, Dollie promptly delivered him to the hospital, where he stayed overnight for observation. A few days later he started to vomit blood. He was rushed to the hospital in Lexington, where doctors declared that his spleen had ruptured, and he was sent into emergency surgery.[6]

Liz remembered this time, and the worry that pervaded the family. "Mom and Dad were extremely concerned, they thought they were going to lose him."[7] Since the fall, he had bled internally. By the time he was rushed into surgery, doctors weren't sure he would survive. He stayed in the hospital for more than a month before finally pulling through and recovering. It's difficult to imagine the worry of two parents as their son lay in bed, fighting for his life, while they still had to care for six other children.

Aside from his asthma, his surgeries, and his frequent injuries, Gatewood was also burdened with an affliction that impacted his self-esteem. Liz remembered the origins of this malady: "When my mom was pregnant

From the very start, Gatewood was a "stand-up comedian" in his large family, always looking for a way to entertain his siblings.

with Gatewood, she got very ill."[8] Some sort of bacterial infection weakened Dollie, which worried doctors as she attempted to carry Gatewood to term. To fight the infection, they administered an antibiotic called tetracycline. What the doctors did not know, but future investigation would show, was that tetracycline taken during pregnancy had a major effect on the tooth development of the child. As he grew up and his baby teeth came in, they were discolored, brittle, and prone to injury.[9]

"They were rotten, they were just rotten," Liz said. "They were so bad that Mom and I often talked. . . . We think that had an impact on Gatewood, because the kids always teased him."[10]

So here was Gatewood, a ten-year-old with six siblings, already too wild for his own good, forced to stay inside and turn inward just as he yearned for acceptance, fun, and adventure. His surgeries stopped him from exploring with his friends, and the kids at school relentlessly teased him for the way his teeth looked. He became more shy and reserved, and found a new passion: reading.

While always a gifted child (his second-grade teacher had Gatewood tested and showed that he could have skipped multiple grades), Gatewood became a voracious reader. He counted Edgar Rice Burroughs, James Fenimore Cooper, H. G. Wells, and Ray Bradbury as favorite authors. One of

Easter 1954. Religion was a big part of Gatewood's family. His parents, Dollie and Henry Clay, raised their children in the Catholic tradition.

his favorite books was *All the King's Men* by fellow Kentuckian Robert Penn Warren. The story of the populist politician Willie Stark ignited Gatewood's imagination and fed his dreams of fame and renown. This, along with his first opportunity to see Governor Bert T. Combs speak at the Carlisle County Fair, may have first drawn Gatewood to the allure of political ambition.[11]

By Gatewood's own admission, his health scares and surgeries gave him an even keener zest for life, and a willingness to take risks. They also forced him to develop his intellect and imagination, always daydreaming that he was somewhere else, fantasizing about a life full of big ideas and bigger accomplishments. The ridicule he received for the appearance of his teeth also gave him a certain shyness and anger. As he grew into adolescence, Gatewood would never back down from a fight, and he would develop a sharp distaste for bullies. He tried to escape from his reality by imagining he was on a trailblazing adventure with *Leatherstocking*, or battling aliens in *War of the Worlds*. He imagined himself in front of roaring crowds, like Willie Stark, people everywhere clamoring for his wit and charm and power.

Still a young boy in Carlisle, he yearned to stand out from his siblings and dreamed of excitement. Little did Gatewood know that his world was about to be turned upside down.

To better understand the changes that came to the Galbraith family in 1959, it's best to have a clear view of the relationship between Dollie and H.C. Young lovers and newlyweds, they embraced their hometown. Both of their families were well-known community fixtures, and their social standing was established. They owned a beautiful home and a small farm. H.C. rose in the social ranks from a truck driver and small-time auto mechanic to a business owner and entrepreneur.

H.C. was a climber and dreamer, with a tenth-grade education. He believed in hard work and enjoyed the fruits of his success: a beautiful and clever wife, a gaggle of talented children, respect from his community, and financial well-being. This was the American dream: living in a beautiful small town and accomplishing anything you aimed for, based on how hard you could work and how badly you wanted to succeed.

Dollie had the hardest job of all: raising seven children while H.C. worked twelve-hour days to make ends meet. Here was a smart, compassionate, and fair-minded woman, who came from a progressive family. She and her two sisters had all completed high school and received college educations, a rare feat in 1930s America. Dollie encouraged her children to explore their interests and to value their educations.

Dollie had her hands full managing a growing household and nearly constant pregnancies. Things would have fallen apart without her care, hard work, and love. But she was also, without doubt, the leader of the family. When a decision needed to be made, H.C. knew that Dollie was in charge. He would regularly tell his children, "Whatever your mom says, goes."[12]

This background is important when looking at the next step for the Galbraith family. They had a comfortable, happy life in Carlisle, and were part of a tight-knit community. They were surrounded by friends and an extended family, and were secure in their lives. But something still ate at Dollie. She was educated, knowledgeable, and had an eye to the future. She knew that as her parents had prioritized education for her and her sisters, the key to success for her seven children would be access to education. While Carlisle was familiar, it didn't provide the opportunities that she saw as so important to her children.

By the late 1950s Judy, the eldest Galbraith child, had followed a boyfriend (and future husband) to Lexington. Judy shared a sense of adventure and sense of humor with Gatewood, and she shaped much of his friendly

Gatewood (*front, in the white shirt*) and his siblings grew up as part of a Catholic family, attending parochial schools and serving regularly as altar boys and church volunteers.

nature. Being the oldest of seven, Judy remained a quasi-parental figure for her siblings while leading the family in striking out on her own. Though it was a short forty-mile drive away, Lexington was a whole new world compared to small-town Carlisle. Dollie's children were growing up, and she began to think seriously about how to provide them with the opportunities that her parents had prioritized for her and her sisters.

One day she decided: the family would move to Lexington. They would leave their life in Carlisle, the business H.C. had built, the family and friends they loved so dearly, and the life they knew.

True to his word, H.C. didn't seem to put up a fight. What Dollie said was what the family did. This tacit agreement underscored their relationship. Without exception, the living Galbraith kids remembered their parents as having a strong and affectionate marriage. They respected each other, and H.C. avoided the toxic paternalism of the 1950s that robbed women of the ability to make decisions for their families or for themselves.

This decision completely altered the future of the seven Galbraith children, and that of Dollie and H.C.'s marriage. Later in life, Gatewood's siblings would look back on this decision as vital to their success later in life. It would also lead to some of the greatest tragedies that the family had to endure.

Whatever the case, Gatewood was twelve years old when the family moved to the big city of Lexington, the Jewel of the Bluegrass. The rambunctious, self-conscious, and often ailing little boy had grown into a gangly preteen, with big ideas swirling in his head and a desire to make a name for himself growing in his heart.

After growing up in small-town Carlisle, the Galbraith kids saw Lexington as a teeming metropolis. Even though all of them had visited once or twice, moving to the big city was its own strange journey. The family found a house on Dantzler Court off Nicholasville Road with three bedrooms, one and a half baths, and a small backyard, just a few blocks away from the outer boundary of the University of Kentucky. The location underscored Dollie's commitment to keeping a college education fresh in the minds of her kids. Since Judy had moved out, the two remaining Galbraith girls shared one of the bedrooms, while the four boys shared another.[13]

Lexington's population was swelling dramatically, from under 80,000 people in 1940 to over 130,000 in 1960, the year after the Galbraiths made their move.[14] Throughout the twentieth century, more and more businesses relocated and consolidated in Lexington, drawing rural families like the Galbraiths out of their communities and into its growing arms. The self-proclaimed Horse Capital of the World, Lexington's own booming population led to the establishment in 1958 (a year before the Galbraiths arrived) of the urban service boundary, an imaginary barrier that barred developers from purchasing the local horse farms, which provided much of Lexington's beauty, and building developments that would lead to urban sprawl.

The transition was quite profound for the whole family: moving from their spacious house and small farm in quiet Carlisle to a cramped postwar house in the heart of Lexington. It also marked a major transition for H.C., who left a successful automobile dealership and garage in Carlisle. When the family moved to Lexington, he bought a restaurant and opened Galbraith's downtown on Main Street across from the Kentucky Theater. H.C. and many of the kids worked long hours to try to make the restaurant a success. H.C. was usually there from six in the morning until nine at night, six days a week.

The kids all enrolled at Catholic schools in town, the younger kids downtown at St. Peter's, and Gatewood, Hank, and Liz at Lexington Catholic Middle and High School on Clays Mill Road. Liz and Hank recalled feeling constricted by the environment of the parochial schools, surrounded by strict nuns and priests at a time when corporal punishment was still the norm. This was a sharp contrast to the laid-back environment they had in Carlisle, and the Galbraith kids bristled under these new rules and dress codes.

After he moved to Lexington with his family, Gatewood attended St. Peter's parochial school, where this photo was made, circa 1960. He was in the eighth grade and a growth spurt left him towering over his peers.

The kids also had to navigate a new social world. Even growing up in Carlisle, the Galbraith boys were taught to never back down from a bully or a fight. Gatewood took this seriously, often getting into scuffles over the smallest of insults. He became locally famous for starting fights with much bigger boys, and then relying on Hank to finish them. Whether it was caused by the self-consciousness over his deformed teeth or by his wild nature, Gatewood carried this tendency into life in the big city, with often interesting consequences.

Hank was a gentle soul who didn't go out looking for fights. But as the oldest boy in the family, he promised to always look out for his siblings. By default, this usually meant protecting Gatewood. The lack of tolerance for bullying lasted into adulthood for Hank, who admitted, "It just sets me on fire and I have to intervene." Gatewood took full advantage of this protection, and he never shied away from a fight once they moved to Lexington, no matter the size of the opponent. "But Gatewood, he never backed down. He would, you know, be spouting off to somebody, and I don't know whether he was ever right or wrong, but he wouldn't shut up. He wouldn't stop. And he was a scrawny little guy at that point and kind of sickly . . . and sure enough he'd get into it, and I couldn't let those guys just beat the shit out of him a couple times, so I'd intervene."[15]

Henry Clay "H.C." Galbraith Sr., 1973. H.C. was the beloved yet flawed patriarch of the Galbraith family. He was an entrepreneur, owning an automobile dealership and repair shop in Carlisle, and he also opened Galbraith's, a diner in downtown Lexington.

In one instance, shortly after the family had moved to Lexington, Hank and Gatewood were playing basketball with a group of boys at a nearby home. As they often do, the game got heated, and twelve-year-old Gatewood started to get pushed around by a nineteen-year-old named Butch. When Butch finally pushed Gatewood down, fourteen-year-old Hank stepped in, and Butch proceeded to push him as well. The fact that this college freshman was picking on his twelve-year-old brother didn't sit well with Hank. He shoved Butch to the ground and straddled his chest, pinning his arms to his sides. He instructed Gatewood to go get a big stick, because he "wanted to teach Butch a lesson." At this point Butch broke down in tears, begging Hank not to hit him with the stick. Hank started to feel bad and let Butch up. The bully grabbed the stick from Gatewood, hit Hank with it across the thighs, and ran home.[16]

As the Galbraith kids struggled to adjust to their new life in Lexington, business at the family restaurant took a turn for the worse. H.C.'s financial prospects began to unravel, and Gatewood and his family were thrown into a turbulent period that would shape his future in strange and unpredictable ways.

The Galbraith kids gradually got used to life in Lexington, with the older children starting to make friends, find jobs, and create their own community. Yet even as his brothers and sisters fell in line, Gatewood kept stepping over it. He worked a paper route on Southland Drive in Lexington, often reading the news stories in between houses. He remained quiet and timid around kids his own age, but had no problem acting out or starting a fight to defend his honor.

He continued to be the troublemaker of the family, outpacing all of his siblings in how often he was chased around the house, ordered to get down off the roof, or told off for urinating in the yard. He was particularly irksome to Dollie. Gatewood was the only child that she would lose her composure with completely, one time trying to swat him with the handle of a broom as he misbehaved.

"My mom would get mad at them, especially when they would fight in the house," Liz remembered, describing the lengths Dollie would go to in order to remain a respectable neighbor in the face of four rambunctious boys. "My mom would run around and put all the windows down and then take the broom after them. . . . You know, being the good Catholic woman that she was, she didn't want anybody to hear this."[17]

Added to the stress of raising their children and keeping up with their hyperactive son, H.C.'s business in downtown Lexington failed. New suburban construction and sprawl was driving business and traffic away from downtown Lexington. Even with his older children pitching in during the evenings and weekends, H.C. couldn't turn a profit and had to close Galbraith's and return to his career in car sales.

This was a devastating blow to H.C., who had built himself a successful career and life from such humble beginnings in Carlisle. The family had to move from the house they rented to a much smaller three-bedroom home just down the street. Dollie's teaching degree came in handy, as she went back to work as a teacher at Mary, Queen of the Holy Rosary Catholic School. Luckily, she was a talented and well-loved teacher who thrived in the classroom.

Aside from the impact it had on the family as a whole, H.C. was laid low by this failure. His children, even nearly sixty years later, still remember him as a loving, dedicated, and gentle father, who loved their mother and the rest of the family. He had always been a social drinker, but the failure wreaked havoc on his mental and emotional health, leading H.C. to the bottle on a regular basis. He would come home from his new job, at a car dealership on New Circle Road, and drink heavily. He never screamed, never was violent, but would often pass out in his chair by the end of the day. On the weekends he would sit outside in the sun and drink beer after beer until he fell asleep.[18]

His behavior had an impact on his children, and more so on those old enough to truly understand what was happening. The older siblings were increasingly disturbed by his behavior, and his disconnect from normal family life. It was especially troubling for Hank, the oldest Galbraith boy, who was tasked with protecting his younger siblings, Gatewood in particular. Hank started to count drinks for his father, and to get in arguments with him about his drinking.[19]

Gatewood was caught in the horrible sweet spot of this family crisis. As a young teenager, he was old enough to realize what was happening, yet young enough to be deeply affected by it. While Hank and Liz were fully aware, they had the ability to escape. They were old enough to drive, were about to graduate, and were thinking about college. Gatewood's younger siblings were mostly shielded from this experience. They were too young to fully grasp what was going on. Some younger siblings remember it as not being too traumatic as kids, or simply chose not to speak about it.

One can imagine how traumatic this series of events was for a boy growing into adolescence. First, a move from his childhood home, where he had established friends and an extended family, to a vastly larger city full of unfamiliar faces. A quest for belonging, to stand out, and to make a name for himself. New schools, a new house, a new way of life. The family business failing, his mother forced to start work, his father's descent into alcoholism. His world had been torn apart, then sewn back together with different thread. In spite of these challenges, or perhaps because of them, Gatewood slowly began to remake himself. Just as he had imagined staring out the window, back in Carlisle.

Things still weren't rosy for Gatewood at school. Like his older siblings, he bristled at the strict and stuffy nature of his new parochial school, Lexington Catholic High School. The nuns and priests who taught his classes quickly grew tired of his hijinks and his constant desire to be the class clown. He was known for fighting, pulling pranks, telling dirty jokes, and bad language. After months of this, Gatewood finally went too far. One day, after being reprimanded, he called one of the nuns "a bitch" and was quickly expelled from school.[20]

Dollie was now a teacher at the parochial elementary school across the street, and this broke her heart. The family had been through plenty of struggles since moving to Lexington, and she was trying to hold everyone together. She had older kids who resented her for moving them from Carlisle, younger kids who needed tending, her husband's illness to manage, and then, on top of it all, Gatewood. Gatewood's younger sister, Edna, remembered that when he was finally expelled, his mother simply went out to the backyard and sobbed, exhausted by this latest twist.[21] The expulsion was even more hurtful to her as a devout Catholic who believed in parochial education. Nevertheless, Gatewood still needed to go to school. So Dollie gathered herself, punished Gatewood as well as she could, and enrolled him at the nearby public school, Lafayette High School, just down the road.

In the midst of this crisis, Gatewood experienced his own transformation. He had finally had enough of his rotting teeth and the social and physical toll they had taken on his life. With the blessing of his parents, he decided to have them removed and to wear dentures for the rest of his life.

The experience was excruciating. His teeth were pulled a few at a time over a number of weeks, and the pain left Gatewood huddled in bed, often crying himself to sleep. His little brother Tim, who shared a bed with him in their crowded house, will never forget the sound of the usually boisterous Gatewood whimpering in bed next to him as the pain kept him up all night.

After the extractions came the fitting of dentures. Like a caterpillar emerging from a cocoon, Gatewood's decision gave him a new lease on life. He was able to reinvent himself in a new school, around a new group of people, and he began to show off the smile that would define much of his public life.

"Once that happened, I believe that it did help," Tim said. "It made him able to do what was bottled up inside him. Which was to be more gregarious, be more out there and be with people."[22]

During this time Gatewood also grew out of his lanky, skinny body and grew taller and physically stronger. Eventually reaching six foot four inches by the time he graduated from high school, he no longer needed Hank to finish his fights for him. He wasn't afraid to physically challenge other boys, as quickly became apparent in the halls of Lafayette High School.

Ferrell Wellman, who would go on to become a member of the Kentucky Journalism Hall of Fame and Kentucky Broadcaster Hall of Fame, and who would interview Gatewood during his future political campaigns, vividly remembered being in Gatewood's presence as a fellow student at Lafayette in the 1960s. "He was this presence, and there was something about Gatewood . . . he had a chip on his shoulder all through high school. I mean he was the guy walking down the hall looking for a fight, and he got into them. He got into trouble constantly because there was no mute on Gatewood," Wellman explained. "If someone looked at him cross-eyed, he not only would say, what are you looking at? He would then provide an evaluation of what he thought of that particular person and their lifestyle."[23]

Lafayette High School, when Gatewood arrived in the mid-1960s, had a reputation as being the buttoned-down, preppy, suburban high school in Lexington. The suburban sprawl that pushed Lexington's boundaries farther south resulted in a new crop of teenagers whose parents had sought out more spacious, newly constructed neighborhoods that were built rapidly in the fifties and sixties, with names like Lansdowne, Garden Springs, Southland, and Open Gates. The students at Lafayette, many coming from solidly middle- or upper-class families, stuck to the customary unofficial uniform of khaki pants, blue button-down shirts, and penny loafers.

Gatewood did not fit into this mold. In an interview with Wellman on Kentucky Educational Television as part of his gubernatorial campaign nearly thirty years later, Gatewood remembered them knowing each other in high school. He immediately brought up the fact that, if one existed, he would be in the "Lafayette High School mean hall of fame."[24] Wellman would later say, "You know, a lot of people just saw him as kind of this redneck who just wandered down from Nicholas County. And in some ways, he was. But he had a way, whether it was in class or whatever it was, of rubbing a lot of people the wrong way." Still, though Wellman remembered Gatewood's reputation as a brawler and troublemaker, he, like many others who knew the adolescent Gatewood, did not think of him as a bully. "Now, Gatewood was, you know, he wasn't a bully. Was extremely smart in high school, extremely well read."[25]

As the Galbraith boys had been taught by their mother and father, and as Hank displayed many times for Gatewood, the family did not suffer bullies. In his autobiography, Gatewood remembers transferring to Lafayette and starting fights with all the bullies he could find at Lafayette, as quickly as he could. "I know I got into 10 fights the first week and developed such an immediate reputation, by whipping the 4 biggest bullies there (one at a time), that soon after, if someone had something to say about my strangeness, they did it out of my earshot."[26]

Gatewood made his fair share of enemies. Wellman recalled that a senior who had been insulted by Gatewood would get up early on Sunday mornings and drive to the intersection of Rosemont Garden and Nicholasville Road. Gatewood maintained a paper route throughout his time in middle and high school, and this was the intersection where the distributors would drop his stack of papers to deliver to the neighborhood. For a few weeks in a row, the unnamed Lafayette senior would wait for the papers to be dropped off, douse them in lighter fluid, and set them aflame before driving off. The distributor would change the drop-off spot, only for the newspapers to be turned to a smoking pyre before Gatewood arrived. Yes, he definitely rubbed some people the wrong way.

This was Gatewood emerging from his shell. He had new teeth, a new body, and a new license to make a name for himself. The experiences in the early part of his life gave him a chip on his shoulder that would remain, and would become his hallmark on the campaign trail. Gatewood was a loud, aggressive, troublemaking teenager who never backed down from a fight. He began smoking cigarettes at fourteen and would often sneak alcohol into the school gym during basketball games. He sought out bullies and taught them memorable lessons, and even though he bristled at the authority of his parents, he took their values to heart: to stand up for the little guy, to never forget where he came from, and to do big things with his life.

In 1965 Gatewood graduated from high school after a makeup summer chemistry class and some good luck. His parents were relieved, after the roller coaster of the past few years. Gatewood was still bright and well read, but he had given up a lot of academic motivation for more exciting pursuits. Nevertheless, diploma in hand, he applied to the University of Kentucky.

By Gatewood's own recollection, he was lucky that this was still during the time when the university had an open admissions policy. Basically, this meant that any student who had graduated with a high school diploma and a sufficient grade point average would automatically be admitted to the state school. This was exactly why Dollie had made the gamble to move to Lexington, and why she felt that the family struggles had been worth it. She was trying to open the door of opportunity for her kids, and the University of Kentucky beckoned, just up Nicholasville road.[27]

Gatewood began his college career at UK in the fall of 1965, and quickly fell behind. Once again choosing more interesting pursuits over studying, he couldn't keep up with his classes. He lacked the maturity and discipline required to maintain his standing, and he soon dropped out. He reenrolled in the spring of 1966, but succumbed to the same temptations and dropped out for the second semester in a row.[28]

This period coincided with the intensifying of the conflict in Vietnam. Gatewood was enthralled by the drama that played out on the nightly news. Even as a fledgling college student, Gatewood resisted any antiwar sentiment on campus, going so far as getting in a yelling match with various antiwar groups. Gatewood was dedicated to his country, and to the U.S. Constitution, firmly believing that part of being a good citizen was being willing to fight

Gatewood graduated from Lafayette High School in 1965, after making quite an impression on his teachers, peers, and administrators.

for those beliefs. Predating the later draft lotteries, conscription began to ramp up just as Gatewood started at UK.

Here he was, a nineteen-year-old college dropout who had no idea what to do with his life. He still dreamed of fame and glory. Pairing that with his convictions about the U.S. intervention in Vietnam, his next move made total sense. Gatewood decided to join the Marine Corps.

What better way to make a splash? To live dangerously, and to push himself to the limits that he had imagined for so long? He was disaffected, distracted, and unmotivated as a student, and was still grasping for how to make a name for himself. Going to war seemed like the perfect answer.

Gatewood's brother Mike recalled this period in his big brother's life. "Well, he wanted to prove himself as a man, like most of us guys do, and knew that perhaps that discipline that the military would require would have been good for him."[29]

Gatewood put it even more succinctly when recalling his motivations behind joining the Corps: "I dropped out again mid semester and did what any other socially, sexually and academically frustrated 19-year-old male would do. I tried to go to war."[30]

There was one major problem holding Gatewood back from this dream: his chronic asthma. He was classified 4F, unfit for military service. Gatewood wrote that he was able to find a few local doctors to convince that he had "outgrown" his asthma, even though he had experienced attacks within the past year. Gatewood got his way and received the medical voucher he needed in order to enlist.[31]

In the spring of 1966, Gatewood took a long bus ride to Parris Island, South Carolina, the site of the Marine Corps Recruit Depot, where all newly enlisted Marines go through basic training. Gatewood relished his chance at a new start, even though he couldn't get his body to agree. He consistently failed the physical challenges he faced during training, mainly due to his breathing problems. One day, when he was cleaning the barracks with another recruit, a cloud of dust was swept in his direction. In seconds his lungs sealed themselves shut, and he experienced one of the worst asthma attacks of his life. After he was checked out by medical personnel, his time in the Marines came to a quick end. Rather than attaining glory on the battlefield, Gatewood was honorably discharged and shipped back home. Betrayed once again by his body, Gatewood still yearned to leave his mark on the world. He was still listless, and searching for purpose.

Back in Lexington, he continued to immerse himself in wasting time and attending parties, drinking beer and trying to get laid. He didn't know what to do with his life, or how to do it. He would reenroll at UK, only to succumb to the same vices and drop out before finishing even a semester. He held a series of part-time jobs and coasted through a life of dark, smoky rooms, failed romances, and sour hangovers. He needed a spiritual journey, and a new start. Influenced by the rise of hippie culture and a sense of adventure, he would soon have it.

Returning to Lexington with his discharge papers in hand, Gatewood had to start all over. He had been building up the promise of military valor in his mind, hoping it would lend some direction and discipline to his life. Instead he ended up hanging around campus, attending parties, chasing women, and drinking as much alcohol as possible.

By his own written admission, he became obsessed with the opposite sex, fully committed to living a life of one-night stands and notches in his belt. He fell in with company who were equally committed to these objectives, and his group became a fixture at many of the local Lexington dive bars between campus and downtown. This was a fast and dangerous way of living.[32]

As Gatewood remembered, he was working at a men's clothing store in the old Turfland Mall on Harrodsburg Road in Lexington in the fall of 1968 when he got a call. He vaguely recognized the voice and soon realized it was one of his old buddies from his days at Lexington Catholic, Teddy Mertens.

Teddy asked if he could come over that night to Gatewood's apartment. He had something to show him. He showed up after Gatewood got off work with a giant bag of marijuana that he had brought back from Thailand, where he had been serving in the air force.[33]

Suspicious at first, Gatewood let Teddy talk him into trying some. Teddy rolled a joint, lit it up, and encouraged Gatewood to inhale deeply.

Gatewood was a committed cigarette smoker and had obviously given himself over to the pleasures and pain of alcohol. But when it came to marijuana, he was inexperienced and nervous. Whether or not this was the first time Gatewood tried marijuana, this was the first time he tried quality cannabis. His life would never be the same.

For the next few months, he and Teddy smoked the entire stash Teddy had smuggled back from overseas, hanging out in Gatewood's apartment, tearing through endless snacks, and, for Gatewood, rediscovering the pleasure of life. In his autobiography he claims that he instantly felt relief from his chronic asthma when he started to smoke quality pot. He wrote that he could breathe more deeply, live more fully, and not constantly experience the anxiety that came along with waiting for his next asthma attack.[34]

His younger sister, Edna, recalled, "I remember smoking with Gatewood for the first time, like in 1968, smoking weed with him. . . . But yeah, my parents were very aware of this. They would never try it, but they knew we smoked weed. And just that it was part of our life, sort of."[35] While it hadn't yet become the major focus of his life, it's obvious that Gatewood instantly took to using cannabis recreationally and medicinally.

When Teddy took off to work for family members in California, Gatewood was right back where he started: working a dead-end job, depressed, and, usually, drunk. He decided that he needed a change of scenery. One of his friends in Lexington suggested he come to Myrtle Beach, South Carolina, where the friend worked summers on the beach. Gatewood followed along, taking a job checking out beach chairs and umbrellas until he had a falling-out with the friend. With no other plans and stuck at the beach, Gatewood was out of options. Then he remembered Teddy. He walked to the highway, stuck out his thumb, and began a truly epic journey.

Over the next forty days, Gatewood would hitchhike across the country three different times. Along the way, he forged numerous transitory friendships and lived a harsh life on the open road. Often he would walk for hours and spend lonely nights on highway interchanges, waiting for a charitable passerby. He ended up back in California and worked with Teddy on his family's ranch and farm before the two eventually took off for San Francisco and lived there for a few months against the backdrop of the psychedelic

Bay Area in 1969. Together with marijuana, this involved Gatewood's first interactions with LSD. He and Teddy spent their days securing work and a roof over their heads and their nights high or tripping.[36]

After months of adventures, they were homesick and decided they needed to head back to the Bluegrass. They hitchhiked across the country, tripping on acid nearly the whole way. Finally they arrived back in Lexington, but Gatewood would never leave behind these experiences. After initially trying to find this type of soul-searching experience through the military, he had found it instead wandering like a vagabond across the desolate highways of America and experiencing an acid- and cannabis-induced awakening in San Francisco during the Summer of Love.

The opening chapter in Gatewood's life is vital to understanding the rest of his story. His childhood in Carlisle and his place in a big, happy, and complicated family always remained central to Gatewood's personality. The paradise he remembered growing up in a small town would inform his views later in life: his passion for rural communities, his distrust of large corporations, and his belief that simple, unassuming people were the best kind. This experience, and his early interest in politics, led Gatewood to the libertarian, populist message that he would later share across the Commonwealth. He always maintained a strong connection to the people and values of Carlisle.

Gatewood's physical ailments as a child would also play an important role in his story. His early injuries, struggles with chronic asthma, and the problems with his teeth influenced his personality during these formative years. When he was healing from a ruptured appendix, he turned inward and lost himself in reading and exploring his mind. His struggles with asthma induced an anxiety and restlessness that led him to try remedies that were out of the box and, as he would often explain, played a major role in convincing himself of the magic of marijuana. The bullying he endured due to the condition of his teeth made him truly despise those who picked on anyone, and made him quick to fight. His physical transformation when he had his teeth pulled allowed him to open up and become the gregarious, center-of-attention, main-attraction character he would revel in as a political candidate.

His family was always the most important part of Gatewood's life. The memories of his brothers and sisters revealed the complicated dynamics of their family, and the struggles that they shared together. Universally, his siblings remembered Gatewood as the wild, energetic, intelligent, and outgoing stand-up comedian of the family. They also revealed the deeper currents of Gatewood's emotional and intellectual life, which would later evolve into an interest in campaigning and political office. Gatewood's parents, H.C. and Dollie, served as role models for all of the Galbraith children and instilled the values of charity, respect, love, and sacrifice that Gatewood and all of his siblings would reflect throughout their lives. All families are complicated. The Galbraiths were no exception. The Galbraith children remembered happy childhoods and their parents' loving marriage, but H.C.'s alcoholism, triggered by the family's move to Lexington and his business failure, impacted his children in different ways.

The Galbraiths' relocation to Lexington was one of the most important events in Gatewood's life. The courageous decision by Dollie to move away from the family and community they had built in Carlisle was truly selfless: she wanted to open up opportunity to her children and to expand the possibilities for their lives. All of her children would attend the University of Kentucky, and they would go on to a range of rewarding lives—Judy as a stay-at-home mother who cared for a growing family, Hank as a child and family therapist, Liz teaching on a variety of Native American reservations throughout the American West, Edna as a certified nurse and consultant, Mike as a successful linguist and engineer, Tim as an executive for Yum! Brands and Frito-Lay. For Gatewood, as we shall soon see, a passion for the law and public service would be fostered in the halls of the University of Kentucky. The accomplishments of their children are a great testament to the choices and sacrifices of Dollie and H.C.

Gatewood's decision to join the Marine Corps and his subsequent discharge also deeply impacted his growth as an adult. Throughout these early years one can see him searching for purpose and meaning, and being thwarted either by his body, his circumstances, or his personal failings. His journeys across the country and his willingness to dabble in hallucinogens opened a new door for his understanding of the world. His love affair with marijuana, and his convictions about its God-given purpose on earth, would go on to color much of his public life.

By the end of the 1960s Gatewood's story was just starting, but to truly understand the person he became, these early years are crucial. After this long, complicated, winding journey, Gatewood was ready to write the rest of his story. And what a story it was.

2

The Model Plan for Legal Marijuana

After a few tumultuous years and the mother of all cross-country road trips, Gatewood was glad to be home. Unfortunately, he was reunited quite quickly with his old vices. He started a job working as a milkman for a Lexington dairy located on Third Street, where he would deliver milk starting at 4 a.m. He fell back into partying, and drinking, and wrote that he would often party all night, show up for work, complete his route, and then sleep all day.[1] He still lacked motivation to pursue his education, and was stuck in a rut. Perhaps most concerning was his own descent into alcoholism. After witnessing the strains that his father's illness put on the family, he couldn't resist this lifestyle. By his own admission, drinking made him rude, overbearing, and frustrating to be around. His own friends started frank discussions with Gatewood during this time, trying to turn around his reckless decisions and disturbing behavior.

Everyone who knew Gatewood during his years around the University of Kentucky campus describes him the same way: a bright, wild, reckless, outgoing, irreverent, center-of-the-universe young man, still seemingly without real direction or ambition, save for making a scene. Kevin Hill, a friend of Gatewood's who participated in various student protests alongside him, remembered in vivid detail a Halloween party that they attended together. Everyone at the party was in costume, with the usual bevy of witches, werewolves, vampires, and ghosts. Suddenly a cry went up, followed by shrieks of laughter. When Hill looked out, he saw Gatewood and his date, both completely nude save for Band-Aids covering their navels. Their costume? Adam and Eve.[2] This was the perfect illustration for Gatewood's personality: he always wanted to be the center of attention, and he usually succeeded. This tendency would soon take a more serious turn, landing Gatewood in the middle of a chaotic period in American history.

The travel of the past year and his time in California had truly changed Gatewood's perception of the conflict at the center of the national discourse:

As a college student, Gatewood was often foiled by his own partying and excesses. He found a voice on the University of Kentucky campus, eventually leading protests against the Vietnam War and what he considered administrative overreach.

the war in Vietnam. In the space of a few years, Gatewood shifted from a gung-ho pro-military hawk to an LSD-tripping antiwar dove. Those antiwar groups he used to argue with on the University of Kentucky campus? Now he started joining them, participating in the marches and protests that were widespread at UK in the late 1960s and early 1970s. Gatewood lived in a rented apartment near campus, and his neighborhood was the center of the student-led counterculture movement in Lexington. They formed a group called the Grosvenor Street Zoological Gardens and filtered student protests and activist groups through a united front. In a 1971 issue of the *Kentucky Kernel*, the University of Kentucky student newspaper, "The Zoo" is described as a group that "provided help with legal services, food stamp information, pregnancy test referrals and as a center to separate rumors from facts during 'emergencies.' The Zoo has also helped people suffering from bad drug 'trips' and has been called upon many times to provide bail."[3]

Beginning in the spring of 1970, protests against the Vietnam War increased in size and frequency on the University of Kentucky campus. Things boiled over on campus following the shooting of four students at the Kent State University campus on May 4, 1970, which sparked protests at the University of Kentucky and across the country. During a meeting of the UK Board of Trustees, UK student government president Steve Bright spoke out against the war, police actions on campus, and what students saw as violations of their rights in the university's student code. Specifically, students wanted troops and firearms kept off campus, especially in the wake of what happened at Kent State. During the meeting, hundreds of students swarmed Patterson Office Tower, where the meeting was being held, in order to take their protest to the ears of the trustees. Chaos reigned, and most student demands were ignored. A. B. "Happy" Chandler, former Kentucky governor, senator, and commissioner of Major League Baseball, punched a student protestor in the face when he was confronted trying to leave the meeting.[4]

Later that day, a massive student-led march erupted on campus, where UK students carried a black coffin and an American flag that read "Four More Dead" in memory of the Kent State students. They marched through campus, across downtown Lexington, and all the way to Transylvania University, a couple of miles away. The protestors finished back on campus and rallied around Barker Hall and the Buell Armory, which was the symbolic center of military action on campus. During the protest, which had halted traffic around campus and downtown, onlookers began to see flames coming from an ROTC annex building on the corner of Euclid Avenue and Martin Luther King Jr. Boulevard. The fire spread and consumed the building, also damaging nearby dormitories. A student was arrested under suspicious circumstances but was subsequently released due to lack of evidence. More protests followed on May 6 and 7, with local and state police and National Guard troops trying to keep peace on campus. Students continued to protest, and were met with tear gas, handcuffs, and no cooperation from campus administrators.[5]

Although other students involved couldn't place Gatewood at the scene, he wrote that he took part in the protests and was in the midst of thousands of student protestors as they faced off with National Guard troops who were attempting to break up the protest. This was a moment of clarity for Gatewood, who realized, in the midst of the chaos, that there were better ways to effect change.[6]

A few months later, Gatewood and other members of the Zoo had the idea of holding a weekend-long rock concert. For the venue, a Lexington physician, Dr. Phillip Crossen, volunteered his farm just outside the city. Crossen was a friend to the counterculture movement on campus and, as a practicing ob-gyn, was outspoken in his support for abortion rights and contraception. The student group named this concert Woodstick, as a tribute to the Woodstock music festival held in upstate New York in 1969. Lexington police broke up the concert, citing Crossen for offenses related to drinking, lewd behavior, and illegal drug use. Viewing the charges as trumped up and a way to lash out at the counterculture movement, the Zoo organized protests, one of which drew around five hundred students and was led by none other than Gatewood Galbraith, who riled the students up with a bullhorn as they marched through downtown and demonstrated outside the courthouse.[7]

Strangely enough, Gatewood's older brother, Hank, was upstairs in the Phoenix Hotel at this time as part of his Army Reserve responsibilities. Hank was also strongly against the war in Vietnam but was driven to volunteer in the Army Reserve to avoid having to go to the front lines. During this required workshop, the attendees were interrupted by the protest going on outside. Walking to the window, Hank looked down and saw his brother in the front row, yelling through a bullhorn.[8]

Though Gatewood continued to struggle with poor choices, drinking too much and partying too hard, the protests on campus and his leadership in these organizations provided him with a small glimpse of the purpose he thirsted for. This was just the beginning of his involvement at the University of Kentucky. As he wrote, "Despite 6 years of on-again, off-again registration and class attendance wherein I had earned 0 credits, I was allowed back in and I started my formal education in the Fall of 1971. I was 24 years old and a milkman. Is this a wonderful country or what?"[9]

Gatewood made a new commitment to himself. This time, he wouldn't drop out, he wouldn't let his vices overwhelm his potential. He was getting older, after all. A six-foot-four-inch twenty-four-year-old in class with eighteen-year-old freshmen, he was imposing, magnetic, and loud. He saw, from the protests of the past year and the political unrest on campus, that he had a purpose. He saw himself at the front of every march, leading every protest, ready to change the world. But to do that, or at least to be effective in these pursuits, he knew that he needed a college degree.

This was also the first time Gatewood had to seriously deal with what would become a lifelong challenge: money, or lack thereof. As a result of his inconsistency in staying in school, his hedonistic lifestyle, and poor decisions, Gatewood declared bankruptcy before enrolling again at UK. "Louis Gatewood Galbraith," read the bankruptcy petition announcement in the *Lexington Herald-Leader*, "117 Dantzler Court, milkman, liabilities $5,099, assets $82."[10] This really was a fresh start for Gatewood.

Prior to his involvement in the protests of 1970, he also had a deeply transformative experience that brought him to grips with reality. He and his old friend Teddy scored some LSD and Gatewood took the equivalent of twenty hits of acid. He had an insightful and painfully exposing trip, surfing the waves of his subconscious and creating hallucinations that showed him the error of his ways. The experience stripped away Gatewood's ego and convinced him that if he continued down his current path, he would soon be too far gone to turn around. Whether or not this was the catalyst for his new commitment to his education, it was clearly a moving experience.

Drugs and the counterculture movement dominated Gatewood's experience during his time at the University of Kentucky. There was a small group of students who regularly used recreational drugs, and who were consequently targeted by Lexington law enforcement. Kevin Hill remembered these experiences vividly. "There was a small community that used drugs extensively, mostly marijuana or some LSD, some psilocybin, and some mushrooms. It was your basic 1960s psychedelic group. Student enrollment was maybe fourteen thousand, and I would say that group was, at the biggest, one thousand students, but maybe lower."[11]

The Fayette County Attorney, Lawson King, the same attorney who prosecuted Dr. Phillip Crossen for the Woodstick concert, and a team of detectives made it their mission to root out drug use and the counterculture on campus. Hill remembered this hostile campus environment, where students attracted to the counterculture and drug use would have to dodge law enforcement. "There were undercover cops on campus who would infiltrate and make busts, and King was just this blazing asshole as a prosecutor."[12]

The squad included Jay Silvestro, Henry Vance, and Drew Thornton, who were widely despised by the UK students they targeted. Thornton would later lead The Company, a drug smuggling ring based in Kentucky, and would die in 1985 when his parachute malfunctioned when jumping from a plane. His body was found in Tennessee, along with a bag containing 88 pounds of cocaine valued at $15 million. His story, along with others related to The Company, was told in *The Bluegrass Conspiracy* by investigative reporter and author Sally Denton.[13] Vance would also find himself in legal trouble, both for his involvement with Thornton and later for supplying a firearm to a young woman in Florida who used it in the revenge slaying of a Florida prosecutor.[14]

This team of law enforcement officials employed deceptive tactics in order to entrap and arrest UK students they suspected of drug use. One of these busts occurred on Tuesday, November 10, 1970. Following investigations by the Narcotics Unit, Lexington police carried out a raid and arrested four UK students, among others. When asked how long these raids would last, a spokesman for the Lexington Police Department refused to say, but he "hinted that it could be several days before the last of the suspects was rounded up."[15]

It was a delicate dance to be a part of the counterculture on campus and yet sidestep the obvious targeting by both the University of Kentucky administration and local police forces.

Gatewood loved being at the center of these conflicts, and thrived in the spotlight. His new commitment to his studies, paired with his deep convictions about law enforcement, military action, and personal liberties, kept him engaged on campus in ways that had failed him in his past attempts to matriculate.

It is about this time that Gatewood's name begins to frequently grace the pages of the *Kentucky Kernel*, as he constantly placed himself at the forefront of demonstrations on campus. In April of 1971, Gatewood led the charge for a campuswide student strike. Among the reasons the strike was needed, Gatewood claimed, was an issue related to the student code, which "represents a scalpel which could castrate every student's rights—I like to call it 'castration without representation.'"[16]

Even before Gatewood was known as a mainstay in the UK student resistance, he gravitated to outspoken characters who were passionate about their beliefs, and who lived up to their convictions. He found an early role model in the figure of Dr. Gene Mason.

Following the campus unrest in May 1970 and his demonstrations in support of Dr. Phillip Crossen, Gatewood was riding high on a wave of political passion. Before enrolling at UK, he regularly audited Dr. Gene Mason's Political Science 390 course. As his concern was provoked in defending Crossen, Gatewood continually spoke out against the investigation he saw as a sham. In Dr. Mason's class, the students discussed the current political climate and what had occurred on campus in the previous months. During these discussions, Gatewood predicted that buildings in Lexington would be bombed or burned due to civil unrest as a result of Crossen's trial. Neither Dr. Mason nor most of the class took this as a threat from Gatewood, but rather as a prediction fraught with emotion.

The comment did not stay in class, though. At some point, word spread about what Gatewood had said. It made its way to the ears and desks of Jack Hall, UK's dean of students, and Robert Zumwinkle, vice president for student affairs. With the unrest and protests of the last year vivid in their minds, Hall and Zumwinkle thought it appropriate to share the class roster with the local Lexington FBI field office, who were also on alert due to the events of the past few months. FBI agents tracked down enrolled students from the class and interrogated them about Gatewood's remarks. In a press release defending this step, Hall and Zumwinkle painted Gatewood's remarks as reckless and dangerous, and contended that "the University was acting in the interest of protecting members of the University community against possible serious physical harm."[17]

Gatewood, along with other student leaders, saw this as an egregious violation of student rights and an attack on academic freedom. In response to the release of these enrollment records, Dr. Mason filed a complaint with the University of Kentucky administration and spoke out against what he saw as a major offense.

Steve Bright, the UK Student Government Association president, was appalled at the FBI investigation. A voice of student leadership throughout this tumultuous period on campus, Bright criticized Hall and Zumwinkle for their failure to protect Gatewood, as well as Dr. Mason's students. In an appearance following the decision, Bright said of the investigation, "Not only does this constitute fear in the classroom, but the most shocking thing of all is that it is all legal."[18]

This wasn't the first time Gene Mason had crossed paths with the administration. He was a devout friend to the counterculture faction on campus and heartily supported protests against the Vietnam War and the UK administration. The year before, he had been investigated and found guilty of receiving a stolen typewriter. This was a felony, and he was convicted in Fayette Circuit Court. For this transgression, among other factors, his contract was not renewed and he did not receive tenure. During the FBI probe he was also arguing his case to the university as to why he should remain on campus, as well as to the Fayette Circuit Court as to why he shouldn't spend two years in prison.[19]

In December of 1970, Bright and other students had gathered more than two thousand signatures on a petition in support of keeping Mason as a professor. In a direct challenge to the University and its administrators, students organized a series of open forums where both the faculty members who were being fired and their students could speak as to why they should stay. An advertisement in the *Kernel* detailed the need for such an event: "Several student petitions protest the termination of faculty appointments. What is expected of University faculty? Do good teachers get fired? Who decides? Is there recourse? Publish or perish?"[20]

This was the first time Bright remembered Gatewood, who "got up and didn't really ask a question as much as he just sort of gave a testimonial about how great Mason was." Bright remembered him as a colorful and passionate speaker, someone who could craft a phrase, someone who could lead and persuade others into action.[21]

Perhaps most notably, Mason also had political aspirations. He knew how to make a splash, and he loved challenging the status quo. When he was eventually convicted of receiving stolen property, he claimed that he was being targeted. "Mason felt his arrest and conviction was the result of a political plot," the campus paper reported. "He had planned to run for the sixth district Congressional seat in 1969."[22]

The students' actions did not stop Mason or the other faculty members from having their contracts terminated. In fact, Mason was later sentenced to one year in prison in Fayette Circuit Court. But this episode reveals Gatewood's new commitment to his life as a student at the university. It also shows his penchant for organizing, speaking, and engaging crowds of people. Hill remembers Gatewood as wanting to be the center of attention and as someone who enjoyed a good time, but also as a young man with serious convictions. "I think he was much broader in his concerns. He was worried about police relations with the Lexington community. He was worried about the war in Vietnam. . . . he cared a lot about the curriculum at the university, what courses were being offered and so forth."[23]

This was a dramatic change for Gatewood. He went from a chronic college dropout to being deeply involved in organizations, protests, and organizing activities on campus. As he tried to be more serious about his studies, he was also drawn to magnetic, outlandish, and colorful personalities on campus. It was no coincidence that Gene Mason was one of Gatewood's early role models. A brash, egocentric, and explosive public figure who loved to challenge authority, Gatewood was also drawn to running for public office. He emulated Dr. Mason's passion and provocation, and these would guide him throughout the rest of his public life.

Thirty-odd years later, Mason would return Gatewood's praise. When Gatewood's autobiography, *The Last Free Man in America: Meets the Synthetic Subversion*, was published, Dr. Mason included an endorsement that was printed on the back cover: "There is more truth, humor and courage in this book than in any book I've read in the last 50 years, and I read volumes. Gatewood Galbraith stands a giant bud ahead of the everyday, thoughtless, gutless, gimme politicians."

In March of 1972 Gatewood had started a job as a bouncer at the Paddock Bar near campus. The Paddock provided him with some income, but it also reinforced bad habits. Gatewood remembered these days, when he would go to classes during the day and spend the rest of the time drinking beer at the seedy bar. It helped that the clientele dovetailed nicely with Gatewood's interests. He wrote, "The longhairs, hippies and leaders of the growing anti-war movement gathered there each evening to plot strategy, drink beer, play football, pursue sexual liaisons, score some good pot, mescaline, LSD, speed or mushrooms and raise hell in general." Gatewood would work all night while downing a dozen beers each shift.[24]

Even though Gatewood wrote about his interest in marijuana dating back to the mid-1960s, his friends couldn't recall him having much interest in it during his early years at the University of Kentucky. His main interest was drinking, and he did it well. Kevin Hill remembered, "I mean, people think of Gatewood and drugs now. Gatewood was seriously into alcohol when I knew him. He drank a lot. He was, I think, living with Les Rosenbaum . . . and they were famous for their drinking and carrying on."[25]

Thomas McDowell was another friend of Gatewood's when they attended UK, and he also remembered Gatewood's somewhat reckless reputation. "Well, he was a real party guy and a womanizer, to be sure. He was kind of loud and brash and didn't hold back with his opinions no matter what it was."[26]

His drinking led to conflict, whether he was on campus or on the clock at the Paddock. As the drug busts and investigations continued, Gatewood always found his way to the middle of it. He somehow got into a fight with two bar patrons, who turned out to be Lexington policemen James Hatcher and Robert Giles. The year before, Gatewood had recognized Hatcher on campus and had his blown his cover as an undercover narc, sent to spy on students and to orchestrate drug busts. Gatewood tried to press charges against the two officers after the fight, to no avail.[27] Hatcher would later resign from the Lexington Police Department.

During his first year back at UK, Gatewood realized his drinking was seriously risking his future. Not only did it often get on the nerves of his friends, but it was getting in the way of his studies. His revelation during the chaos on campus in May of 1970 was still his guiding principle. He knew that he needed a degree. He also realized that studying the law and politics would allow him to take part in the future of his commonwealth and his country. This lesson took longer for Gatewood to learn than it does for most. Here he was, a twenty-five-year-old freshman, with not much to show in the way of life accomplishments. Already a former paper delivery worker, a clothing salesman, an honorably discharged Marine, a milkman, and now a bouncer, he didn't want to continue a life of underachievement and inaction. He saw now that drinking was only getting in the way.

Finally he quit his job at the Paddock and forced himself to stay in his room and study. He began working full time at a restaurant on campus, working 40–48 hours a week while maintaining a full course load. It was difficult—not only the full schedule, but tearing himself away from the world of carousing and fellowship that he so enjoyed. Throughout his entire life, Gatewood always wanted to be the center of attention. The sacrifice he made to commit to his studies must have been painfully difficult.

This is the point in time where Gatewood decided that the only intoxicant he would use was marijuana. This decision also coincides with when he became more deeply interested in cannabis and hemp, and it would guide the rest of his life. While Gatewood framed this as a purely noble decision to focus on his studies, his family's past must have played a part. Gatewood was drinking a dozen beers a day. When he looked in the mirror he saw bloodshot eyes and an impressive beer gut. How could this not remind him of the struggles of his father? Surely this was in his mind when he decided to nix drinking: that perhaps he had inherited more from this father than just his smile and wit.

No matter the inner workings of Gatewood's mind, this decision had far-reaching implications. Gatewood's discipline allowed him the time and space to succeed where he had failed, and to sail toward graduation. It also turned his interests more fully to cannabis and issues related to marijuana activism and reform. These views would shape the rest of his time at the University of Kentucky and pave the way for his captivating public life.

Guided by his involvement in student organizations and his renewed commitment to his classes, Gatewood was able to graduate with a bachelor's degree in General Studies from the University of Kentucky in just three years, in 1974. Nearly a decade after he had first enrolled, and after a variety of jobs, a bankruptcy, and a trip to Parris Island, he finally had his ticket to the life he envisioned. Ever since his involvement in the May 1970 protests, Gatewood knew his future was in the law and politics. He saw only one path forward: law school. Luckily the University of Kentucky College of Law agreed, and even with his checkered academic past, he was accepted. His grade point average and high Law School Admission Test (LSAT) score showed the admissions board that he was serious.

Gatewood took the difficulty of law school in stride and claimed that he studied more than fifty hours a week for his entire first year in order to catch up to his peers and keep his grades up. He lived on the corner of 4th and Upper Streets in downtown Lexington, in the building that formerly housed the YWCA. Gatewood lived in one massive bedroom and rented out the rest to friends and family. Since he had sworn off alcohol, during his time in law school he started to increase his use of marijuana, which came to inform his thinking and studies.[28]

Gatewood's younger sister, Edna, remembered this building and this time well. Depending on when they were in school and what else was going on in their lives, multiple members of Gatewood's family would rent rooms in his downtown headquarters. Edna remembered it as a fun and exciting time. "We kind of cycled through this one bedroom and it was great to live with him. It was exciting, it was fun. And my mom said she didn't sleep a wink for many years. She'd wake up and think, oh my God, what's going on at that house?"[29]

Future Lexington mayor Theresa Isaac attended law school at the same time as Gatewood, and remembered that even though he was more serious and committed as a student, he still wanted to be the center of attention. "He was just, you know, a larger than life personality!" Isaac recalled that at gatherings that seemed to draw the entire cadre of law students, Gatewood would often hold court, telling one-liners and stories that made him the life of the party.[30]

In addition to using marijuana for recreational purposes, this was also the period when Gatewood became more deeply interested in national movements related to marijuana. The country's most prominent marijuana rights organization, the National Organization for the Reform of Marijuana Laws (NORML), was founded in Washington, DC, in 1970 by attorney Keith Stroup with funding from Hugh Hefner's Playboy Foundation. After merging with a variety of other national and regional organizations in the early 1970s, NORML was actively lobbying politicians and lawmaking bodies while Gatewood was in law school.[31]

Gatewood wrote that the work of NORML and other organizations was a good start, but it did not go far enough in addressing the issues he saw at the core of the marijuana issue. "However, this group's goals were described as effecting 'decriminalization,' which I felt was very limited and did not provide solutions for the questions of where would people get their herb if they didn't or couldn't grow their own and who would make money off the market as it emerged from under its criminal status."[32]

Throughout the 1970s, NORML played a major role in helping marijuana to be decriminalized in ten states. With President Jimmy Carter in the White House and a signal from his administration that decriminalization would be more widely considered, pro-marijuana advocates and groups like NORML seemed to be turning the tide. Carter advocated for more fines and moral suasion in discouraging people from using marijuana, in lieu of stricter penalties or jail time. In 1977 he famously said, "Penalties against possession of a drug should not be more damaging to an individual than the use of the drug itself."[33] With a somewhat reluctant ally in the White House, and a list of successful lobbying campaigns, NORML's work seemed to be making a real impact in the country.

But Gatewood's concerns remained. While decriminalization was a good step, it stopped short of the full legalization that he desired. What's more, NORML and other organizations did not consider the implications of their advocacy, namely who could access marijuana, how it would be regulated or taxed, and how they could stop corporations from taking control of yet another valuable industry.

Gatewood never let go of his childhood in Carlisle. He always thought first of the little guy, of the farmer, and of the families living in poverty who could potentially benefit from marijuana decriminalization and legalization. Of course, he was a naive third-year law student in 1976, but his unwillingness to compromise on marijuana reform is what made him a revered national advocate as well as a political candidate with relatively little hope of ever winning an election.

Gatewood decided that since others weren't addressing these questions, he would have to do so himself. This was the birth of his Model Plan for Legal Marijuana.

In August 1976, Gatewood published a three-part series in the *Kentucky Kernel* detailing his plan for the legalization of marijuana. It was scheduled for the first week students were back on campus, and Gatewood was champing at the bit to share his thoughts, ideas, and research. Throughout the three articles, Gatewood displayed his deep and intense knowledge of the history of marijuana, its uses, and the issues surrounding the idea of legalization. This was Gatewood's coming-out party, albeit in the pages of the student newspaper. He was approaching the end of law school, and he knew that this was one way to make a splash. As we have seen, not many of his close friends in college remembered him being too interested in marijuana while an undergraduate. He was much more invested in beer and liquor, and was famous for his rabble rousing. His decision to give up drinking in favor of smoking marijuana led to a blossoming interest in the crop. In law school his study of laws and regulations led to an even more intense interest. It was time to share his ideas with the world.

The first article was published in the Editorials & Comments section of the *Kernel* on August 25, 1976. Titled "Marijuana: Laws, Views Must Change," it introduced the issue to his readers, particularly claiming marijuana's historical use as a justification for addressing the drug laws of the United States as "repressive, totally unrealistic in their portrayal of its dangers and obviously unenforceable."

Gatewood addressed the changing landscape of marijuana laws in America, even referencing then-governor Jimmy Carter's support for decriminalization as part of his presidential candidacy. Aside from claiming that decriminalization would not go far enough, the article further addressed the future of marijuana by discussing the implications of legalization. Always with Carlisle and the small farming communities of Kentucky in mind, Gatewood wrote that there must be a plan in place to be certain that a future cash crop as valuable as marijuana would not benefit major corporations or the rich alone. Writing a line that he would later adapt and use often on the campaign trail, Gatewood explained, "However, if we leave this movement to [chance], it will be a very familiar story in that those interests with large sums of money to spend will control the rules as usual and, just as usually, the small landowners will be left to fight among themselves for the leftovers." He argued that the "inevitable" legalization of the drug needed to be addressed so that there could be thousands of farmers making "$15,000 a year from the growing of pot" rather than a few privileged corporations making millions.[34]

In the second article in the series, Gatewood investigated the history of marijuana persecution. He reviewed the long and sordid history of how cannabis was policed in the United States, and pointed to the racist roots of the practice. Startlingly anticipating the same arguments made nearly fifty years later in the midst of the Black Lives Matter movement, Gatewood detailed how marijuana laws were mainly created to punish certain segments of society. Discussing the passage of the Boggs Act of 1951 that ratcheted up criminal penalties for drug possession, Gatewood wrote, "This increased the criminal sanctions against the use of marijuana by sentencing to 10 years or more in the federal penitentiary those users caught possessing. These were mostly black, a very repressed people in those years."

He also used this article to discuss the Drug Enforcement Agency and the federal War on Drugs. Even in 1974, the DEA budget was $135 million. "That averages out to $64,285 per agent for one year. That's great pay to prosecute anyone, much less the quite unthreatening marijuana user." Previewing arguments that he would make for the next four decades in public life, Gatewood predicted that these laws would soon change. He would be continually disappointed in this prediction.[35]

Gatewood used the final article in this series to discuss the details of his plan, and to advocate for the small farmer over large corporations. Aside from the large marijuana plant graphic that rendered much of the article illegible, Gatewood reiterated the value of his plan: that this cash crop perfectly suited the Kentucky climate and soil and could conceivably enrich nearly every farmer in the commonwealth who was just trying to scrape by. He broke down the mechanics of his model plan, discussing an allotment, closed market, and tax system that would make the state government responsible for regulating the sale of marijuana while raising revenue for the state as well as for the farmers who participated.[36]

Gatewood's "Model Plan" is extremely important in understanding the rest of his life pursuing public office. From 1976 on, he basically never wavered from this proposal, dreamed up as a young law student. He would repeat these ideas and theories for years to come, on concert stages, in bingo halls, in political forums, and on television, at every opportunity. The plan also speaks to the contradictions in Gatewood's political ideals. He was often portrayed as a libertarian, but in favor of intricate state regulation.

Where Gatewood saw common sense, experts and politicians saw naiveté. Much of Gatewood's argument focused on a conjecture that he had already accepted for fact: that marijuana was not harmful and that it did not warrant criminalization. While the history of cannabis in the United States is covered at length in a variety of studies, suffice it to say that Kentucky, a socially conservative state, was not fertile ground for this reasoning.

Following this publicity, Gatewood even gave his plan a new name: the Kentucky Marijuana Feasibility Study. He also filed articles of incorporation for a new organization, calling it the Future Marijuana Growers of Kentucky, Inc.

In the articles of incorporation, Gatewood introduced the organization: "Kentucky Marijuana Feasibility Study, Inc. is a Lexington-based non-profit organization which has studied the possibility of marijuana as a cash-crop, specifically in Kentucky and generally in the South. As a result of our efforts, we have derived a model plan adoptable on the state level for the growth and marketing of marijuana in a manner which will benefit the most people in the greatest way."[37]

In the pages of the 1976 *Kernel*, Gatewood laid out the political reasoning, strategy, and passion that would guide his relentless pursuit for political office. This would bring him some measure of fame and popularity, yet it would also doom any real chance he had of accomplishing his goals. But was this a trade-off that Gatewood willingly accepted?

Gatewood had doubled down on his future, giving up on partying and drinking, and by all accounts he worked hard to make it through law school and to pass his classes. By the spring of 1977 he had finished classes and it was time to sit for the Kentucky Bar Exam. As part of this process, Gatewood needed three people to endorse his application. In his memoir, Gatewood wrote about approaching various local judges, politicians, and even the current president of the University of Kentucky, Otis Singletary, for their endorsements. Because of the Feasibility Study and his outspoken views on the issue of marijuana legalization, he wasn't able to secure any of their signatures. So instead Gatewood did something completely in character. He approached two of the housekeepers at the law school and an electrician who worked on campus. Since he had spent years talking with them, they were quick to offer their endorsements, and Gatewood was able to sit for the bar exam.[38]

By his own admission, Gatewood's grades in law school weren't stellar, but they were firmly good enough. He took a review course, sat for the exam, and waited for the results. Since the names of students who passed the bar were published in the local newspaper, Gatewood would find out with the rest of the world whether or not he could practice law. Unfortunately, he was disappointed. His name did not appear with those who passed the bar, and he was back to square one.

Gatewood would later fail the bar exam a second time, and he was always suspicious of the anonymized procedure for grading the exam. He believed that because he had garnered some measure of infamy for the Feasibility Study and his outspoken stance on marijuana, he was being targeted. It's safe to say that this amounted to paranoia and some inability to accept the reality of his failures. Whether through their protective instincts or a genuine belief in a concerted conspiracy, much of his family seemed to side with him.

His sister, Liz, agreed with the assessment that his public interest in marijuana prevented him from fair treatment when sitting for the exam. "He took the bar two or three times, not because he wasn't smart enough to pass it, but because he got involved in marijuana. I mean, that's my own feeling."[39] This distrust of public institutions, and of the status quo, stuck with Gatewood ever after.

Gatewood's legal career was on hold, and he was trying to figure out his next steps. Most of these plans revolved around studying even harder for his next attempt at the bar exam. This didn't stop him from the occasional social dalliance, and on one of these occasions he "smiled at the beautiful, long-haired woman sitting over by the bandstand" at the Jefferson Davis Inn in downtown Lexington. Luckily, his "heart perked up considerably when she smiled back."[40]

"I think I had met Gatewood several times, at parties or whatever, but I do recall talking to him for the first time, for a long time, at the Jefferson Davis Inn, probably late one afternoon," Sears recalled. This was in June of 1978, and Susan Sears was a twenty-four-year-old UK graduate student who was teaching philosophy at the university. Gatewood was smitten immediately, and the feeling was mutual.

Gatewood Galbraith with his parents at his wedding, 1978. Gatewood maintained a close relationship with his parents and siblings. His mother always defended her ambitious son.

"I was really interested in what he was doing. We were both politically active." Susan remembered how important social issues and activism were in their attraction and relationship. "He was certainly political, but he was incredibly, we were both incredibly, passionate about social justice and people who were disadvantaged."[41]

Susan was raised to take a keen interest in social justice issues, and to pay attention to politics. When Martin Luther King Jr. and other members of the Southern Christian Leadership Conference organized a 1963 march in Kentucky's capital, Frankfort, Susan's mom pulled her out of school so that they could attend together. Her father was in the military and was charged with notifying families in the Owensboro area and the tristate region of deaths during the Vietnam War. Susan grew up with the reality of the war, as well as the social injustices that plagued the country. This was someone who was committed to changing the world, who was ambitious, intelligent, and deeply interesting. To put it simply, Susan checked all of the boxes for Gatewood.

"I think, though, the connection that we had, just right away, I think the word we used for it . . . was unimpeachable, just undeniable and unimpeachable, and it was there. So we spent a lot of time together between June and August, and by August we had decided we wanted to get married that fall."[42] Gatewood's ambition and Susan's intelligence and passion made this decision a no-brainer for both of them. They were fascinated by one another, and it didn't take long for them to decide that they should spend their lives together.

They were married the Saturday after Thanksgiving, a date chosen because Susan and Gatewood agreed that their lives shared a common theme of gratitude. They had spent time discussing their values and what was most important in their lives. Gratitude was the value at the top of the list, and practicing it was the critical family ethic they would later prioritize with their children. They were young and in love, and Gatewood and Susan fed off one another's energy.

While their marriage and new relationship was a bright spot in their lives, reality set in soon after. As was often the case, Gatewood still felt adrift. He tried and failed to pass the bar exam a second time, and needed to find some way to make money. He briefly held various jobs to try to make a living, including selling encyclopedias and vacuum cleaners door to door. Because the Kentucky bar had a three-strikes rule, he only had one more chance to pass. The future he envisioned while raising hell on UK's campus hung by a thread. He wanted to change the laws he saw as unjust, and already he was feeling a desire to run for public office. These decisions, these twists of fate, would also have implications for his marriage and his soon-to-be-growing family.

Susan and Gatewood wasted no time in starting their family, welcoming a daughter just over a year following their wedding. She was nearly a month late, and was delivered by the same Dr. Phillip Crossen whom Gatewood had defended all those years earlier on the steps of the Fayette County courthouse, and whose farm had hosted the Woodstick concert. While Susan was pushing, Gatewood played "Here Comes the Sun" by the Beatles on a small cassette player they had prepared. They had planned on playing the song in preparing for the birth of their first child, for they felt that it embodied the joy about to enter their lives. Even though she was born in the midst of winter, they already had her name picked out: Summer. To the young parents it signified warmth, light and the brightness of their future together.

Susan remembered how enamored they were with Summer. "But, you know, having this baby, I remember we, we couldn't, we just sat and watched her even when she was sleeping. We couldn't take our eyes off her." In the midst of the chaos and anxiety of trying to scrape together a living, Gatewood and Susan were given the most precious of gifts. They loved their young family, and built a tight community of friends in Lexington.[43]

The Galbraiths, circa 1979. Gatewood married Susan Sears in 1978, and the couple welcomed their first child, Summer, in 1979.

While he was trying to patch together enough money to support his family, Gatewood demonstrated his entrepreneurial spirit and vision for innovation. A Canadian businessman named Bill Spence contacted Gatewood about a new invention. Called the Quadractor, it was an all-terrain four-wheel-drive mowing and towing machine. In his autobiography, Gatewood described it with passion: "a four-wheel drive, four-wheel steering machine that looks like a table with a motor and seat on top and same-size wheels at the bottom of all four legs. It was belt driven, sending power to the legs, which were, in effect, vertical axles." The real draw of this machine was its versatility and safety when working on steep slopes and hillsides. It could be used anywhere from forests to rice paddies.[44]

A July 1979 article in *Mother Earth News* also lauded the contraption, calling it "half tractor, half June beetle on casters" and listing its impressive features: "[a] turns on a dime, [b] pulls *eight times* its own weight, [c] climbs a 42 degree slope, [d] maneuvers over rocks or through streams, and [e] logs, plows, discs, cultivates, and mows."[45]

Gatewood spent two years traveling to discuss the wonders of the Quadractor, and he secured partnerships with businesses throughout Tennessee and Kentucky. Envisioning this as a path to a secure living, he put his ambitions for a law career on hold to try to develop the prospects for this

Before he passed the bar exam, Gatewood invested his time and money in the JAC Quadractor, a farm implement for which he saw great promise.

miracle machine. He invested all of his savings in the project, and he was desperate to make some money for his family. He saw the machine as perfectly designed for the steep hillsides and unforgiving terrain of Appalachia. It also held great potential, in Asia and throughout the world, for mitigating the hazardous working conditions of farmers who were routinely put at risk of dangerous falls during their labor.

In 1981 Spence gathered his group of investors to inform them of some bad news: after negotiations to have the machine built in China, he had lost control of the company and had sold it to business interests overseas. Gatewood's dream was gone in an instant, and with it his only hope for scraping a living. As he put it, "I had hoped this would be the way I could make my living. Now it just vanished into thin air."[46]

During this dramatic turn in Gatewood's fortunes, he and Susan welcomed their second daughter, Abby. Susan recalled Abby being born "screaming at the top of her lungs." This arrival foretold Abby's future role as an independent, take-charge young woman who was "always the most vocal to some extent."[47]

Gatewood was once again blown away and overjoyed by this new addition to their family, writing, "This time I got to cut the cord and the miracle of birth amazed me a second time. You cannot watch this happen and not believe in miracles. I certainly can't."[48]

Once again, Gatewood was out of options, and now he was responsible for two young daughters. After he turned back to selling encyclopedias, he received some great news. A legal challenge had overturned the three-strikes rule for the Kentucky Bar Exam. Gatewood took the bar review for the third time, then sat for the exam for the third time in three years. Eleven years after his revelation standing between protestors and National Guard troops on Limestone Street next to UK's campus, Gatewood finally did it: he became a practicing attorney.

It must have been one of the biggest thrills of Gatewood's life to open the pages of the *Louisville Courier-Journal* on Sunday, May 10, 1981, and to finally see his name listed in a simple article headed "Here is a list of the people who passed state bar exam."[49]

In recalling this personal achievement, Gatewood couldn't help defending his failed attempts of the past. "I truly hope it had nothing to do with the fact that they had replaced the Chief Bar Examiner who had graded my last two attempts. But I'm pretty sure it did."[50]

These eleven years, from 1970 to 1981, laid the groundwork for the rest of Gatewood's life. From a bankrupt twenty-three-year-old milkman to a practicing attorney, Gatewood matured, albeit much later than his family, or he, expected. Gatewood came to grips with some of his failures, and allowed his passions and beliefs to shape his life. It took him a while, but he did mature. Giving rein to his vision of the future, he shook off some of the demons that had haunted his path in life: the inability to stay in school, a wild, alcohol-fueled lifestyle, and a lack of commitment to his life's purpose.

Gatewood had recommitted himself to a promising future and transformed from a Marine recruit to an avid antiwar activist. After spending years hanging around the University of Kentucky campus, he became a twenty-four-year-old freshman in 1971. Witnessing the protests of May 1970, Gatewood had realized that in order to change society, he needed to take part in its most sacred institutions: the law and politics. He would be a thorn in the side of the UK administration for the next seven years. This was Gatewood's first real taste of fame, and he relished the spotlight. He was certainly sincere in his beliefs about Vietnam and how UK was run, but it was also undeniable that he reveled in leading protests, speaking in front of hundreds of his colleagues, and being the center of attention.

Without yet realizing it, he was in the process of creating the blueprint of his future political aspirations. Drawn to irreverent and rebellious figures like Dr. Gene Mason, Gatewood despised authority and used controversy as a tool to draw attention to the causes close to his heart. Practicing the lines and speaking style he would echo for the next four decades on the public stage, Gatewood perfected his gravelly baritone and quick one-liners. Whether leading a protest, challenging professors in class, or stealing the spotlight at student meetings, his time on campus was in shaping his future.

In the midst of this transformation, Gatewood realized that his self-destructive lifestyle was getting in the way of his life and negatively affecting those around him. Haunted by the constant reality of his father's alcoholism, he showed determination and maturity by quitting his work at the Paddock and giving up alcohol altogether. This was the second decision that paved the way for his future political fame. While he had experimented with marijuana ever since that fateful day when Teddy showed up on his doorstep, his use amped up while on campus.

After graduating with outstanding grades in just three years, Gatewood was accepted to the University of Kentucky law school and nearly exhausted himself to keep up with his classmates. He spent this time starting to evangelize for cannabis regulation and legalization, most notably in his Marijuana Feasibility Study, which made a splash throughout the commonwealth. His articles announcing the plan in the *Kentucky Kernel* and his incorporation created political ripples across campus, in Lexington, and even in Frankfort. He struggled to pass the bar exam, finding out the hard way that his intelligence and cleverness weren't always enough to get by.

In the midst of this struggle he met a beautiful woman and beautiful person in Susan Sears, and their whirlwind romance changed the path of Gatewood's life, always for the better. He became a father, and with mouths to feed he felt the pressure to live up to his dreams. After pouring his heart, soul, and wallet into the failed Quadractor, Gatewood was still selling encyclopedias door to door to try to make ends meet. On his third attempt he finally passed the bar and qualified to be a practicing attorney.

Much like his years as a child and teenager, his time at the University of Kentucky was full of setbacks, passion, and a determination that eventually paid off. His time leading protests and student organizing efforts at the University of Kentucky whetted his thirst for public recognition, a feeling he would constantly chase for years to come. Here he was, on the brink of public fame and scrutiny, now with higher stakes: a family to support, a future to build, and a vision to realize.

3

A True Pioneer in the Kentucky Spirit

"Lexington political activist Gatewood Galbraith outraged some, caused some to start thinking and garnered national publicity a few years ago when he proposed that Kentucky legalize marijuana. . . . He's practicing law—'mostly marijuana cases'—and still advocating pot as a Kentucky product."

These lines in the June 8, 1981, issue of the *Lexington Herald-Leader* are the first mention of Gatewood beginning to practice law. They reference his model plan for marijuana in Kentucky and the relative measure of fame it brought him. "'It's not a morality issue,' says Galbraith. 'It's an economic issue. Right now, Kentucky-grown marijuana is selling for $2,500 to $3,000 a pound in New York City. Look at how much farm income and tax revenue the state is losing.' Galbraith already is being rumored as a candidate for Kentucky agriculture commissioner in 1983."[1]

Gatewood was looking to make a splash as an attorney and as an increasingly public figure in Kentucky. He was, without a doubt, somewhat responsible for those rumblings about the 1983 election. Before we follow Gatewood down the path of politics, it's worth understanding the beginning of his legal career, and how he was seen in Lexington. As this article makes clear, Gatewood cherished the spotlight he had garnered while in law school. But he also needed to make some money.

Gatewood had tremendous promise as an attorney. Many of his early mentors encouraged him to focus solely on the law, and to develop a career based on civil rights and legal cases that spoke to his convictions. Gatewood did have a passion for the law, but he could never fully turn away from a life in politics.

As he tells it in his autobiography, his start in the law was fairly uneventful. His first job was in a small office right next to the old Lexington courthouse. He went into practice with a Lexington attorney named Jim Early, who had served as a public defender and was mainly a criminal defense attorney, something Gatewood was drawn to.

A quick survey of Early's cases throughout the 1980s paints a fascinating picture of his law practice. In 1984 he successfully defended court typist Marlene Halsey, who was accused of conspiracy in passing off carbon copies of secret grand jury testimony in a case involving Lexington socialite, horse breeder, and celebrity Anita Madden.[2] Later that year he defended Sung Hahner, who was accused of prostitution when a police officer said that she offered to have sex with him in exchange for forty dollars during a massage at a Lexington massage parlor. Hahner was found not guilty after a quick trial.[3] During a 1987 fundraiser for the American Cancer Society and the Markey Cancer Center, Early contributed his legal services for a full divorce to the auction.[4]

Early was clearly a character himself, which explains why Gatewood was attracted to his practice. Even with an outsized reputation, business was often hard to come by early in Gatewood's legal career. This led to even more stress. Gatewood's law license was supposed to relieve his financial issues. Instead it often just left him waiting for work to appear: "In 1981 I had a wife and two children and money was nonexistent, so I sat beside my office phone, for days at a time, hoping it would ring, and I could make grocery money for the week. Sometimes, I didn't."[5]

When he could get work, Gatewood had a natural talent in the courtroom. He was personable, and a talented speaker. All of that practice speaking out on campus, leading marches, and publicly advocating for his beliefs paid off once he was finally allowed to practice. Susan recalled his talent throughout his career, specifically his ability to connect with the humans in a courtroom. "What he was just extremely, extremely good at, and that is, speaking to a jury, speaking from the heart, looking a witness in the eye, and speaking the truth."[6]

Even though it was still difficult to make a living, Gatewood relished his work. In describing the feeling of hearing a "not guilty" verdict when he was defending clients, Gatewood found bliss. "Maybe it's just me but next to the love of my daughters, a forty-foot putt and sex, it doesn't get much better than a Not Guilty verdict."[7]

Fed by the attention he had received as a law student for his Model Plan for Legal Marijuana, Gatewood was already thinking about running for public office. It was now clear to him that the issue of hemp and marijuana legalization was his key to planting his foot in the door of Kentucky politics. What's more, he wasn't going to wait in line for this opportunity. He had big, bold ideas, and he loved the attention they brought. Gatewood was already becoming famous in Kentucky political circles.

In January of 1983, Gatewood declared his intention to run for public office for the first time. In a short news snippet in the *Lexington Herald-Leader* it became official: "Well, heh, heh, some thought it was a joke last year when Lexington lawyer Gatewood Galbraith said he planned to run for Kentucky agriculture commissioner on a platform that included legalization of marijuana—and a heavy tax on the weed to fatten up lean state coffers. Since then, Galbraith's been raising an illicit crop of supporters. 'I'm setting Jan. 24 as my target date for announcing,' says he."[8]

If his Model Plan was the first hint of his political aspirations, this was his coming-out party. The rambunctious, self-conscious, comedic young child from Carlisle had found his calling, some thirty years after being inspired by Governor Bert T. Combs at the Nicholas County Fair. What would be his first campaign slogan? "Galbraith—A True Pioneer in the Kentucky Spirit."[9]

To better understand his decision, it's worth taking a broader view of the political landscape in Kentucky during this time. It's obvious that Gatewood was considering a run for public office as far back as 1977, while still in law school. The small fraction of attention and fame that he garnered in response to his Model Plan made him thirsty for more. In fact, if we take his words at face value, much of his motivation to complete his undergraduate studies and attend law school stemmed from his desire to become part of the very system he wished to change. He decided to enter that system during an interesting time of transition in Kentucky's history.

Gatewood may have chosen this time to enter state politics in large part due to a recent example of success by a splashy and controversial figure. In March of 1979, with only a few weeks left before a crowded May primary, John Y. Brown Jr. flew into Louisville and announced his intention to run for governor. He proceeded to spend much of his personal fortune on the campaign, drawn from the deep coffers of his success promoting and expanding the Kentucky Fried Chicken restaurant chain throughout the country. A tall, handsome, and well-groomed businessman, he and his wife, the former sportscaster and Miss America winner Phyllis George, campaigned across the state. He eked out a victory in the Democratic primary and then soundly defeated former governor Louie B. Nunn in November's general election. This was not much of a surprise: Brown benefited from a state that then boasted 2.5 Democratic voters registered for every Republican.[10]

Gatewood assuredly drew inspiration from Brown's run, as he was also seen as someone from outside the political establishment who made a splash in newspapers and on the local news stations during the campaign. Here

Gatewood was, trying to justify a run at state office with no past political experience, as an outsider trying to subsist on media attention over a splashy and controversial issue.

Al Cross is a member of the Kentucky Journalism Hall of Fame and served as a reporter for the *Louisville Courier-Journal* for over twenty-six years. He was the chief political writer for the *Courier-Journal* for fifteen years and covered most major political campaigns in the commonwealth. Cross currently serves as the director of the Institute for Rural Journalism and Community Issues and is a prominent writer, commentator, and author on issues related to political history in Kentucky. Cross pointed out that Kentucky was already in the midst of a massive shift by the early 1980s. "This change hasn't been fairly quick. It's been going on for a long time, and it began in the 1950s." In a series of state and national elections, the longtime stronghold of Democratic politics in Kentucky shifted right pretty much constantly for the next seventy years. "Liberal Democrats in Kentucky have always been in a minority. And as cultural issues came to dominate, people were driven by their culture and their backgrounds into the Republican Party."[11]

This process, among other trends, spurred on Republican candidates to slowly win more and more federal, statewide, and local elections in Kentucky. The shift to cultural issues resulted in many of these victories, included Ronald Reagan's victory over Jimmy Carter in the presidential election of 1980, when Kentucky voted for the Republican challenger over the Democratic incumbent by a mere 17,000 votes. A few years later, in 1984, Reagan won the state in a landslide, helping to elect a young political hopeful named Mitch McConnell to a vacant U.S. Senate seat. "Now, McConnell likes to argue that Reagan's coattails didn't elect him, but that is just poppycock. Yeah. If you hadn't had such a strong Republican candidate on the ballot, then McConnell wouldn't have won by five thousand votes or so," Cross explained. "You know, Kentuckians are culturally conservative. And as the Republican Party embraced these issues of cultural conservatism, people in Kentucky found a more comfortable home in the Republican Party."[12]

Deep in the midst of these transitions, Gatewood decided to throw his hat in the ring. It's fair to wonder, was he serious about this run, or was this simply a ploy for publicity and fame? In fact, questions like these would follow Gatewood for the rest of his life. They didn't come just from Kentucky voters or political operatives, but from his own family.

"It happened pretty quick," his sister Edna remembered. "It was just like, whoa, that's interesting, right? It was a Saturday and he was dreaming of 'Where do I start with this life as a politician?' You know, we often thought, why don't you put that much passion into your law practice and build that up so you'd have some security, financial security?"[13]

His sister Liz echoed this sentiment. "What we were in favor of was to start a little bit lower than the agriculture [commissioner], you know, get on the city council or something like that and then work up to it. He never wanted to start there. He wanted to start at the top."[14]

Liz remembered that their mother, Dollie, was always a steadfast supporter. Some Lexington residents regarded Gatewood and his candidacy as a joke, and did not have kind words for him. When Dollie in a restaurant or a store would sign her name, often the clerk would ask, "Are you related to Gatewood?" After a few uncomfortable run-ins, when people asked this, Dollie would often retort, "So why do you want to know?"[15] She might then go on to explain her support for her son, and the passions that drove him to politics.

Gatewood's little brother, Mike, saw a different reason for his first campaign. Mike remembered Gatewood going on and on about the benefits of hemp, from motor fuel to paper, and he saw his brother's first attempt at statewide office as an affirmation of his deeply held beliefs. "And so seeing those kinds of practical applications for what Kentucky farmers could do with a handy crop kind of spurred Gatewood to take up that cause and then challenge the political establishment through running for office to try to advance that vision. So that was just another thing that kind of drove Gatewood."[16] Mike understood this as a natural progression for Gatewood, a choice that had to be made.

Susan strongly supported his run for office and knew it was important to Gatewood. "Agriculture made perfect sense to me, given what he wanted to accomplish and the manner in which he wanted to accomplish it. And I was all in at that point." Even though they were scraping by on Susan's teaching stipend and the small amount of money Gatewood was managing to generate in his law practice, times were still tough. Susan worked twenty hours at a week at the local food co-op in Lexington so that they could get their groceries at a discount.[17]

While Gatewood was preparing for the campaign, he and Susan experienced loss and heartache. Susan was eleven weeks pregnant with twins when, on September 20, 1982, and their daughter Abby's first birthday, she started to experience extreme pain while grading and studying at the University of Kentucky M. I. King Library. She lost the babies that day, and she and Gatewood were left to grieve during an already stressful and worrying time.

While experiencing crisis in his personal life, Gatewood was still convinced of the need to run for office. His youth in Carlisle was still near to his heart, and he yearned to test his ideas on the campaign trail. The answer to why he ran for office in 1983 is somewhere between these two realities: it was neither a purely altruistic choice to help farmers, nor only to seek some measure of personal renown. Gatewood had the knowledge and motivation to start his political career, and that was all he really needed to justify the decision. He felt he had no other choice than to take the public's temperature and to see how his ideas played out in an election. He had the support of his wife, even while they were struggling to raise two young children without much money. No matter the internal reasoning, he was on the brink of his political future and was thrilled to be in the game.

After Gatewood formally filed to run in the Democratic primary for the office of agriculture commissioner in January 1983, he began to take stock of the race and his competition. Gatewood faced three other hopefuls in the 1983 May primary for the privilege of running against whoever the Republicans nominated. David Boswell was a member of the state House from western Kentucky but was relatively unknown on the statewide stage going into the election. Tom Harris, from Carrollton, was a fixture in state politics who had served as agriculture commissioner from 1975 to 1979. Ward "Butch" Burnette was a farmer and Kentucky state representative from Fulton who, by the early 1980s, had already been in legal hot water for shady financial decisions while in public office.

From the outset, Gatewood received a fair amount of media attention, nearly all of it focused on one thing: his support for legalizing hemp and regulating marijuana. This was, after all, Gatewood's sole reason for getting involved in the race. Throughout public forums, debates, and media interviews, Gatewood stuck to his guns and focused on the same components that he published in the Model Plan seven years earlier.

"Galbraith, 36, is running the most unusual campaign, built around a call to legalize marijuana, or hemp, as a cash crop for Kentucky farmers. Before being outlawed as a drug, hemp was widely grown in Kentucky for its seed and fibers, which were used in a variety of applications. While admitting that his views on marijuana may antagonize some voters, Galbraith says that, 'after hearing me speak many people who never before were associated with marijuana agree that the present laws are unworkable.'" The *Lexington Herald-Leader* reported on Gatewood's ideas somewhat skeptically, noting that Gatewood also made medical claims about the potential uses of marijuana. "In addition, he said that the chemicals in marijuana have been proven to have medicinal value. If those chemicals are to be widely used, he said, they should be produced from Kentucky grown plants and not by large pharmaceutical houses."[18]

In a 1983 candidate forum hosted by Kentucky Educational Television before the primary, Gatewood defended his stance and ideas and showed an impressive command of the other issues facing Kentucky farmers. Sporting a tan suit and wearing his brown hair in youthful curls, Gatewood was confident and austere. The very first question, as it most likely had to be, was asking Gatewood about his support for legalizing marijuana. The commentator framed this issue as the "main" platform of Gatewood's candidacy. Showing some defensiveness at being written off based on one issue, Gatewood responded, "I would disagree a slight bit. That is not my main platform. My main platform is to make farming profitable again. And the way I see making farming profitable again is to recapture the markets that the farmer used to have before the synthetic manufacturers came in and displaced them from their heritage of farming." Echoing arguments from his past that would go on to guide the rest of his time running for public office, Gatewood rattled off his understanding of how large corporations and businesses had ruined the practice of farming and agriculture for the state. "A hundred years ago the farmer produced all the fiber, all the medicine, and all the food. Today he produces little fiber, no medicine, and, if you go into a grocery store and look at the ingredients on a package, you'll find out that he's being displaced from his heritage of food production."

Pressed more on his stance, and facing an obvious disrespect of his views, Gatewood defended his knowledge on the subject. "I suggest that, given our heritage in growing hemp, that Kentucky be the leading state in producing marijuana as a medicine. I do not believe that the legislators will bury their head in the sand and avoid or ignore the potential hundreds of millions of dollars in the current legal markets that potentially exist for the Kentucky farmer right now." The forum hosts would not let up on Gatewood's controversial stance on using marijuana recreationally, continuing to question him about it. He finally responded unequivocally, "I do not believe the current marijuana laws are working. I don't believe anybody can make any argument that they are working. They are not keeping it out of the hands of the children, they are not taking it out of the hands of the criminal element."[19]

Having the benefit of forty years of history, we know that Gatewood's stance was naive. The potential profits to be derived from medical or recreational marijuana were not enough to draw this through Kentucky's legislature. But Gatewood proved throughout the forum that he was no joke. He knew his issues, marijuana or not, and seemed just as qualified and well versed as Boswell, Harris, or Burnette.

In an editorial published a few weeks before the primary election, the editorial staff of the *Herald-Leader* endorsed Boswell in the race, lengthening Gatewood's already long odds. The article framed the election as a battle of attrition, where Boswell was the proper choice for office simply because he did not have anything to disqualify him. "Boswell hasn't attracted great attention in the legislature. He has worked hard and done a competent job, though. And, more important in the context of this race, he has done nothing that would keep him from being either a viable candidate or an acceptable state official. That sets him apart from his opponents in this race." The piece spent most of its ink attacking Harris, mainly for erstwhile low-interest student loans given preferentially to his children. But it also made clear the obvious distaste and lack of credence given to Gatewood's ideas by the media. "One of his opponents, state Rep. Ward 'Butch' Burnette, pleaded guilty last year to a misdemeanor charge of misusing $41 of a federal loan. Another candidate, Lexington lawyer Gatewood Galbraith, is basing his campaign on a proposal to legalize marijuana."[20]

The *Herald-Leader*, by taking one line to write off Gatewood's candidacy, perfectly reflected the predominant national sentiment regarding hemp and marijuana. It certainly illustrated Kentucky's reticence to accept hemp and marijuana legalization as a serious political idea. This was the beginning of an important contradiction and conflict in Gatewood's political life. The one issue that provided oxygen to the proverbial fire of his political aspirations also left him as the butt of many jokes, and as a candidate not to be taken seriously. Again, the question remains: Did Gatewood understand this, or did he truly believe that the issue would get a fair shake in the culturally conservative landscape of his native Kentucky?

In this way, Gatewood did live up to his campaign slogan. He was a true pioneer for a radical idea that, as he maintained vehemently, would actually help Kentucky farmers. He had in mind those friends and families he had left back in Carlisle, and he recognized their faces in every bingo hall, fraternal lodge, and office park throughout the campaign. While some saw him as a joke, he was not a buffoon. He defended his position expertly, was knowledgeable about how his ideas could actually help people, and was well versed in what life was actually like for these families. This didn't make the issue any easier for Kentuckians to endorse, but it also didn't allow the other candidates to write him off. He was clearly well prepared, quick witted, and encyclopedic regarding the issues that he advocated for. As Gatewood wrote of that election, "Sure, I got laughed at, but never to my face. And no one proved me wrong. That was extremely important to me."[21]

On the night of the May 24 primary, Gatewood and Susan huddled with close friends in a Lexington bar to watch the election results. Gatewood fared poorly in the crowded four-person field. David Boswell scored a resounding victory, winning by more than 30,000 votes. Gatewood finished a very distant fourth, racking up just over 40,000 votes, some 50,000 behind third-place Tom Harris.[22] He did finish second in Lexington's Fayette County, his best county result of the night. This spoke to the fame and reputation he was building in his home city, which would be key to encouraging him to run for future political offices. While Gatewood hoped he would fare better in the race, he still found the results encouraging. He had raised little money and had still made an impression on more than 40,000 voters.

Gatewood claimed that he spent $8,500 on his campaign, while Boswell had spent hundreds of thousands. He also touted his 11.5 percent vote share as something that shocked the political world. It's easy to see that this was overstated. In a four-way race for a fairly minor state office, he finished last by a good 50,000 votes. But the experience did give Gatewood a taste for future ventures in politics. He had campaigned. He had debated, and shaken hands, and driven across the commonwealth in every direction to reach voters. He was in love.

The race also had the effect of improving his name recognition. The newspaper stories and shots of Gatewood on local news channels had accomplished something, at least. People had heard of him, and publicity was invaluable to a new attorney hustling for business. He wrote, "My first year of practice, 1982, I grossed $17,252. During the year 1983, when I spent the first four months campaigning, I grossed $24,531. In 1984 it jumped to $54,541. I may not have won my first race, but business had definitely picked up."[23]

Gatewood got back to practicing law and supporting his family, and Susan continued her work at the university. Susan recalled the feeling of relief they both had following the campaign: "We made it, you know, we just were through this . . . and I felt like I could breathe again." But in this moment of blissful relief after a stressful few months, tragedy struck once more. Susan was about five months pregnant in May 1983 when, just a week after the primary election, she started to feel unwell while Gatewood was appearing in court in nearby Winchester. "And it wasn't long after he left when, um, I gave birth to that baby." Extremely premature, the baby did not survive, and Susan was on the verge of losing her own life. "As I recall, they were pretty close to coding me, I lost so much blood by the time we got there."[24]

Gatewood rushed to the hospital as soon his family contacted him. They grieved this loss together, especially because they were never able to hold their baby. Both miscarriages had an impact on Gatewood and Susan, but this loss was especially difficult because of how far along she was. They were told the baby was a boy and they didn't get to name him or properly say goodbye.

This crushing loss, coming on top of the stress and frustration of Gatewood's run for office and their difficulty in providing for their family, pushed Susan, and soon Gatewood, to seek therapy and counseling for grief and for their marriage. This continued for five years, and during it Gatewood owned to the stress that he had put on his wife and his family. Referencing the most recent miscarriage, Gatewood said, "Susie, I don't know why this happened . . . but I will not run for political office again until we are financially stable enough for me to do that without all this stress. I promise you."[25]

Financial stability would nearly always remain out of reach for Gatewood. This promise, and the inherent difficulty, stress, and trauma brought on by his first run for office, would overshadow his marriage. For the next seven years, Gatewood kept his word. He would work as an attorney and support his young family. But his initial taste of political fame and attention did little to quench his thirst for the limelight. Even as he grew his practice as an attorney and his presence in the Lexington area, he constantly sought out a platform to spread and test his ideas on the public, and to become the unifying voice for hemp and marijuana throughout the commonwealth.

Following the primary, Gatewood did return to his law practice, but he also found time to interject himself into every public conversation regarding the debate over the regulation or legalization of marijuana. Boswell had cruised to victory in the general election, as did the other Democrats running for statewide office. Even though Gatewood couldn't find a way to the general election that November, his name remained in the newspapers. Throughout the mid-1980s the conversation about limiting the production and sale of illegal marijuana focused a lot on one little-known chemical: paraquat.

Paraquat was a powerful herbicide first used by U.S. troops in the jungles of Vietnam. Extremely toxic, the chemical could kill marijuana plants in a single day. As part of the effort to cut down on the importation of marijuana from Mexico, President Gerald Ford's administration negotiated with Mexico to provide funding to spray Mexican marijuana crops with paraquat from aircraft, a practice that persisted through 1978. The public caught wind of it after articles appeared in *High Times* and *Time* magazine later that year. Suddenly cannabis users across the country were up in arms about this toxic chemical and the effect that it might have on smokers. Some reports stated that the inhalation of paraquat could inalterably damage human lungs in just a few months of use. They described a painful, slow suffocation that quickly incited panic across the country. Later reports debunked many of these claims, showing that actual paraquat exposure and harmful effects were vastly overstated by various publications.[26]

The stigma around the use of paraquat survived this public trial, and the herbicide continued to elicit panicked responses whenever it was offered as a potential solution to illegal growing. The controversy reached Kentucky shortly before the general election of 1983, when it was reported that federal officials were considering using paraquat to destroy illegal cannabis crops being grown in the Daniel Boone National Forest in eastern Kentucky. The DEA had already started spraying marijuana fields in northern Georgia and were eyeing other potential targets. When a U.S. district judge issued a temporary restraining order on this practice, Gatewood saw his chance.

"Gatewood Galbraith, a Lexington lawyer who favors legalization of marijuana as a cash crop in Kentucky, said yesterday that the Georgia action could set a precedent to halt paraquat spraying," reported the *Herald-Leader*. "He also said that he 'will be fashioning a suit before the federal court' in Lexington to prevent paraquat's use in Kentucky."[27]

Public outrage did little to dissuade the DEA, and they actually did do some limited spraying of paraquat on illicit marijuana plants later in 1983. That decision was derided by Kentucky politicians, including then-governor John Y. Brown Jr., Senator Wendell H. Ford, and Congressman Hal Rogers, who represented eastern Kentucky in the House of Representatives. In 1985 the DEA once again threatened to spray 15,000 acres of non-federal land in Kentucky, California, and Georgia. Even though the Kentucky State Police could not use paraquat as the DEA could, they still reported destroying 120,000 marijuana plants throughout the commonwealth on 559 separate small plots. When asked his opinion on this latest development, Gatewood offered, "If they do that, I don't know how I will be able to protest, but I will sure try."[28]

Further cementing his role as the leading voice on the issue, Gatewood weighed in anytime that marijuana or hemp would make the news. Often Gatewood was used as a foil by the Kentucky State Police, who increasingly focused on eradicating marijuana in the rural areas of the state. In a 1984 investigation, the Kentucky State Police estimated that marijuana was the second most profitable crop in Kentucky, second only to tobacco. "There's no doubt marijuana is a booming business in Kentucky. The illicit crop brings in anywhere from \$167–\$600 million a year, according to available estimates. At that volume, pot has become the second- or third-biggest cash crop in the state."

This study shows the remarkable financial impact that marijuana had in Kentucky. It was proof of what Gatewood had been saying since the mid-1970s. Farmers in Kentucky were suffering. Marijuana, even with the risks its illegality entailed, was one way to scratch out a living. "Lexington attorney

Gatewood Galbraith, who ran for state agricultural commissioner last year on a platform calling for the legalization of pot, views marijuana production as the way to overcome the 'absolutely desperate plight of farmers.'"

Given this "desperate plight," ideal growing conditions, and a long history with the crop, Kentucky punched above its weight in marijuana cultivation and production. Kevin Zeese, then national director of NORML, claimed that Kentucky was third in the country in marijuana profit, trailing only California and Hawaii. While not all public officials or agricultural bureaucrats believed these figures, Gatewood saw proof of the claims he had been making for a decade. "People will do damn near anything to stay on their farms. If it takes growing marijuana, that's what they'll do."[29]

This is also when Gatewood cemented his legacy as a national expert on marijuana and hemp. Since he began attending protests, festivals, and meetings in the mid-1970s, he had been building a network of activists in this controversial field. Starting in 1988, he and H. Paul Stanford, an activist and future entrepreneur of medical marijuana and hemp, forged a friendship based on their mutual interests. "Initially we would gather in Washington around these conferences," Stanford recalled. "You know, we'd have a hotel room and Gatewood and I would get together and smoke cannabis and talk about how to legalize it." As Stanford worked throughout the 1980s and 1990s to lobby the Oregon state legislature to legalize medical marijuana, he would often rely on Gatewood's expertise in drawing up legislation or working through public arguments. Referring to a recreational marijuana bill that failed in 2012, Stanford said, "We started drafting the wording for our initiative that made the ballot in 2012 in the late eighties, and Gatewood had quite a bit of input into that. We had input from about a hundred different experts around the world based on international law and federal laws and civil liberties rulings by the courts, specifically in Hawaii and Alaska and Michigan. But Gatewood was very helpful in that."[30]

Another member of this network who ended up being close friends with Gatewood and Stanford was Jack Herer. Herer, one of the most famous cannabis and hemp activists of all time, connected with Gatewood and Stanford at those same conferences. Beginning as a glass pipe entrepreneur and head shop owner in California, Herer quickly became one of the loudest and smartest voices for legalization in the country. In their first meeting, Gatewood mentioned being from Kentucky and that state's long history with hemp. Herer blew him away with encyclopedic knowledge of the plant, its uses, and what he perceived as its medicinal benefits.

Herer sparked an enlightenment and interest in Gatewood from this first meeting in the 1970s, and his work and activism guided Gatewood's beliefs and political persuasion. As Gatewood remembered, this initial meeting set in motion much of what he would publicly espouse for the rest of his life, and in his upcoming failed run for agriculture commissioner: "My mind raced in several different directions. If what this man was saying was true, how come it wasn't common knowledge where I came from, Kentucky? The world's largest producer of hemp for over one hundred years, and there was not a word of this spoken in any history class within the state."[31]

Herer's most influential work was a book titled *The Emperor Wears No Clothes*, in which he laid out a historical argument for the uses of hemp and marijuana and detailed their agricultural development, including their denigration and vilification by government and big business. Crafted for a certain audience, the book has drawn huge acclaim since it was published in 1985. While some experts disagree with some of Herer's findings, his book made him famous. Gatewood was a big fan, and Herer clearly showed that the feeling was mutual.

Filmed in the late 1980s, Herer and Gatewood were interviewed together. Referring to Gatewood's bona fides, Herer said of the Marijuana Feasibility Study, "This man wrote a book that I read that was one of the really . . . some of the greatest work on hemp long before I even really understood hemp." Herer heaped praised on Gatewood, who must have been delighted to hear from one of his heroes, "He wrote it in '77. . . . The Feasibility Study fucking blew my mind away. . . . He is not somebody who needs to come to me to learn about hemp. I learned a lot of my hemp from him."[32]

This relationship illustrates Gatewood's standing in the world of marijuana and hemp, but it also speaks to some important realizations about Gatewood's interests and motivations. He was clearly seen as one of the leading experts in this field, and crafted a vast network of like-minded experts, activists, and, yes, hippies, who admired him and his ideas. It also shows some of the appeal of Gatewood's beliefs. Even if he was not getting serious political attention at home in Kentucky, he expanded his vision to become a renowned expert among a community of similar believers. This reinforced the value of his ideas, and it also made Gatewood feel good about himself. He craved attention, and often public approval. If he couldn't find it at home, he needed to find a wider audience. In doing so, he happened to solidify his role as one of the heroes of the legalization movement across the country.

As Gatewood embodied the public face of the marijuana movement in Kentucky, he also began to think bigger. He began to court friends from across the country and build a network of experts, activists, doctors, and even the rare politician of similar mind. Rather than trying to evade being labeled "the marijuana candidate," Gatewood fully embraced his role and based much of his public and professional life on the fame he received for this issue. At the same time, he still had a family to provide for. The next few years would be a dizzying dance of legal cases, national activism, and fatherly responsibility. Gatewood's family was still growing, and he had to deal with the push and pull of everything that demanded his time and attention. His decisions over the next few years would alter his life and determine much of his legacy.

While Gatewood practiced law and maintained his public image, Susan was pregnant once again. Following the medical issues she had experienced, Susan's doctors were extremely cautious during this pregnancy. After four months of complete bed rest, Susan gave birth to their third daughter, Molly, a happy and healthy baby girl. Gatewood and Susan were overjoyed after the sorrow of the past couple of years, and Gatewood needed to buckle down even more to provide for their family. His small measure of fame did increase his revenue, but it never seemed to be enough. Gatewood's name continued to make news stories, and the variety of cases he handled gives some glimpse into his work as an attorney.

One case involved a man named Edgar Wallace, who represented Lexington's 1st District in the mid-1980s. Wallace had served six years on the Lexington Urban County Council when he was arrested on drug charges. Convicted of two misdemeanor drug offenses, for trafficking a simulated substance and marijuana, he was sentenced to a year in prison. After serving half his time, he applied for shock probation, by which inmates can be released early and put on probation for an extended period. Gatewood represented Wallace, arguing that he had worked admirably during his time in incarceration and had counseled younger inmates. Gatewood had a special interest in cases involving drugs and marijuana, and went out of his way to defend as many such people as he could.[33]

Much of the time, these clients couldn't pay. As Gatewood recalled in his memoir, "I couldn't say no to anyone in trouble, whether they had any money to pay me or not. I gave away hundreds of thousands of dollars in legal work and for three years averaged more than 30 appearances a week in the local courts at a cost of almost nothing to my clients."[34] Gatewood was frequently generous, sometimes to a fault, and truly cared about the people he represented. He also took cases that reinforced his standing as Kentucky's expert on marijuana and hemp issues and broadened his reputation as an effective trial attorney.

His cases and interests were also sometimes eccentric. In one case he represented a couple who couldn't make a down payment after purchasing a large horse farm at auction, and who were being sued by the auctioneer.[35]

Galbraith family, circa 1984. Gatewood and Susan's family expanded after Summer was born, welcoming Abby and Molly, while Gatewood also focused on passing the bar exam, practicing law, and launching his political career.

When two teenagers were charged with burglary and arson of Garden Springs Elementary School in Lexington, Gatewood defended them in court. They were initially convicted, but on appeal a Lexington judge threw out the conviction and dismissed the charges. Echoing the over-the-top rhetorical style he was already famous for, Gatewood commented on who was really at fault. "I'm convinced that the police and the prosecutors were under such pressure to find a culprit that they were willing to sacrifice this young man on the altar of retribution, even though they knew the evidence showed Carter didn't do it."[36]

Gatewood was obviously talented as an attorney, and as a speaker, but it sometimes appeared that his extracurricular interests and lack of preparation hurt his performance in court. Judge Ernesto Scorsone, a future state representative, state senator, and circuit court judge, began as a trial attorney operating in Lexington at the same time as Gatewood. He remembered seeing Gatewood in action: "I saw him in the courtroom and I would say he was one of those attorneys that would be, you know, kind of from the seat of his pants kind of thing. . . . He wouldn't come prepared with, you know, memorandums of the law or anything like that." Gatewood never failed to bet on himself, however, and would depend a lot on his rhetorical talents. "He was hoping that his personality would prevail, you know, and there's some attorneys that rely on that rather than preparation and doing their homework. . . . So I never thought of him as a meticulous, careful attorney. A bright guy, great presence, wonderful voice."[37]

Gatewood's friend from college, law professor Kevin Hill, echoed these sentiments. Before qualifying that his comments would be hearsay, Hill continued, "The story I heard was that he was a very sloppy lawyer, OK? He missed deadlines, he counted on his ability to speak to get people out of trouble rather than doing the hard work. He probably wasn't a bad lawyer for misdemeanors and some felonies, but I wouldn't have given him a will to draft or write articles of incorporation or anything like that."[38]

Bob Treadway, who was disbarred and worked with Gatewood on writing for his cases, agreed with these estimations, but also emphasized what Gatewood was really good at. "He was great at communicating with people and particularly with jurors and with, you know, kind of working class people, if you know what I mean. I think the lawyers themselves didn't think all that much of him as a lawyer."[39]

Even though his attention was divided, usually at the cost of his legal practice, Gatewood did have his fair share of victories in court. In one 1987 personal injury case he represented a woman whose husband had been severely injured, and almost killed, due to the alleged actions of a semitruck driver. After working with a Louisville personal injury attorney, Gatewood got the insurance company to settle for a seven-figure sum. This was a huge windfall for Gatewood, and assuaged a few of his family's financial fears.

The reprieve didn't last long. Gatewood's failure to manage his money or to prioritize his legal career had devastating consequences for the rest of his life. He wrote, "The check was big but hardly big enough. Sometimes I think that my only hope for money is to out-earn my capacity to mismanage it."[40] This hope never came to fruition. Financial issues came to a head as Gatewood began to look forward to future political campaigns.

Finances continued to be a burden for Gatewood and Susan, amplified by raising three bright little girls whom they tried to provide with top-notch educations and opportunities. The girls all attended a Montessori school, where they excelled and mirrored the talents of their intelligent parents. Gatewood's split attention and inability to either make or manage money continued to stress his marriage. It also put him in awkward situations with his siblings, whom he regularly came to in order to borrow money.

Gatewood and his daughters, circa 1984. Even as Gatewood's political aspirations grew and he juggled work and life, he always expressed love for his daughters and valued his time with his girls.

"Gatewood was always a poor money manager, and my grandfather said once about Gatewood that Gatewood would take your last nickel or give you his last nickel," his big brother Hank recalled. As far back as the mid-1970s Gatewood had consistently borrowed money from him and failed to pay it back. Gatewood's financial mismanagement created such animosity that Hank eventually had to cut him off. In one particular case, Hank remembered, Gatewood had asked him for money in order to buy the girls some shoes for school. Hank had no choice but to stand firm and to try to change the pattern of Gatewood's behavior. To his credit, Gatewood never derided Hank for this decision, or even criticized him for it. For Gatewood, money existed in a different dimension. It was a means to an end and not something he could plan for.[41]

Edna echoed this approach, having been burned by Gatewood's borrowing habits one too many times. "There were no hard feelings," she remembered. "But the thing is, if you give them a lump sum of money, then all of a sudden they're going to a hotel to have a night out, you know?"[42]

Gatewood wasn't devious or conniving in looking for help from his siblings. He just simply did not comprehend the fact that money was something to plan for. This was not to say necessarily that he was selfish. He donated his time and money constantly. This was part of what his grandfather was expressing in the quote that Hank remembered. Gatewood would give money away just as easily as he would take it from others.

While he was experiencing some measure of success in the courtroom, Gatewood never put his heart fully into building a profitable practice. He had promised Susan that he would not pursue public office again until they were financially stable. Remembering the extreme stress it had put on their family, he did stick to this promise, at least for a few years. He didn't throw his hat into the ring for any office in the statewide elections of 1987, but shortly thereafter he began to consider making an even bigger splash than his run for agriculture commissioner.

By 1988 Gatewood had already decided that he wanted to run for Kentucky governor in the 1991 race. He and Susan were still going through therapy, trying to raise their girls, and navigating all of the intricacies of marriage. But while Gatewood had promised Susan not to seek office, he could not turn away from this inward calling. Gatewood was now truly a public figure, known throughout the commonwealth and throughout the country for his positions on hemp and marijuana. He didn't want to remain primarily a criminal defense attorney. He loved the law and saw that as part of the same mission: to fight against what he saw as government overreach against personal liberty.

On August 7, 1989, the *Lexington Herald-Leader* published an article headlined "Lawyer Who Favors Legal Pot May Run for Governor." All of Gatewood's media availability paid off in this announcement nearly two years before even the primary would be decided for the 1991 governor's race. The article was datelined Fancy Farm, the site of Kentucky's most famous political spectacle and now one of Gatewood's favorite places to be seen, to shake hands, and to shake up the popular political conversation. It also covered the speeches of other political candidates at Fancy Farm, including Wendell H. Ford, Jim Bunning, and Mitch McConnell. It must have been obnoxious to those prominent politicians to not make the headline. Gatewood soaked up media attention, even in years when he wasn't actually running for office. "'I plan on announcing within 60 days,' Galbraith said as he shook hands at the annual Fancy Farm picnic, the summer's biggest political event in Kentucky."[43]

As he ramped up public appearances and started to generate buzz for his campaign, Gatewood even began to make news outside of Kentucky. Media outlets had not really cared about his run for agriculture commissioner, but running for governor was a different story. Reportage on Gatewood's appearance at a Washington, DC, conference that included representatives

Gatewood with his children on his fortieth birthday, 1987. Gatewood struggled to balance supporting his family and running for office. His decision to run for governor in advance of the 1991 election further strained his marriage.

from NORML as well as his friend Jack Herer's organization HEMP (Help End Marijuana Prohibition) noted that he criticized President George H. W. Bush's War on Drugs, claiming that there was an easy way to pay for the policing of actual harmful, hard drugs like crack cocaine and heroin: "While Democrats jawed with the White House on Wednesday, about how much should be spent on the drug war, Gatewood Galbraith proposed a novel way to finance the crusade. Galbraith's solution: Make marijuana legal, license and tax it—and then use the $35 billion generated each year to wipe out the real bad stuff, like crack."[44]

Gatewood went into this campaign full force, even before it really began. This was his next big step, and the media attention fed his belief that he could succeed and make a difference in the status quo of Kentucky politics. From the outside, it appeared that Gatewood was choosing this over his family and his commitments. Susan understood that he couldn't deny himself what he saw as his life's calling, but from a simply practical standpoint she also couldn't live with the implications of this decision. She had to find ways to feed, clothe, and educate her children. His decision to run for governor was what effectively ended their marriage, and they divorced in 1989. With three young girls at home, this was heart-wrenching for both of them. Looking back on it, Susan seemed to have some depth of understanding about why it happened. "Neither one of us wanted to divorce, but there wasn't any way for him to do what he did and for us to stay married. . . . And I couldn't do what he needed me to do if running for office was what he was going to choose. So we made that decision. We told the girls in his office, we walked straight down to comprehensive care to a counseling session we had set up for the five of us. And it was just incredibly, incredibly painful."[45]

Susan and Gatewood prioritized the well-being of their children, and would go on to live as true partners. Gatewood never suffered an ill word to be said about Susan, and by all accounts they were outstanding parents to their girls.

"I think they were much better friends than husband and wife," said Gatewood's sister Edna.[46]

Gatewood's little brother Mike agreed. "His priority was to make that difficult time easier for their children. And the way you do that is to demonstrate that you still have a shared commitment." Speaking thirty years after the event, Mike's estimation of Gatewood's and Susan's maturity had certainly come to fruition in how they raised their girls. "And, you know, his girls are great. They're dynamic . . . I mean because of those kinds of values that Susan and Gatewood instilled in them."[47]

The 1980s, in sum, were turbulent, exciting, and unsettling for Gatewood and his family. This was the time he came into his own, when he passed the bar and started to practice law, a profession that he pursued with passion if not always with preparation. He overcame the hurdle of the bar exam and proved to himself that he had what it took to be an attorney. He mixed this professional attainment with the lessons he learned in law school, namely his growing interest in and passion for marijuana and hemp reform.

This also had a positive side effect for Gatewood: people cared. They were interested in what he had to say, either because they agreed with him and celebrated someone sharing their view, or because they thought he was a curious attraction and held outrageous views in a culturally conservative state. Driven by the political example of John Y. Brown Jr. and his commitment to seeing these ideas played out on a bigger stage, Gatewood began his search for public office.

While he wasn't elected agriculture commissioner, his last-place showing didn't dissuade him. He was disappointed, but he saw it as the natural starting point for his future political aspirations. Hearkening back to his time daydreaming as a young boy in Carlisle, Gatewood had learned from an early age to dream big, and to live that way, too. Instead of running for city council, or getting involved in local politics, he made a splash throughout the state, running as a relative unknown with some very controversial ideas. Those ideas brought with them media coverage, even if they sacrificed his ability to actually win the election. He was also operating from outside the political establishment, and his contentious ideas about hemp and marijuana ensured that he would remain on the outside looking in when it came to public support or fundraising.

This was also a period of time when his family was growing, in number and age. Summer was joined by sisters Abby and Molly, and the three Galbraith girls would always remain the proudest achievement of Gatewood's life. He saw right away that it was tricky to balance his work, his political aspirations, and his family, as he and Susan consistently struggled with financial issues. The stress caused by these issues, and the tragedies they had experienced earlier as a family, set Gatewood and Susan on two different paths.

As Gatewood became more widely known for his role as an activist and leading voice on hemp and marijuana across the country, he simply could not put political aspirations out of his mind. He decided that he had to run for office, and threw his hat into the ring for the 1991 election for Kentucky governor. Susan could not live with this decision, and the broken promise that Gatewood had made. Even through their divorce, their love for each other and their girls shone through, and they prioritized family and their children's well-being over any quarrels. This dedication would dictate their lives together over the next twenty years.

The election of 1991 and Gatewood's future political efforts would bring more hardship, heartache, and drama. The next chapter in his life was one based on politics, and his growing fame throughout the country. A variety of circumstances and chance encounters would shape Gatewood's life, all stemming from his first run at major office. Reflecting on this decision and the end of his marriage, Gatewood wrote, "By definition, everyone's obsessions are his or her very own. No one else should be made to bear the burdens that a true believer can put on them as the believer follows their commitment through the thickest and the thinnest of times."[48]

4

Spectacular Bid

The next two years in Gatewood's life were spent campaigning as much as possible. He was trying to scrape together enough money from his law practice to support his run for governor, and to meet his obligations as a father, ex-husband, and employer. In an exhausting period of just a year and a half, Gatewood crisscrossed the commonwealth, participating in any forum, town hall, or media event where he could share his ideas and vision for the commonwealth.

On November 21, 1989, Gatewood held an event at Heritage Hall in Lexington to officially kick off his campaign for the Governor's Mansion. The focus, as always, was on Gatewood's main issue: hemp and marijuana. He detailed his plan to regulate and tax marijuana, saying that it would raise $700 million in tax revenue to fill the fiscally starved state coffers. While this garnered most of the attention of the press, Gatewood also laid out his longer list of priorities if elected to public office. According to the *Lexington Herald-Leader*, "his campaign also would focus on protecting the state's environment from landfills and waste dumps, promoting hemp as an industrial and cash crop, curtailing police powers and improving the state's educational system. He suggested an international sweepstakes tied to each year's Kentucky Derby. He said such a move could yield tens of millions of dollars a year in additional state revenue."[1]

Here, again, was the delicate balance for Gatewood. Being known as the "marijuana candidate" brought with it media attention. It was the oxygen he needed to feed the fire of his campaign. He would take this attention, but he also tried to inject his campaign with other political ideas that were important to him. The campaign for the Democratic nomination allowed Gatewood to spread his wings. Unlike his run for agriculture commissioner in 1983, Gatewood didn't have to focus only on issues related to farming or how hemp and marijuana would benefit Kentucky's agricultural sector. The office of governor has oversight over all areas of state government, and Gatewood needed to prove that he had a fuller grasp of the issues facing Kentucky.

In explaining his stance on these issues and his ideas to address them, Gatewood's political philosophy came into focus. The 1991 campaign served to solidify his political beliefs, as he became known not only for his progressive stances on marijuana reform but also for his belief in libertarian principles. He was an advocate for marijuana and hemp reform, and supported new tax structures that could provide Kentucky with a fiscal advantage. He was in favor of environmental protections, seemingly promoting more government oversight and regulation. But he was also in favor of limiting the power of Kentucky law enforcement and the overall breadth of government involvement in the lives of Kentucky citizens. One issue, in particular, indicated his preference for limited government and illustrated his contempt and distrust of broad international agreements and treaties.

In his memoir Gatewood points to trade agreements as a major reason for his run. This was surely overstated, as he had long set statewide office as his political target. The concept of "free trade" surfaced most prominently in the late 1980s. It is based on the idea that in order to encourage economic expansion and activity, countries agree to pacts that eliminate or severely limit tariffs, quotas, subsidies, or prohibitions that reduce the trade of goods or services.

President Reagan began negotiating what would become the North American Free Trade Agreement (NAFTA) while in office. His vice president and successor, George H. W. Bush, strongly supported the measure. In 1989 President Bush took steps to encourage free trade, including the elimination of human rights considerations when agreeing to trade agreements. This made it possible for the United States to increase trade with countries like China, and was seen as the next logical step in the free market economy movement in the wake of the fall of the Soviet Union.

Gatewood found this reprehensible. "That signaled the abdication by the United States of their stance on Human Rights and replaced our policy of Fair Trade with the Corporate profit-driven policy of Free Trade. In short, America went from representing the interests of human beings to representing the interests of corporations, even when they trounced Human Rights."[2]

For Gatewood, always holding memories of Carlisle in his heart and constantly empathizing with rural communities in Kentucky, this was truly the beginning of one of his most deeply entrenched and widely shared political beliefs. He distrusted corporations and saw the radical shift to free market capitalism as a malignant force in Kentucky society. This became one of the cornerstones of the rest of Gatewood's political career. It also colored his understanding of how corporations, as he saw it, cut off farmers and small communities from the very resources that had allowed them to flourish throughout much of the nation's history. This was a wider push-back against Reaganomics, and the massive upswell in corporate profits that defined much of the late twentieth century in America. Gatewood hearkened back to an idealized, simpler time, when even small communities got a fair shake.

Even as he broadened his platform and exhausted himself on the campaign trail, Gatewood still faced an uphill battle. In a crowded 1987 primary field, Wallace Wilkinson had prevailed over former governor John Y. Brown Jr., Lieutenant Governor Steve Beshear, former governor Julian Carroll, and Kentucky physician Dr. Grady Stumbo. Bolstered by a young political operative named James Carville, Wilkinson's campaign focused on instituting Kentucky's first statewide lottery. In what turned out to be an effective strategy, this popular issue propelled Wilkinson to victory in the primary, and in the general election in November 1987.[3]

Although Wilkinson would have liked to run for reelection, Kentucky's constitution still prohibited a governor from being elected to consecutive terms. Wilkinson tried to change this with a constitutional amendment, but it remained in place. Instead Wilkinson's wife, Martha, threw her hat in the ring leading up to the primary season. Brereton Jones, the lieutenant governor and presumptive Democratic nominee, had an immediate head start in both notoriety and funding. He, Martha, and Gatewood were eventually joined in the race by Dr. Floyd Poore and Lexington mayor Scotty Baesler. There was increasing speculation that another former Kentucky governor, Senator Wendell H. Ford, would also run in the primary, but he eventually bowed out and remained in Washington.[4]

The towering odds against his candidacy did not deter Gatewood. Throughout all of his campaigns he was always determined to carry on to the end. This was doubly true in the 1991 race. He pushed forward in the face of lack of funding, and tracked back and forth across Kentucky to take his message to the voters. He still had a lot to figure out, especially at home.

Gatewood and Susan were blessed with three brilliant, beautiful, and resilient daughters, but their parents' divorce was still a complicated challenge for them to navigate. It was even more difficult when one parent was a prominent public figure. Gatewood had made the decision to run for governor and had begun campaigning at the very time the family tried to heal from the divorce. Susan and Gatewood were committed to not speak ill of one another, and to remain close partners and involved in the lives of their children. But the girls did not have an easy road. Their father's decision to pursue public office must have seemed, at times, a statement on what was most important to him. He charged ahead with his campaign plans even as his personal life was in turmoil.

Because he had the greater earning capacity, Gatewood was responsible for child support for his family. As the main breadwinner in the marriage, he had a responsibility to care for his children and to provide them with a secure place to live and basic necessities. It was also vital to both Gatewood and Susan that their daughters continue in the school they had attended nearly all their lives. Still, Gatewood began campaigning tirelessly, working only part time as an attorney. This was an unbalanced equation, as he needed to provide Susan around $1,700 per month to cover child support, the home mortgage, and Montessori school tuition. Gatewood did feel it was his responsibility to follow through on these payments, but he did not always live up to his end of the bargain. Gatewood's inability to make timely child support payments put Susan in a very difficult position: trying to provide for her family while also shielding her daughters from public scrutiny of Gatewood's choices.

Summer, Gatewood and Susan's oldest daughter, had a better understanding of these circumstances than her two younger sisters. When her parents informed her that they were getting divorced, within twenty-four hours Summer came to Susan and asked if she could have a hyphenated last name, Sears-Galbraith. She saw this as consistent with her parents' approach: they were still a family, just a "different kind of family." She sought to continue to unify her family during a turbulent and emotionally fraught time.

As her parents were going through the divorce, and as Gatewood's profile rose in advance of the 1991 election, Abby decided that it would be better to be known by her mother's last name. She was starting a new high school and was afraid of constantly having to answer questions about her dad and marijuana. This didn't sit well with Gatewood. It surely hurt to hear that his daughter wanted to drop the Galbraith name completely. But more importantly, as he told Susan, "This is not how we do things in our family." They weren't meant to hide from life's difficulties. They were there to help Abby work through them. He finally acquiesced, once again prioritizing his daughter over his own preferences.

On one occasion, Summer and her classmates were waiting on a teacher in the school gym, and the boys in her classes surrounded her and began to tease her about marijuana. They had heard about Gatewood and the campaign on the news, and now were using his notoriety to poke fun at her in school.

On another occasion, Summer's talent for writing was on display. As part of the Drug Abuse Resistance Education (DARE) program taught in schools throughout the country, Summer's essay on resisting drug use won her a prize, and a $50 savings bond. She proudly read her essay at a city council meeting. This struck many as odd, but the award committee was blown away by Summer's ability to reconcile her father's support for marijuana with her own condemnation of the more dangerous and often lethal synthetic drugs. "And I don't think I would have seen any contradiction between that and his views, because in my mind, marijuana was a different kind of drug."

Summer felt exposed due to Gatewood's notoriety, but she also had a mature understanding of the drugs that could actually ruin lives and destroy families. She recalls that, even before the 1991 campaign, her father focused on the issue of opioids and heroin in Kentucky, long before it became the salient political talking point it is today. He was ahead of his time in identifying the dangers of addiction to prescription painkillers, and the destruction they were already causing. "Dad was talking about the opiate issue way before any of the other politicians, the opiate issue . . . I remember him telling me that the Democrats and Republicans both didn't want to talk about it."[5]

Gatewood and Susan continued to keep their daughters in counseling, just to be sure that they had the support they needed during this time of radical change and transition. "Gatewood and I may have overplayed this a little bit," Susan remembered, "but we just wanted to make sure, you know, that they had somebody to talk to."[6]

In hindsight, it's easy to see why the girls were sometimes reticent to be associated so clearly with their father. Gatewood was growing into a political fixture and local celebrity, showing up more and more in newspapers in advance of the 1991 campaign. Not all of this coverage was related to politics, or at least explicitly focused on Gatewood's platform. Framed in the context of the gubernatorial race, one 1990 *Herald-Leader* article detailed Gatewood's financial shortcomings: "The Fayette County government has filed three misdemeanor criminal charges against Galbraith for non-payment of employee withholding taxes, allegations he does not dispute. Galbraith also routinely falls behind on child support and maintenance obligations and made a $2,352 past-due payment recently."

Published in the midst of his campaign, this article pointed out Gatewood's mixed-up priorities. He was in deep trouble with Lexington's Fayette County, where he had failed to properly meet his tax obligations while operating his practice. As the article also made clear, he was having trouble keeping up with his child support obligations, which put an obvious strain on Susan and his girls. Gatewood simply kept falling behind in his finances, though he still found ways to ensure his ability to run for public office.

Environmental concerns were a constant theme of Gatewood's political campaigns. This sign, part of his run for governor in 1991, points to this issue and his campaign's 1-800-866-HEMP hotline.

"Despite his personal financial troubles, Galbraith has lent at least $6,775 to his campaign finance committee and promises to go even deeper into debt to pay for his race for the Democratic nomination for governor."[7]

Gatewood was facing an uphill battle in the election, and simply could not raise the money he needed to be competitive. Leaving out the more dubious details of his financial life, Gatewood wrote, "I was hitting the campaign trail whenever the opportunity presented itself but it came in second to fulfilling my commitment to my law practice. Sometimes I might have a case in one part of the state, then have to drive 200 miles to attend a campaign forum in another part. Even gas money was a concern as every bit of income went to Susan and the kids."[8]

Quotes like this illustrate Gatewood's ability to reframe these events in his own mind. His law practice was not coming first. If it had, he would have dropped what seemed like a hopeless campaign in order to find his way out of debt and back into the good graces of the law. This is just one example of the cognitive dissonance Gatewood allowed himself in his memoir, and often in his own life. He saw the election as a higher calling, and he was obviously willing to sacrifice a lot for a chance to be successful. In serious legal trouble in a variety of contexts, he still kept finding ways to loan money to his campaign. But at what cost?

The *Herald-Leader* quoted Gatewood as saying, "I've gone into debt over this campaign and if necessary I'll go further into debt," and "I think the people out there living paycheck to paycheck understand."[9] One of those people was at home, struggling to raise her three kids and constantly seeing her ex-husband in the news.

Gatewood was increasingly out of options and was backing himself into a corner with his financial decision-making. His campaign flailing, he needed a Hail Mary to bolster his chances. It came in the form of a long-haired, pot-smoking country music star from Texas.

As Gatewood told it, midway through his campaign he was out of money and getting desperate. He had caught up with his child support payments for the time being but was behind on rent for his law office in downtown Lexington and didn't even have enough money to pay the phone bill. His campaign was floundering. It was starved of money and time, and Gatewood was not making a big impact across the state, even though he spent every extra moment at various events throughout Kentucky. This looked like a repeat of the 1983 election, and he couldn't even find campaign donors to support his continued efforts. His biggest donor was himself. He hoped to raise enough funds in the future to pay himself back for his campaign expenditures. It wasn't sustainable, and Gatewood was running out of time.

He managed to wrangle together $700 and, in typical Gatewood fashion, rather than do the safe thing like pay rent or restore his phone service, he took a risk. He paid a local television station to record his campaign message. Gatewood sat in front of the camera for thirty minutes and made an impassioned plea to the residents of the state he loved. He talked about the need for a voice to represent those hurting, unappreciated, and taken advantage of. He spoke of his passion for rural communities and for farmers, and how corporations were encroaching on their ways of life. He discussed his Model Plan and how revising marijuana laws in the state could unlock the potential for farmers to make a living once again, and how it could rejuvenate communities that were hurting.

He used what was left of the money to pay for it to be broadcast, and promptly forgot all about it. He continued to campaign and tried to scratch out a living with various cases across the state. When he returned from a trial to his office, he panicked when he saw a piece of paper taped to his door. He thought for sure it was a vacate notice from his landlord. Instead it read:

Gatewood leaned into his marijuana and hemp advocacy during his first run for governor in 1991, labeling himself a Green Democrat.

"Gatewood, Willie Nelson is trying to get hold of you. Call your ex-wife for details."[10]

By 1990 Willie Nelson had risen to be one of the most famous singers and songwriters in the world of country music. Beginning in the 1950s, Nelson had grown in fame and acclaim, working as a disc jockey, honky-tonk singer, and then joining the Grand Ole Opry in Nashville. In the 1970s, from what would become his adopted hometown of Austin, Texas, he would release a series of wildly successful albums that captured the attention of the nation and helped to make Austin famous as a destination for live music. He eventually joined the country supergroup the Highwaymen, with Kris Kristofferson, Johnny Cash, and Waylon Jennings.

He and Gatewood shared some interesting similarities. Since before Gatewood was born, Willie Nelson had been a vocal advocate for marijuana, and he became interested in several progressive social causes. By the 1990s he was widely known for his marijuana use, as well as his music. Nelson also shared a genuine passion for farmers and rural communities, like the one he had grown up in in Abbott, Texas. In 1985 Nelson began a benefit concert series called Farm Aid along with fellow musicians John Mellencamp and Neil Young, raising millions of dollars for family farms throughout the country.

Nelson also had his fair share of financial difficulties. Even though he was a successful musician, he often found himself short of money through a mix of bad investments, poor financial decisions, and what he claimed was "bad advice from accountants." In 1990 the IRS hit Nelson with a tax bill for $16.7 million.[11] Before the judgment, he was touring the country and happened to be flipping through TV channels as his bus rumbled through Kentucky. He settled on a stark scene: a local politician speaking directly to a news camera in an empty studio. The message resounded with Willie, and he encouraged his staff to try and contact Gatewood.

After finding that Gatewood's office phone was not in operation, Nelson got in touch with Susan, who called the office on the floor below Gatewood's to leave the message taped to the door. Gatewood returned the call, and within a few days he was driving away from Dallas/Fort Worth Airport in the backseat of Willie's Mercedes-Benz. They spent a few days together, and a friendship blossomed. The two men discussed their similar affinities and struggles, and Gatewood came away from that meeting with an important win for his campaign: Willie agreed to play a benefit concert for Gatewood in the lead-up to the 1991 primary.

This was a major boon to Gatewood's hopes. Willie Nelson was a celebrity, who by pure chance took an interest in Gatewood. It gave him some measure of legitimacy and made his campaign an even bigger spectacle. It revved up interest and media coverage and built some excitement leading up to the primary. What Gatewood didn't realize was the trade-off in this bargain.

Jack Brammer, who covered political campaigns as a reporter for the *Lexington Herald-Leader* for forty-three years, remembered how the popular perception of Gatewood shifted even farther into the obscure once he became publicly associated with Willie Nelson. "You know, in the media, that was an easy peg to label Gatewood," Brammer said. "Gatewood would associate with Willie Nelson . . . it was easy for the media to peg him as the marijuana candidate."[12]

Al Cross pointed to an even bigger obstacle for Gatewood. He had a campaign style that made him relatable, and quotable, and popular, but his outspoken advocacy for marijuana and his lack of a serious nature made it difficult for mainstream voters to support him. "Gatewood never took himself completely seriously. Because he didn't, a lot of the voters didn't take him seriously. They saw an entertaining guy who made useful points and gave them stuff to think about."[13]

Gatewood and Willie scheduled the benefit concert for October 14 in Louisville. Before Gatewood returned to Kentucky, they also made plans to stage a publicity tour in advance of the benefit, visiting cities throughout the commonwealth to spread his message. Gatewood was reenergized and, for the first time in his political life, had the wind at his back. He doubled down on his campaign and began to work harder than ever to make his dreams of the governor's office a reality.

Even though he had been campaigning since late 1989, Gatewood's campaign began in earnest in the spring of 1990. One notable event was a rally held in Woodland Park near downtown Lexington, sponsored by NORML. Gatewood was a headliner of the rally and spoke to the assembled crowd of more than three hundred. Gatewood's message had changed since his run for agriculture commissioner in 1983. His words were sharper, his accusations more pointed.

Comparing the War on Drugs with a "Nazi point of view," Gatewood lashed out at the current climate of marijuana persecution in the United States: "They're implementing a police state, and a police mentality, and a police procedure, and they're putting it under the auspices of a drug war."[14]

In his campaign for the Democratic nomination, Gatewood turned up the fiery rhetoric. Rather than only trying to justify his ideas about marijuana and hemp with dollars and cents, he framed the struggle as a kind of holy war. He compared the federal government and state police forces to fascist regimes who were eager to stomp on your rights and destroy your lives. A police state masquerading as a moral quest: this would be the defining message of his campaign.

These lines are now quite familiar to any who followed Gatewood's public life, but the leadup to the 1991 election was where they were tried on, polished, and bent to his political will. The media coverage kept coming. Reporters enjoyed Gatewood, who was on easy terms with them and who was always good for a quote.

"Well, I think that Gatewood dealt on a personal basis with me and other reporters. And, you know, there was a degree of mutual respect there and regard even," Al Cross remembered. "And he also, I think, as a practical matter, knew that it wasn't a good idea to piss off reporters." From covering Gatewood's appearances, Cross recalled that Gatewood did have a particular gift for connecting with voters, by identifying what their worries were, and what their hopes were for the futures they envisioned. "Gatewood appealed to your head and your heart and occasionally to your gut. And I think in doing that, he was a fairly effective politician."[15]

Part of this connection was applying his ideas about marijuana, and its enforcement, to government as a whole. Reading his statements now, his ideas are clearly identifiable as libertarian, a movement that gained more steam in the mid to late 2000s. Libertarians were seen as being fiscally conservative, yet socially liberal. They held that government spending and bureaucracy should be shrunk as much as possible, while the government should keep its nose out of social or ethical concerns.

"I'm the most conservative candidate in this race," Gatewood declared. "When I grew up, 'conservative' meant you kept the government in a little box. When you opened up that box and let the government grow exponentially, it got out of control and got too intrusive. What I want to do is put government back in that box." In interviews he didn't shy from his past or his beliefs about hemp and marijuana, but he did try to connect them to these larger principles of freedom and constitutional rights. In his eyes, he had been fighting these same battles since his time at the University of Kentucky. "There's no doubt that I'm an old hippie, and I don't apologize to anybody for that. Certainly those are the same people who came together to stop the slaughter in Vietnam, and I'm proud of that. Compared to 'Republican,' I'll take hippie every time."[16]

In an appearance at a Kentucky bingo hall, Gatewood explained these beliefs even more succinctly: "It is our view that government has gotten too big and too intrusive, and we think that government ought to keep their hands off your bedroom, your bloodstream, your back pocket, your brain, your bladder, and your bingo hall."[17]

Gatewood was banking on a fairly hopeless political strategy: convince enough of the Kentucky voters who were disenfranchised and disconnected from the political process to vote for him. He was relying on a precarious personal calculation: that there were half a million Kentucky voters who smoked marijuana and would be driven into his camp based on his ideas and outspoken support of the plant. He continued to repeat the proposals from his Model Plan. Just like tobacco and alcohol, marijuana should be regulated by the state government through an allotment system. Farmers would be able to grow a certain amount, for which they would be paid a standard rate by the state. The state would then oversee its sale and distribution, making a handsome sum as the middleman and eliminating the black market for marijuana that currently existed.

He was also trying to prove that marijuana did not make you lazy or stupid. He was a busy practicing attorney and made sure that reporters and voters knew about his work. "People say, 'How can you be a practicing attorney and smoke Marijuana?' My response to that is: 'Hey, if slavery were still legal, I'd be heading the underground railroad. If the Vietnam War were still going on, I'd be out in the streets demonstrating. If segregation were still intact, I'd be sitting at a lunch counter somewhere."[18]

Unfortunately, Gatewood's passion and media coverage did not result in campaign donations. By early April 1990, Lexington mayor Scotty Baesler had already raised more than $600,000 for the primary race,[19] and Lieutenant Governor Brereton C. Jones had topped a million.[20] Gatewood was in dire financial straits, falling even further behind in his tax obligations and trying to keep up with his child support payments. Through September 28, 1990, his committee had raised a meager $38,208 and spent $49,512, leaving itself, and Gatewood, in debt.[21]

In a candidate closeup on Kentucky Educational Television, Gatewood sat down with his old high school acquaintance Ferrell Wellman to get his message out to Kentucky voters. He cited the money flowing into the governor's race as proof that he was running for the people and not for special interests. "Well, I'm not beholden to any special interests. . . . I haven't raised the kind of money these other folks have raised. I haven't had to approach those kinds of people. I've been a very people-oriented and person-to-person campaigner," he said.

Wellman countered with a question based on Gatewood's own precarious financial position. "You've talked about not raising a lot of money, you've had personal financial problems that have been well documented. You've made a lot of personal sacrifices . . . has this race been worth it?"

Without skipping a beat, Gatewood answered in the affirmative. "Oh, it's absolutely been worth it. My race substantiates the sacrifices of millions of people, past generations, and this generation who have sacrificed and given . . . up a lot, maybe even their life. . . . I'm taking advantage of what is the American system's strongest point. And that is the ability to put an idea in the marketplace through the process of an election and allowing the people to accept or reject it."

This was Gatewood's holy fight, his most sacred obligation, and an opportunity for him to try out what had driven him to run for public office in the first place. He needed to try out the ideas that made so much sense to him, that drove his passions, that defined his life.

When Wellman moved on and asked Gatewood about his ideas for legalizing and licensing hemp and marijuana, Gatewood defended his position while also pointing out the drugs that were beginning to cripple communities in Kentucky: "Let's make one thing straight. I'm not talking about your white powder or pills. I'm not talking about your processed and synthesized cocaine. I'm not talking about Dilaudid, Valium, Librium, and all these prescription medicines. Those are not natural. They are man-made and synthetic. I'm talking about any green natural plant that a person wants to raise and consume, I think it should be their God-given right."

Once again, Gatewood saw the future. The frame in his mind, the struggle between the natural and what he called "the synthetic subversion," was the guiding principle for how to think about marijuana, your ethical and moral judgments be damned. Many interviewees for the oral history project mentioned that Gatewood was "ahead of his time." Most were referring to his insight about marijuana and the spread of its medical and recreational legalization. Few remembered that Gatewood saw, years before others, the harm that prescription opioids and painkillers would inflict on rural communities in Kentucky.

He also proved forward-thinking in discussing the implications of the drug war that was going on. Mass incarceration was picking up steam, with harsher drug penalties causing a quick uptick in those housed in prisons throughout the country. "I do not believe that doubling the prison population over the next twenty years is a solution to the present-day drug problem. I feel like if we can attack the poverty, the malnutrition, the non-education, the medical impairments, if we can attack those we can cut out a lot of the basis of crime. . . . I want medical treatment and rehabilitation to work. I do not want to use the law enforcement unless we have to. I want to take the money out of corrections and put it into public health and mental health."

When asked about his description of himself as conservative, Gatewood doubled down on his opinions. He had often said that Ronald Reagan and George H. W. Bush were not conservatives, they were "aliens." He reiterated his ideas about keeping government in a box and then explained that he stood for what he saw as true conservatism: removing barriers that disadvantaged small communities and family-owned businesses. Reagan, he said, "took it off the backs of big business, big industry, and let them run wild. But the people who paid for that were the middle class and the individual. . . . that's not conservatism!"[22]

Scotty Baesler remembered being with Gatewood on the campaign trail as they vied for the nomination. "He actually made pretty good arguments. I always thought he was very interesting. . . . But he did a good job. I thought he was very engaging with the public. You know, probably if Gatewood had come on a little later and had a little more money, you don't know what he would have done. He was actually a pretty good candidate. He was very witty, gave a good speech. . . . I always enjoyed Gatewood."

Gatewood was getting his message out every way he knew how. His campaign, while still struggling financially, was at least making waves and gaining interest both within Kentucky and around the country. With every appearance, every interview, and every campaign event, he tried to fire up his small but loyal base while broadening his message. He was not just the marijuana candidate. In his eyes he was a righteous crusader, someone fighting on the front lines for public policy that made sense and that worked for normal people. Through financial difficulty, long nights, and an exhausting campaign and work schedule, this mission kept him going.

By early 1990 Gatewood had left (or been forced to vacate) his law office on Short Street. He secured a two-story brick house on the corner of Nicholasville Road and Waller Avenue near the University of Kentucky hospital, which served as his home, his law office, and his campaign headquarters. Gatewood was working himself to the point of exhaustion, getting little sleep and struggling with the balance of work, campaigning, family, and finances. He refused to take his foot off the gas.

His oldest daughter, Summer, remembered the days of the 1991 campaign, more specifically how Gatewood's girls experienced his hectic life. On days that he had custody, they were surrounded by the race, and the media attention that it drew to their father.

When Summer won the DARE essay contest, a female reporter contacted Susan to ask if she could do a story in the *Herald-Leader* about Summer's award. Susan's response was a blanket refusal. It was quite obvious that reporters were trying to seize on the irony of Gatewood's daughter winning an antidrug essay contest.

"And so," Summer remembered, "she had a meeting with the editor and the reporter and said, no, you will not do this to an eleven-year-old child. . . . She is her own person and she does not need to have publicity around this."[23]

Gatewood would pick up Summer, Abby, and Molly, take them out to eat, and then end up back at his home and headquarters so that he could work on his law cases or on the campaign. They would ride for hours in the backseat of his car so that he could visit fairs, forums, and meetings across the state. Not wanting to be shown up by his bright and precocious daughters, he wouldn't allow the girls to ask questions of him during the Q&A portion of his campaign events.

It was becoming more and more obvious, as the girls grew older and as Gatewood's fame grew, that this was not a normal family. They felt loved and valued, but they also felt their father's shadow everywhere they went. When they were with him, they were sharing him—with the campaign, with his clients, with the worries that kept him up at night.

Willie Nelson was scheduled to play a concert in Maysville, Kentucky, the day before Gatewood's benefit. When the promoter who set up the concert began to read news stories about Nelson's support of Gatewood in the 1991 race, he put plans for the concert on hold.[24] While he eventually agreed to go forward, this illustrates the biggest fault in Gatewood's plan for the campaign: sentiment against marijuana was still widespread and deeply held, especially in the more socially conservative parts of the state. Some might question whether the promoter did not already realize that Nelson was in favor of legalizing marijuana, but the local stakes of the election brought this to the forefront. Once again, Gatewood was overestimating his own state's ability to be progressive on this controversial social issue.

Ever since Gatewood had struck up his friendship with Willie Nelson, word had spread about his campaign, and he began to draw national interest. Because of Gatewood's outspoken position on marijuana, along with the celebrity that Willie Nelson brought, *High Times* magazine decided to cover the state tour and benefit concert planned for that October.

High Times was founded in 1974 on a bit of a lark. Funded by the sale of illegal marijuana, it was meant to be a joke, an issue of *Playboy* that focused on marijuana instead of nude women.[25] Each issue even had a centerfold. Instead of a centerfold photo in the traditional sense, it was a zoomed-in, high-resolution photograph of a bud of marijuana, a different strain for each issue. *High Times* was the widest-reaching outlet for marijuana enthusiasts, decades before the internet made it possible to link those interested in pot.

John Holmstrom, a reporter and future editor of the magazine, drew an interesting assignment. In the fall of 1990, *High Times* sent him to Kentucky so that he could cover Gatewood and Willie Nelson's tour and concert.

Holmstrom, a New Yorker, arrived in Kentucky the day before the planned events. He drove from the East Coast and was struck by an unfamiliar landscape of rolling hills and vast horse farms, cordoned off with miles of black wooden fences. "And so, you know, I wasn't aware of what Kentucky was about with the horses and everything. . . . Lexington itself is a beautiful city. I mean, I loved Lexington, you know, and that's where I spent most of my time. That's where Gatewood's campaign was based, out of the house where he and his volunteers lived."[26]

By this time, Gatewood's Nicholasville Road base camp had expanded to be a volunteer camp, where those working on his campaign would often spend the night or even take up brief residence. Holmstrom immediately liked and connected with Gatewood, impressed by the same features that Baesler remembered from the campaign trail. Speaking about the trip thirty years later, he had no trouble remembering Gatewood. "He had such an expression-filled face, and he wore his emotions on his sleeve. You know, that's one of the things that was so charismatic about him. He felt so passionately about legalizing hemp and helping Kentucky and getting the right

Leading up to Willie Nelson's concert in support of Gatewood's 1991 gubernatorial campaign, the two staged a tour throughout Kentucky.

thing done, you know? So that's why when I called my article 'Spectacular Bid,' it was more about, like, how far he tried to reach."

With a gaggle of press in tow, including Holmstrom, Gatewood and Willie Nelson began their tour on Main Street in front of the Fayette County Courthouse, just a few blocks from where Gatewood's father's restaurant had been, and mere feet away from where he had led protests during his days at the University of Kentucky. They stood in front of Gatewood's diesel-powered bright red Mercedes-Benz and poured a gallon of pure hemp seed oil into the gas tank. Shortly after, they set off on a driving tour from Lexington to Frankfort and eventually to Louisville, where the concert would be held that night.

Before departing, the *Herald-Leader* noted, Gatewood addressed the crowd and then handed out "press kits," which included "hemp product samples, seeds and something called 'hemp cake,'" which seemed to be ground-up hemp in pouches.

"Our relationship with Mother Earth is the most basic relationship that we have in this birth-death cycle," Gatewood began. "And when a government tells us that we cannot go to our mother source that is Earth, and plant a seed in God's green earth, and utilize the green plant that comes up out of there in its natural form for our fiber and food and medicine needs, then that government is awry and that government no longer represents the best interests of the citizens of this country."

Nelson followed with some comments of his own: "Once again it's up to the farmers of America to save the planet. Not only to save the state of Kentucky, but the farmers are going to have to save us all. And we're going to have to give them a way to do it."

They took off from downtown Lexington, Willie's tour bus following behind, along with cars filled with Gatewood's supporters and reporters just along for the ride.

"With Nelson sitting beside him in a red Mercedes station wagon that Galbraith himself dubbed the 'hempmobile,' the candidate was seen lighting what looked like a marijuana cigarette as soon as he pulled onto Newtown Pike. When he noticed a reporter and photographer driving beside him, Galbraith lowered the thin, hand-rolled cigarette below the car's tinted windows and lifted an unlit cigar above the steering wheel. He and Nelson then waved and grinned broadly for the camera."

The caravan briefly stopped in Frankfort to speak at a Democratic Party rally at the State Capitol. During the speech, Gatewood didn't even bring up marijuana, but introduced his friend Willie Nelson and explained that

Gatewood Galbraith onstage with Willie Nelson, 1991. Despite last-minute difficulties, Nelson staged the 1991 benefit concert and provided some lifeblood and press for Gatewood's faltering campaign.

his campaign was about fighting for farmers throughout the commonwealth. The other candidates denounced Gatewood's views on marijuana and brought it up constantly in their speeches. The arrival and presence of Willie Nelson had obviously made them a bit squeamish about Gatewood's chances.

Not least of these was then-governor Wallace Wilkinson, who took the stage after Gatewood and his entourage had departed, and whose wife had also recently eclipsed the million-dollar fundraising mark for her own campaign. "We Democrats do not condone the legalization of marijuana or any other mind-altering drug," said Wilkinson, who conveniently forgot about the multiple distilleries currently in operation within minutes from where he was speaking. Gatewood, he said, would "have a damn sight more success running a car on it than he will a campaign on it."[27]

At Louisville Gardens, the venue for the show, attendees had already paid $17.50 for a ticket, not a small sum in 1990. About an hour before Willie was set to perform, the venue approached Gatewood and Willie with a problem. The fee for lights and sound for the show had never been paid, and they were short about $6,500. Gatewood's latest financial misstep became the story instead of a triumphant benefit concert.

Gatewood took the stage and explained the situation to the crowd. He and his staff passed blue buckets around the venue, asking everyone to chip in a few dollars so that the show could go on. It was embarrassing, and chaotic.

Even worse, one of Gatewood's friends and supporters, Winston Hardy, was arrested at the concert venue for carrying a concealed deadly weapon. Hardy, who had served previously as security for Gatewood, was caught with two .38 caliber pistols and was promptly escorted to the Jefferson County Corrections Center.[28]

In the end, it turned out all right. The concert wasn't well attended in the first place, but Willie played his show. At the end of the concert Gatewood went out on stage, his arm around his new friend. There is a photograph of the concert, Gatewood looking youthful and exuberant in the face of that day's setbacks. He wore a red bandana around his forehead and his usual business suit, Willie holding his hand up high.

Gatewood was betting everything on media attention, and the passion that he shared with his supporters. But, much like his planning for the benefit concert, he ignored the details that made campaigns successful. Holmstrom remembered this with a particularly troubling example: "Gatewood really thought he was going to win. But I saw the first problem when I was at the house. . . . you wake up and some of these campaign workers did not bother to register to vote. Yes, campaign workers. Are you kidding me?"[29]

It is telling that Gatewood did not record any of the hiccups of the benefit concert in his own memoir. Surely he remembered going on stage and asking people to "pass the hat," so that the concert could go on. He remembered it as a success, and it surely was astounding that a campaign run by his shoestrings had drawn such a big celebrity and so much media attention.

The *High Times* article came out in January, and Gatewood and Willie Nelson appeared on the cover together. "Spectacular Bid" detailed Gatewood's candidacy and campaign, as well as the media blitz surrounding Nelson's Louisville concert. Gatewood was still proud of the article years later, writing, "That story and Willie's benefit for me that evening made both the front and back cover of the January 1991 issue of *High Times* magazine. Damn, I looked good."[30]

Unfortunately, this attention was not resulting in the kinds of outcomes that he hoped for. He particularly set his sights on the *Louisville Courier-Journal*, which refused to cover his campaign or to take him seriously as a candidate.

Al Cross, who covered the campaign, didn't remember this the same way. "Yeah, I think he would argue that we were engaging . . . in a self-fulfilling prophecy. And yes, he wasn't getting a chance because they weren't giving him a chance."[31]

As Cross recalled it, what kept Gatewood out of the state's biggest paper wasn't a coordinated conspiracy but rather limited column inches and the irrelevancy of Gatewood's campaign. Just as Gatewood had seen a conspiracy when trying to pass the bar, he saw one now in his lack of coverage. The *Courier-Journal* hadn't even covered the benefit concert with Willie Nelson. "The publishers of these newspapers really didn't have much influence over what coverage Gatewood and other minor party candidates got. That was a decision left largely to the editors. But at the initiative of the reporters, I mean, that's one reason you have a political writer. Somebody can make gatekeeping judgments on the front end and not inundate editors with a lot of decisions that need to be made in that regard."[32]

To put it plainly, there was only so much space to cover the governor's race, and editors and reporters at the *Courier-Journal* didn't feel that his long-shot odds of winning the race merited much coverage.

Gatewood received more attention from his hometown *Herald-Leader*, which provided some oxygen to his campaign. In the days following the concert, reporters continued to question Gatewood's stance on marijuana, and especially his personal use of it. The article, titled "Galbraith Says He Has Smoked Marijuana Regularly for 22 Years," focused on just the most controversial issue of his campaign, quoting Gatewood as saying, "I'm a responsible adult in a free society, and I exercise my responsibilities in discreet ways. I don't mean to alarm or annoy anybody. Certainly marijuana doesn't have any properties that makes a person act in a criminal matter, so since I'm not a criminal in any other respect, I just don't draw attention to people who are out looking for criminals."

His financial shortcomings and lack of funds to support this campaign continued to dog any reports that might have provided him some publicity. Besides being in legal trouble for owing occupational taxes, he was still falling behind on his child support payments to Susan and the girls.

"On another legal matter," the article went on, "Galbraith had a hearing scheduled yesterday in Fayette Circuit Court because he was behind on alimony payments to his ex-wife. According to court records, he was given an extra 24 hours to make arrangements to pay $2,352 in overdue payments to his ex-wife and three children. Galbraith said he would make payment arrangements."

Gatewood agreed with this assessment, and admitted the bind he was in. "'There's no doubt about it, I'm broke,' Galbraith explained. He said he had put 'everything I've got' into the campaign."[33]

Gatewood thrived at the annual political gathering known as Fancy Farm, one of Kentucky's premiere political events, which is held every August in Graves County.

These problems never went away, and Gatewood constantly tried to shuffle campaign expenses and legal work to make ends meet. Susan also went to great lengths to make sure that the girls didn't see these news reports, or to see the negative portrayals of their father. This period was incredibly difficult for her, as she tried to raise their daughters in a stable environment, including keeping them in the schools they loved and needed for consistency in their lives. Susan made sure that they knew that Gatewood's failures in the financial aspects of his life were not a reflection on his love for them.

"There was a lot of child support arrearage, a lot of debt. There were times that were very, very hard. . . . And it was never a question of whether he wanted to pay it or not," Susan remembered,[34] becoming emotional as she recalled the hardships that she led her family through. She still loved and trusted Gatewood, and she knew that he wasn't being devious or withholding, but was following his passion and reasserting his most deeply held beliefs. The cost, however, was often destructive and difficult for those around him.

He even failed to show up for his court date in December 1990 when he was to answer for the occupational tax issue. The judge had already continued the case nine times, and finally issued a summons for him to appear.[35]

Things were getting serious, and Gatewood's campaign continued to be hampered by these news stories.

He missed another court date in January, and an arrest warrant was issued. He turned himself in on January 30, 1991, and spent an hour in jail for his transgressions. The next day he pleaded guilty of failure to pay his taxes. He was fined and required to pay the full balance he owed by March 20. He blamed the failure to appear on his daughters being sick, and owned up to his mistakes. When asked about how this would impact his campaign, he demurred: "I will not disappoint my supporters and call off my campaign because of a personal financial setback. Money is like sex and politics—it's all a matter of timing. I still plan to break every voting record ever set and my views haven't changed whatsoever."[36]

At times Gatewood's paranoia bordered on the spectacular. In the few months leading up to the May 1991 primary, he was still crisscrossing the state, fighting his way into every event, forum, or press conference that he could. In late March he thought he heard strange noises when speaking on the phone with his campaign treasurer, Frank Lucchese.

On March 27 he held a press conference in downtown Lexington, claiming that a private security firm he hired found wiretaps on both his and Lucchese's phones. Gatewood said that the one on his phone was put on by the phone company, so it would have been a legal action taken by state or federal authorities. The one on Lucchese's phone, however, he claimed was blatantly illegal, and he asked that his claims be investigated. "I call upon Mr. Fred Cowan, attorney general of Kentucky, to exercise his official powers to the fullest extent to ensure that this election is not stolen from me on Election Day by voter fraud, machine malfunction or governmental skulduggery."[37]

The U.S. Attorney's office did not comment on the accusations. Federal Bureau of Investigation records requested via the Freedom of Information Act show a clearer picture of the accusations and the investigation into Gatewood's claims.

The FBI began by interviewing the person who had inspected the phone lines for Gatewood and who confirmed that they were tapped. Although the person's name was redacted from records, a murky picture begins to emerge. "[Redacted] advised that early March 1991, while at the Louisville campaign office, he had contacted the Lexington office. He stated that during the course of that conversation, his call was put on hold and while he was in the hold pattern, he heard a transmission and the words 'PV49.' He then stated that the telephone went dead."

Gatewood's diesel Mercedes-Benz was dubbed the Hempmobile, and Gatewood demonstrated the promise of hemp oil as a fuel by adding it to his tank. He drove Willie Nelson to Frankfort in the Hempmobile before the 1991 primary election.

The campaign worker who was interviewed then let Gatewood know about this suspicious event, and Gatewood and Lucchese decided to have the phones inspected: "[Redacted] knew a campaign volunteer, [redacted], who also worked for a security company, [redacted] offered to provide a machine that could check phone lines for taps and provided a movie to illustrate the use of the machine."

This campaign volunteer and amateur security specialist confirmed to Gatewood that there were taps on both his and Lucchese's phone lines. Gatewood determined to get in touch with local authorities, and to plan the press conference. If these circumstances were not already questionable, the story unraveled even further as the FBI continued to investigate. After interviewing those involved, they had the phone company check the lines for Gatewood. "On April 25, 1991, [redacted] General Telephone Company, Security department, Lexington, Kentucky, advised that a check of the telephone service at the Gatewood Galbraith headquarters, 1307 South Limestone Street, Lexington, Kentucky, was negative in detecting any type of tapping device or any other evidence indicating any prior taps."[38]

At least according to the phone company, no taps were ever put on Gatewood's line. The story got even shakier once the investigation was underway and the phone company had thoroughly inspected the line that Gatewood was suspicious of. The campaign volunteer who inspected the lines, a few weeks after the press conference, sold the wiretap inspection machine at a swap meet in Louisville for $3,000 and claimed that he had no way to find out where it was.

Whether from genuine suspicion or just a desire to generate some sensational media coverage, Gatewood made this another headline attached to his campaign. It was seldom his ideas that made the front page, but rather unsubstantiated claims, court appearances, brief trips to jail, and questions about his drug use.

A few days after the press conference, Gatewood attended a pro-marijuana rally on his old stamping grounds: the University of Kentucky campus. He spoke at the event, and told the students gathered why he was the right person to lead the state. At least one student questioned whether Gatewood was really qualified, given his financial mismanagement and other campaign gaffes. Mark Rucker, a first-year UK graduate student, challenged Gatewood before the crowd: "I just have a considerable amount of doubt that if you were elected that you would be able to handle the finances of the state if you can't even control your own."

Gatewood, not used to this kind of criticism in a crowd of like-minded individuals, explained his predicament, saying that he was giving up a large income as an attorney in order to make his campaign promises a reality, and to build a better life for Kentuckians. "If I stayed in there working the way I did, I'd have had no problem meeting all those obligations. But as it is right now, there are principles that need to come out and be fought for. And all I do is owe it to them. I mean, I owe a lot of people. And everybody always gets paid."

The exchange continued, Gatewood and Rucker arguing back and forth in the middle of the crowd. Rucker brought up Gatewood's recent night in jail, and Gatewood bristled. "I'm down here on the bottom like the rest of us." He then added, "Son, I'll tell you, a day in jail might do you a lot of good with your attitude."

Another student, speaking to the reporter covering the event, delivered another stinging dismissal. "I think he's born to lose, personally. He doesn't have the money to win any sort of campaign."[39]

Gatewood was drawing a lot of attention, but these recent events had negatively impacted his campaign, even in the eyes of the young people he still identified with, and who he expected would be some of his most ardent supporters.

Around this time, a poll conducted and released by the *Courier-Journal* claimed that he had about 1 percent of public support in the May primary, which infuriated Gatewood. He claimed that the result of the *Courier-Journal* not covering his campaign was to "exclude a legitimate candidate and their issues from a statewide race. It arbitrarily excludes what may be viable issues from being examined in the marketplace of ideas and is a disservice to the people and the political process." Gatewood claimed that if his vote total did not exceed the 1 percent from the poll plus the poll's 3.5 percent margin of error, he would permanently retire from politics.[40]

Constantly trying to find ways to raise money and pay off his campaign debt, Gatewood came up with a new idea for an event: GateWoodstock. He announced the three-day concert with yet another press conference in downtown Lexington. The event would be held on April 26–28, 1991, in rural Bath County in eastern Kentucky, and would involve eighteen local and regional bands. The idea was to raise money, but also to mimic the famous Woodstock music festival held in rural New York in 1969 by bringing together creative, imaginative, and open-minded people. Gatewood told the press: "We believe we represent that generation, many of whom believe that Woodstock stood for individual rights, personal privacy, pro-choice and individual choice, and an outlook on life that seeks to make a reality of those thousand points of light and a kinder, gentler nation that I think George Bush misappropriated for his own mentality and perspective."[41]

Gatewood arrived at GateWoodstock with nine-year-old Abby and six-year-old Molly. A news photograph showed Gatewood in a dress shirt and slacks, holding Abby's hand and carrying Molly in his arms as they walked through the fields at the site of the concert. The reporter recorded that Abby asked Gatewood an interesting question as they toured the grounds: "Is there any TVs here?"[42]

Although attendance was lighter than Gatewood wanted, the show went on without many hitches, and Gatewood spoke at the event, trying to rally last-minute support for the campaign. Suddenly, while on stage, he began to have severe chest pains. His limbs were numb, and something didn't feel right. He had some friends drive him straightaway to a hospital in Lexington, where he was admitted. The toll of the campaign was clear: Gatewood had lost thirty-two pounds over the last year and was diagnosed with exhaustion and bronchitis. Between the stress and anxiety of the campaign and Gatewood's various legal and financial issues, his immune system and mental health were fraying and at risk of collapse.[43]

This was the first, but would not be the last, time that Gatewood's campaigns took a toll on his health. Eerily foreshadowing a future campaign in 2011, the bronchitis and exhaustion should have been a stark warning to Gatewood about the costs of life in politics.

By the time the May 28 primary rolled around, the Democratic nomination was a four-person race. Kentucky's first lady, Martha Wilkinson, had dropped out. Lexington mayor Scotty Baesler, Lieutenant Governor Brereton Jones, and Dr. Floyd Poore remained in the race along with Gatewood, and continued to vie for Democratic votes. Gatewood tried to rest following his brief stay in the hospital, but continued to campaign when he could.

The day of the primary finally arrived, and the result was never really in doubt. Jones had been the leading fundraiser of the remaining candidates and was the presumptive favorite to win the nomination. He did so, topping the second-place Baesler by 35,000 votes. Gatewood finished a very distant fourth, tallying 25,834 votes in the election. The only county he didn't finish last in was his home county, Fayette, where he eked out a third-place finish over Poore.[44]

To Gatewood's relief, he had made good on his promise to the *Courier-Journal*. Rather than 1 or even 4.5 percent, he had garnered the support of 5.3 percent of the Democratic voters. His political career could continue, and he already set his sights on the future.

The period from 1989 through the 1991 primary was a chaotic, exciting, turbulent, and busy time in Gatewood's life. He had continued to practice law, and tried to support his children and ex-wife with the money they needed to ensure a secure and happy life. He was a young and newly single father, who was trying to be present for his kids while also supporting his own ambitions.

The 1991 race was when Gatewood truly broke out on the public scene. He began what would become a lifelong friendship with Willie Nelson, who injected excitement and interest into his campaign. He was always a favorite of at least Lexington political reporters, with whom he enjoyed a productive relationship: he would receive at least some coverage of his campaign activities, while they always found something interesting to print from Gatewood's events and appearances.

From the beginning, his campaign was beset with financial, legal, and personal issues. When Nelson's endorsement and appearance were making headlines and lending some momentum to the campaign, Gatewood had to literally beg for donations in order for the fundraising concert to go on. When he couldn't fulfill his financial obligations to Susan and his girls, or pay the taxes he owed, he didn't settle things quietly. He missed court appearances and continue to spend every cent he could on the campaign instead of digging himself out of the hole he had created. Rather than playing by the rules and making logical choices about his political pursuits, he instead spent a night in jail. Taking the word of campaign volunteers and thinking conspiratorially, he made sensational claims about his phones being tapped, or newspapers callously leaving him out of their coverage of the race.

These missteps became the story of his campaign. Gatewood was haunted by his faults, which were amplified by the bright lights of an important statewide race. In this, some will see hubris and carelessness. Others see a willingness to pursue passion and purpose with little regard for the consequences.

The 1991 race made Gatewood a local political celebrity in Kentucky, and it also cemented his populist message. With Willie Nelson he focused on the well-being of rural communities and farmers. His campaign message about marijuana and hemp was controversial, but the facts were mostly on Gatewood's side, as we have seen in the ensuing three decades. He brought up issues in the campaign that showed he was intelligent and had insight into what would become some of the most important topics in American society. He discussed opioid and heroin addiction, mental health, mass incarceration, environmental protections, and the hollowing out of rural communities left behind in the twenty-first century. In a world of international free trade agreements, rapid technological development, and economic globalization, many were left hopeless.

He didn't see his financial struggles or missteps as a character flaw. Instead, he claimed that they proved two things: first, that he was not part of some elite class but was rather a normal citizen who had the same hardships and shortcomings as those that he sought to represent in Frankfort, and second, that his choices proved his passion for what he believed in. He was giving up what might be a lucrative career in order to fight for his fellow Kentuckians and to build a better future for the commonwealth he loved so dearly.

The chaos of his 1991 campaign would have dissuaded some from continuing in politics. For Gatewood, it was just a taste of what was to come. He decided that his health, his finances, and his name were worth the scrutiny, worth the insults. By the time of the primary, he had already decided what to do next: run for governor again in 1995.

5

The War on Drugs, the Militia, and the Fourth of July

Following the bitter disappointment of the 1991 primary, Gatewood watched the rest of the election unfold under the burden of a heavy depression. He was still recovering from his collapse. The campaign, on top of the legal and financial troubles he found himself embroiled in, left him weak. The anxieties of his future were difficult to tamp down. While defying expectations, he had still lost, and he found himself in debt to Susan, his creditors, the local government, and the Internal Revenue Service. After giving so much of himself to the campaign, he had little to show for it, other than the convictions that kept him and his hopes for the '95 election alive.

Gatewood had to give up his office and home, and, for a brief period, lived in his car. A friend who owned a Lexington hotel allowed him to camp in a room there and to pay what he could when he could. As he meandered his way through this funk, he continued to search for ways to speak out about his beliefs. Brereton C. Jones won the 1991 general election handily, defeating Larry Hopkins in the biggest landslide in the history of Kentucky gubernatorial elections. Gatewood continued to show up in the news as he planned for his political future.

Shortly after the 1991 election, the *Herald-Leader* reported on the activities of the Kentucky State Police and others in the newly formed Governor's Marijuana Strike Force. "Before the onset of cold weather curtailed the growing season, efforts by federal, state and local officials—working as the Governor's Marijuana Strike Force—destroyed 823,088 plants. That is enough marijuana to make 202 cigarettes for every man, woman and child in Kentucky."[1]

The numbers were staggering. They also proved what Gatewood had been saying for years: Kentuckians were good at growing marijuana. The report showed that of Kentucky's 120 counties, authorities found marijuana plants growing in 118 of them. The nearly 8,500 plots that were located were double those of the previous year. While the report celebrated the destruction of the plants, Gatewood saw only the possibilities. Marijuana was already growing in nearly every corner of Kentucky. What if, instead of destroying it, the government supported its cultivation and used the funds available from its taxation to bolster an ailing state government and welfare programs?

"I think it is obscene to count any of that as a victory. It's well known that where marijuana is accessible, hard drug use goes down," Gatewood said. Pointing out the irony of the situation, Gatewood bemoaned the government programs suffering from this waste, including education, health programs, and human services. "There's a hell of a lot of money in those hills, folks. Instead of burning it we ought to be taxing it and spending it."[2]

Gatewood eventually found a new office in downtown Lexington, and business seemed like it was picking up. By early 1992 he was already trying to build support for his run for governor in 1995. He decided that a change in tack was necessary if he wanted to be more successful in politics. Rather than focusing on the benefits of recreational marijuana, he pivoted to focus on hemp. Pointing out that the marijuana issue had been the sole focus of the media during his first run for governor, Gatewood vowed not to pursue recreational legalization of the drug. If he focused on hemp and medical marijuana, Gatewood felt, his other ideas wouldn't be so obscured during the race.

He also made a public promise not to put himself or his family through the same financial and emotional tolls as the previous election. A new law passed in 1992 gave "2-for-1" public financing to candidates for governor and lieutenant governor. If the ticket could raise money above the threshold of $600,000, then they would receive a $1.2 million match. Gatewood planned to spread this fundraising out over the three years leading up to the next primary, mainly through musical and public events, including repeat GateWoodstock concerts.[3] The first of these took place in May 1992, nearly a year after Gatewood had collapsed onstage at the same event. This time, 250 supporters attended, and Gatewood hoped this was the beginning of a new political chapter.[4]

In his memoir, Gatewood devoted an entire chapter to the letters that he received from supporters following the 1991 election. He admitted that much of this new support was due to his association with Willie Nelson. With his new friend's help, his story was spreading and he was quickly becoming a cult hero to people across the country. He received letters from supporters of all kinds: from a group of police officers who saw marijuana laws as a pathway toward a brutal police state, from those incarcerated for growing a handful of plants on their property, from a Vietnam veteran who used marijuana to improve his quality of life, from a woman caring for a husband who was suffering from AIDS and had months to live with only marijuana providing any respite from his terrible symptoms. These letters, and the voices of those suffering, gave Gatewood new strength. No matter the odds, he would fight for what he believed in.[5]

As Gatewood kept up his law practice and set lofty goals for fundraising in service of the 1995 campaign, he always had an eye out for making the news and drawing attention to the race. Even as he shied away from evangelizing for recreational marijuana, he continued to promote its use as a medicine, fully convinced that it had benefited his health and that its prohibition was hurting the lives of millions of people who had to turn to opioids or opiates when searching for relief. Finally he decided that this debate should happen in the open, so that everyone could learn more of the truth, as he understood it, about marijuana as medicine.

In January 1993 Gatewood rented space in the downtown Lexington Hyatt Hotel, just off the main square and next to the famous Rupp Arena. He invited three individuals to participate in the event, which he named the Science & Truth Hearings. Gatewood, along with a cadre of public health representatives and doctors, were set to evaluate the opinions of three experts who had agreed to participate. They were Dr. Lester Grinspoon, who was an associate professor of psychiatry at Harvard Medical School, Dr. John Morgan, professor of pharmacology at the City University of New York and at Mount Sinai Hospital, and Dr. Tod Mikuriya, a psychiatrist from Berkeley, California. These panelists were already in favor of medical marijuana and were recruited by Gatewood both for their expertise and for their opinions. The panel also heard from multiple patients who used marijuana for its pain-relieving properties and who shared stories about the power of marijuana in relieving symptoms of cancer, glaucoma, multiple sclerosis, and AIDS.[6]

In the lead-up to the event, Gatewood expounded on the possibilities of the medical marijuana movement. He promoted the plant's ability not only to heal the ills of disease and to help patients avoid powerful pharmaceuticals but also to cut into the profits of pharmaceutical companies. "I believe the answer to the question is going to be, yes, marijuana as a medicine could cut the cost of health care in the Commonwealth of Kentucky significantly in various areas."[7]

While this was an event to draw publicity to his campaign and for his own passions, it was also an intellectual exercise for Gatewood. He had long been formulating his own ideas about the ways in which the United States economy and society had evolved, forsaking agriculture and local economies in favor of corporations and synthetic materials. The "synthetic subversion," as Gatewood styled it, was in no way better evidenced than in the production of synthetic painkillers. He could not square this in his mind. Here was, as he and his experts saw it, a perfectly safe, responsible, and beneficial natural plant that could treat patients gently and without side effects. Instead, it was illegal, while pharmaceutical companies across the world were quickly generating a wave of new opioid painkillers that would be a scourge for decades to come.

A mere three years after the event, the company Purdue Pharma released its new pill, OxyContin. The drug was a revolutionary extended-release capsule containing the opioid oxycodone, which mirrored the euphoric and addictive effects of morphine and was created to treat only extremely severe pain in cancer patients, or to provide palliative relief for those on the verge of death. Somehow Purdue Pharma was able to finagle approval from the FDA to prescribe OxyContin to a much wider group: anyone experiencing pain. The company's ruthless marketing tactics and high-pressure sales contests allowed it to drive up profits and to flood the country with Oxy or OC, as it was commonly referred to on the street. Journalist and author Patrick Radden Keefe explores this development and the history of the powerful Sackler family, who founded Purdue Pharma, in his award-winning book *Empire of Pain.* Other authors have also identified this development as the birth of the opioid crisis in America, which continues to have devastating effects in Kentucky in particular. Gatewood was prescient in his insistence that synthetic pharmaceuticals would have a ruinous impact on American society.

Quite simply, his predictions came true. Sales of OxyContin rose from $50 million in 1996 to $1 billion by 2000. By the new millennium, oxycodone (the active opioid in OxyContin) became the most prescribed drug in the United States. Going for as much as $120 a pill, OxyContin ravaged rural communities, where its use became widespread, and where sales incentives led Purdue Pharma to focus its distribution efforts. In one particularly egregious example, a drugstore in the 400-person town of Kermit, West Virginia, received nine million hydrocodone pills (another synthetic opioid) in the span of two years. As patients became addicted and prescriptions became harder to find, they would turn to heroin or the even more powerful synthetic opioid, fentanyl, which ignited a new explosion of addiction and death.[8]

Gatewood saw the hearings as a way to strike back against the efforts of pharmaceutical companies and to share what he considered common sense opinions about the role of marijuana in medical treatment. In his recollection of the event, even though he invited all the news and media outlets in Kentucky, none of them showed up. He took this as a willingness to keep the wool pulled over their eyes, and an indication that they had a vendetta against him and his views. He was wrong. Bill Estep, a reporter for the *Lexington Herald-Leader*, was in attendance and recorded the testimony of some of the patients who spoke. Thomas Hart, a man from Covington, Kentucky, who suffered from AIDS, testified that he was taking $800 worth of prescription drugs for his disease, while marijuana worked better to help with the problems he experienced sleeping and eating. "The marijuana has been the only benefit that I have come across as far as making me feel better," Hart explained.

The doctors involved in the panel were still hesitant to explicitly endorse medical marijuana and explained that there were plenty of unanswered questions about how much money it could save patients, or if its effects were truly not harmful. They made clear that even though the gathering was billed as the "Science & Truth Hearings," no scientific evidence or controlled studies of marijuana's benefits were presented.[9]

Their skepticism was fair, but also evidence of the real problem at hand. Gatewood had most certainly recruited medical professionals who were already in favor of marijuana to take part in the event, but the issue itself merited further discussion and investigation. Because of its status as a federally scheduled drug with no medical uses, no scientists had the ability to study marijuana or to fully explore its therapeutic benefits.

Gatewood decried the lack of coverage and viewed this as part of the corporate conspiracy to keep his views out of the mainstream. Even though the event was obviously designed as a form of political publicity, with impartial participants, he framed the alleged media silence as willful ignorance. "They are incapable of considering the merits of any view alternate to their corporate agenda. They have given up relying on science and truth as a compass. They have morphed from voluntary ignorance to intellectual eunuchs, unable to erect thought processes on their own. They have no shame."[10]

As he began to raise money and to plan for his next race, the reality of marijuana prohibition would hit close to home. The movement for medical marijuana was going nowhere in Kentucky. The Kentucky State Police and federal authorities were redoubling their efforts to destroy as much illegal marijuana as possible. Encouraged by an increase in funding from the federal War on Drugs, state police and local authorities were able to employ new technologies and manpower solely dedicated to tracking down and punishing those who continued to cultivate, import, and use marijuana throughout the commonwealth.

This conflict came to a head in 1993, with bloody consequences.

Gatewood continued to campaign and struggled to raise money for the '95 race. He kept up his law practice and remained busy with his cases. Even with the uptick in fame and notoriety from the '91 race, and the increase in business it brought to his practice, he struggled to make ends meet. Finally he was out of options. In April 1993 he filed for Chapter 7 bankruptcy protection in federal court. In the filing, he listed total assets of $18,252.60 and debts of $285,572.74. These debts included more than $65,000 owed to the IRS.[11] Gatewood never mentions this second bankruptcy filing in his memoir.

As his political hopes clung to life and bankruptcy afforded him some measure of relief, trouble brewed in nearby Brodhead, Kentucky. Tragedy would soon give Gatewood a renewed sense of commitment to the causes he believed in, and new fodder for decrying the war on drugs and the efforts of the Kentucky State Police in their crusade to rid the Commonwealth of illegal marijuana.

Sunday, August 8, 1993, was a sunny summer morning that started like any other for four-year-old Jacob Jones. He rolled out of bed, got some breakfast, and started playing video games in his family living room. As he was playing, he noticed a strange vibration shaking the trailer where he, his mother, and his father lived together in rural Brodhead. The vibration started as a subtle sensation but grew stronger and stronger. It shook the walls, and Jacob felt it through the floor where he sat. It got so strong that he remembers it penetrating his body and filling him with a sense of foreboding.[12]

Today Jacob often masks the traumatic events of his past with a friendly and soft-spoken manner. His long and curly chestnut hair falls over his shoulders, and his kind eyes hide the pain of his past, something that he has had a long time to practice.

Back then he didn't understand what was happening. He didn't realize what the helicopters meant. He certainly didn't know that the dramatic events of the next few hours would shape the rest of his life. He didn't know that he had so little time left with his father.

Jacob's father, Gary Shepherd, grew up on a family farm in Brodhead and served in Vietnam, earning a Purple Heart for injuries he sustained in action. Throughout the rest of his life, his left shoulder and arm were immobilized by these wounds. After returning from war, he worked in a nearby pet food factory, and twin passions shaped his life: religion and cannabis.

He first discovered cannabis while serving in Vietnam, when his follow soldiers offered him a joint. Growing up hearing about the evils of drug use, Shepherd was suspicious at first. These suspicions quickly receded, and he became a regular user. He realized that marijuana had medicinal properties. When he returned to Brodhead, he openly talked of his experience with the plant to anyone who would listen. He started growing his own marijuana, usually in remote wooded areas away from the prying eyes of neighbors or law enforcement. As he grew older and relied on the plant more and more, he defiantly grew it in his backyard; plants surrounded his trailer, and seedlings grew under the protection of an old satellite dish on his property.

According to Jacob, his father openly shared that he was growing the plants on his property with the Rockcastle County sheriff. More than a year prior to the events of August 1993, troopers from the Kentucky State Police had visited the property in Shepherd's absence and found seedlings growing in his garage. They didn't remove any of the plants or arrest Shepherd. When Shepherd returned home and found evidence of the troopers' visit, he went to the county sheriff's office and protested. The fact that Shepherd grew marijuana on his property was not a secret, and law enforcement officers in the area were obviously aware of this activity.

Even aside from Shepherd's reputation regarding marijuana in the community, he was seen as a passionate and animated man. He had a deep and abiding passion for religion, often uniting his belief in Jesus Christ with his marijuana advocacy. His views and zealous manner led to social isolation in the traditional community he called home. By 1993 he had been banned from multiple churches in the area due to disagreements with local preachers and congregations. By the time Jacob was four, his father had instilled in him a great respect for the teachings of Jesus Christ. Jacob recalls spending time with his father fishing and hiking, and the long conversations they would have about Christianity, personal liberty, mathematics, and God. So widespread was Shepherd's reputation for outspokenness regarding religion that local law enforcement had a special code name for him: "Jesus."

It is with these tensions in mind that the events of August 8 remain so troubling. Jacob's mother, Mary Jones, had met Gary years earlier while trying to find her way out of a conflictive previous marriage. Gary showed her kindness and peace, offering a place for her to heal. Their relationship bloomed.

On that summer Sunday, Shepherd realized that the circling helicopter was scaring his young son and his wife. It hovered over his property, now violently shaking their trailer. He told his family to stay inside. He went outside into his family's front yard and motioned for the helicopter to land so that he could talk to the officers. He carried a rifle and approached the helicopter as it landed in an adjacent field, behind a chain link fence. Shepherd walked to the fence and spoke with the law enforcement officers about why they were there. They told Shepherd they had received a call that there were marijuana plants on his property, and they were there as part of the Governor's Marijuana Strike Force. The helicopter they used was on loan from the Kentucky National Guard. They informed Shepherd that they would need to enter his property and cut the plants down. Shepherd quickly replied, "Over my dead body." Law enforcement would later point to this statement and the fact that Shepherd was armed to claim that he was prepared for violence and to explain the horrific events of that day.

The Governor's Marijuana Strike Force had started its work in 1989, when the Kentucky State Police received a grant of $250,000 from the U.S. Bureau of Justice Assistance.[13] Kentucky law enforcement had long targeted the illicit marijuana trade before the task force was established. From 1985 through 1991, the Kentucky State Police and related law enforcement eradicated 4,601,795 marijuana plants and arrested 1,681 individuals on charges related to growing marijuana. In 1991, Kentucky ranked first in the country for number of marijuana plants eradicated.[14]

It is difficult to comprehend these numbers or to put them in proper perspective. Suffice it to say that Kentucky, one of the poorest and least populated states, for much of the twentieth century wallowed at the worst levels of most measures of well-being: public health, preventable disease, poverty, child poverty, tobacco use, educational attainment, and more. But it led the country in marijuana eradication and arrests.

Troopers involved in these efforts used cutting-edge technology—helicopters, video cameras, infrared monitors, and night vision goggles—to find and destroy marijuana crops that had long dotted the landscape in Kentucky and to prosecute growers. Troopers didn't need to use this technology to find Gary Shepherd's plants: he had strolled into the sheriff's office and told him exactly where to find them.

Once Shepherd confronted the troopers on that sunny August morning, they boarded the helicopter and flew off. What he and his family could not know was that the four words "Over my dead body" set off a massive law enforcement operation. State police troopers, in coordination with local law enforcement, created barricades on the roads approaching Shepherd's property. Over thirty officers converged on the property, where Shepherd had gone back to playing video games with Jacob, playing outside in their sandbox, and working on his truck in the driveway, always keeping his rifle within arm's reach.

News quickly spread about the encounter. Charles Shepherd, Gary's cousin and a county deputy who had recently completed hostage negotiation training, tried to make it past the roadblocks to defuse the situation. The officers wouldn't let Charles through, and refused access to concerned neighbors who knew Gary and were familiar with his eccentricities.

As midmorning stretched into afternoon, regional news networks started to cover what was now labeled a hostage situation. An armed standoff between a drug-crazed Vietnam veteran and police made for splashy headlines. Jacob saw it a different way. He began to understand that the troopers surrounding the property meant harm to his father.

"They sort of already knew at this time, that they were going to execute my father. It was around this time that I actually realized that as well. And that was a changing moment in my life," Jacob recalls. His protective instincts took over. "There was pretty much a war happening to my family. So I went inside and I grabbed a toy sword. I ran back outside and waved it through our chain link fence."

Using a megaphone, the troopers ordered Shepherd to approach the fence that bordered his property in order to negotiate for his surrender and arrest. It was at this point that Shepherd may have inadvertently sealed his fate. He walked to his porch, picked up his rifle, and set it in the crook of his disabled left arm. The troopers ordered Jacob and his mother to stand with their hands in the air next to the trailer. Shepherd approached the gate, still carrying his gun, and was also ordered to stop and put his hands in the air. As he stood hardly six feet from his family, and about twenty feet from the nearest troops, the situation went to hell. From Jacob's memory, at this point Gary reached over and held the rifle in his right arm and started to raise it into the air. He wasn't able to raise his left arm above his shoulder, and he responded to the troopers' demands that he drop the rifle by shouting, "No, I don't believe like you do!"

This is where Jacob's memory gets blurry. And for good reason. A concussion grenade was thrown and exploded in the few feet between where his mother stood, holding him, and where his father remained in the driveway. A deafening bang. A cloud of smoke. A flurry of gunshots as all three fell to the ground.

As the cloud settled, and Jacob's ears rang with echoes of the volley, his mother's screams pierced the air. His father lay in a pool of his own blood, killed instantly by nine gunshot wounds, many to his head and neck. A bullet fragment had grazed his mother's skull, and she dropped Jacob, who lay in the dirt. As his senses returned, he looked down at his father's body. Blood speckled Jacob's face, crimson red on pale white.

News quickly spread about Shepherd's death, as all the local news outlets reported on the dramatic standoff and the shooting. As Jacob's family reeled from their loss, questions about police conduct began to spread. Why use such draconian measures for a small patch of twenty-five marijuana plants? Why send the National Guard and State Police when Shepherd himself had told local authorities what he was doing on his land? Most of all, why inflame a situation that could have been resolved with the help of friends and neighbors? Gary's brother, Bill, wasn't even allowed to approach the scene or communicate with Gary. The family remained confident that Bill could have deescalated the situation and counteracted Gary's brashness in the moment. As Bill later said, "He needed help. He didn't need to be killed. Is it worth killing somebody over some pot?"[15]

The state began an internal investigation into Shepherd's killing. As the investigation progressed, the case was also presented to a grand jury in Rockcastle County. Records from the Kentucky State Police internal investigation received via an Open Records request show the detail and fastidiousness of bureaucratic reporting.[16] The records are thorough, and include lists of all of the officers involved as well as time-stamped reporting of the incident. It's clear from these records that the officers involved truly feared for their lives and saw Shepherd as unstable. He refused to lay down the rifle that he carried around his property, and he seemed intent on defying the orders of the officers involved. He continued to utter statements that convinced the officers that he was serious about his willingness to die before they would step foot on his property.

This, along with constant refrains from Shepherd that he was willing to die for his beliefs, appears to have convinced the troopers that he was serious. As the standoff stretched into early afternoon, Shepherd left his rifle on the porch and approached the negotiators. When he finished speaking with them and turned back toward the trailer, where Jacob and his mother were standing, two Kentucky State Police officers emerged from the tobacco field next door. One of them threw the distraction device in an effort to keep Shepherd away from his family. Shepherd picked up his rifle and walked toward the two officers. As they yelled at Shepherd to stop walking and drop his weapon, he yelled, "No, I don't believe like you do!" Convinced that he was preparing to shoot, the officers fired on him. As the report states, "Almost simultaneously," the two troopers "fired at Shepherd with their MP-5 nine millimeter assault rifles. Shepherd did not have an opportunity to discharge his rifle before being struck by the state police rounds."

One of the Kentucky State Police officers who took part in the actions that summer day, now retired, was reluctantly interviewed about what happened in Brodhead. "They put my family through hell. I'd rather not dig it up." When asked about that day, he was adamant: "Gary Shepherd was not killed because of marijuana. He was trying to shoot us."[17] Part of his reticence was due to what happened next. Following the internal report from the Kentucky State Police and the grand jury's decision not to indict the officers, Jacob's family weren't satisfied. With the county attorney dropping the case, they decided to file a civil suit against the Kentucky State Police, initially asking for $23 million. A rush to secure an attorney directed them to a lawyer from New York who went on to commit a series of legal blunders. These included failure to personally name the involved officers in the suit, which was dismissed in 1996, then reinstated, then dismissed again.

Jacob recalls these painful years, growing up as he continued to appear in court and be a part of a protracted legal battle. What bothered Jacob most of all was how his mother was depicted: as unreliable and unstable, too emotionally wrecked by the ordeal to be a valid witness. "They really ridiculed her in court a lot, the bullet fragment that she took in the head. They asked her what she saw, that she just didn't hit her head on a cabinet or something."

While Gatewood was never their lawyer, Jacob remembered how he visited the family and lent a compassionate ear. "My family met Gatewood after my father was killed. . . . Gatewood also went around to some neighbors here, which was mainly family members and cousins, and just tried to get a real firm grasp on the case. He never was our lawyer, but he acted more as . . . a friend and someone who kind of came and consoled us in the way he showed empathy, and he connected with my family in a tragic time."

In the days following the shooting, Gatewood was one of many who showed up in Rockcastle County to protest the actions of the Kentucky State Police. Gathered at the courthouse, a bevy of protestors took turns speaking and decried the actions of the police. Speakers included representatives from the Black Panthers, as well as Richard Cowan, the national director of NORML. Of course Gatewood was a driving force in the protests and spoke his mind to the reporters and television crews gathered for the event. "Gary Shepherd's death was the product of a misguided, misdirected and insane policy against the people of this country."[18]

Gatewood lent a sympathetic ear to Jacob and his family, but he also committed himself to getting something done out of this horrific tragedy. He promised from the outset to take organized action against the state police and to right this injustice. "We believe that Gary's death illustrates the increasing militarization of the war against marijuana. It's going to result in more of these tragedies. We seek to [ensure that] Gary Shepherd was the last victim of this misdirected policy."[19] He promised to deliver a petition to Governor Brereton C. Jones to "take those damn helicopters out of the sky."[20]

The Kentucky State Police trooper who was recently interviewed thought that Gatewood was using this public incident for political gain, even while he had personal admiration for him. Echoing the words of so many who remembered him, he recalled Gatewood as a "cut-up. He was an entertainer, and a politician, probably before his time." Even thirty years later, the retired trooper defended the work of the Kentucky State Police and the Marijuana Strike Force: "The flyovers were very successful." He also mentioned the fact that many of the patches they found and destroyed were booby-trapped. A favorite tactic of marijuana growers who were trying to keep out prying eyes was hanging fish hooks from trees so that any wayward visitors would leave with more than they bargained for.

Gatewood found the task force's military tactics and advanced warfare technology to be overblown and extreme. After spending much of his public life defending the crop, he finally had a face to put on his efforts. He united protestors and activists and organized their criticism of these police procedures into actual change. In the days following the protest, Gatewood and a group of activists delivered a petition with more than two thousand signatures to Governor Jones and threatened to file a lawsuit blocking the raids.

Gatewood's actions became a valuable example for Jacob. Much like his father, Jacob became passionate about marijuana, and worked as an activist in protests, marches, and demonstrations. In his late twenties, Jacob enrolled at the University of Kentucky, where he specialized in creative writing and poetry.

While Governor Jones shrugged off the petition and the threats, Gatewood's involvement made a true impact on Jacob and his family. It also provided new fodder for Gatewood's upcoming campaign. He painted a picture of the Kentucky State Police as aggressive, overly powerful, and militaristic. This was another way he could frame himself as a protector of personal liberties against forces out to strip Kentuckians of their freedoms.

The death of Shepherd was a tragic chapter in Kentucky history. While most of the arguments in court and in public opinion centered on the actions of Shepherd and the troopers involved, most people missed the point. Shepherd most certainly acted in a threatening manner that endangered the lives of his family and the troopers involved. The troopers used deadly force and blocked efforts from friends and family to deescalate the situation. While they were cleared of wrongdoing, their actions that day have had a traumatic effect on their lives.

Gatewood, Jack Herer (*second from left*), Kim Eisner, and an unidentified man. Hemp and marijuana activist Herer was a longtime friend and mentor of Gatewood's; he was the author of *The Emperor Wears No Clothes*. He often said Gatewood was among the most knowledgeable individuals he knew with regard to industrial hemp and its uses.

Perhaps the biggest tragedy was a failure of policy. This is why Gatewood focused his efforts on action rather than only words and protests. What ended in Shepherd's death began with the prohibition of marijuana. As Gary's brother pointed out, was the elimination of marijuana plants worth the death of even one man? If these dangerous situations could go bad, were they worth it at all? Gatewood was willing to bet the rest of his political life that they were not, and that more people would agree with him when shown the light of truth.

While the Gary Shepherd tragedy and the ongoing campaign took most of his attention and energy, during this time Gatewood was also enjoying a new romance. Referred to in his autobiography by the name Daisy, Kim Eisner met Gatewood at GateWoodstock in 1992, and he was immediately enchanted. While Gatewood continued to struggle with finances and with meeting his child support commitments, he and Susan still shared a relationship characterized by friendly respect. Yet Susan had now begun her own studies to become an attorney, and even though he still spent time with his ex-wife and daughters, Gatewood was lonely and ready again for love.

Kim recalled her first encounter with Gatewood. She hadn't really smoked pot before, but at that initial meeting she found herself with a group that included Gatewood, passing a joint around a circle. At one point Gatewood thought that a young man was taking too long with it and he said, "Young man, that ain't no microphone!"[21]

Kim remembered that there was an attraction between the two of them from the very start, even though Gatewood was older than her. "I think there was a spark right in the beginning, but I remember thinking, this guy's too old for me. I mean, he was nineteen, twenty years my senior, but there was something about him that I really was drawn to."

This natural attraction led to a blossoming romance, but Kim also became a partner in Gatewood's political and organizing efforts. She recalled coming to the first few meetings for his 1995 campaign, and noticing the same things that John Holmstrom saw when he came to cover the '91 campaign for *High Times*. Things were disorganized, out of order, and underfunded. The campaign didn't even have a list of volunteers, or phone numbers where they could reach supporters. Kim became the de facto organizer and administrator. She was enthusiastic about Gatewood's ideas and his passions.

Gatewood's daughters took to Kim easily, and she became a new constant in their lives. As she and Gatewood continued as a couple, she became entwined in their family, as well as a major supporter and organizer for his campaign. She and Susan became friends, consciously working together to cultivate a close relationship. From Susan's perspective, "Having Kim in Gatewood's life gave our daughters a female presence that was important to the girls when they spent time with their dad. Having Kim in our lives was a positive in all respects, and it was a relief to me that she was there for the girls and loved them."[22] The two women continue to show great respect and love for one another. Kim echoed this sentiment: "From the very beginning . . . just how nice she was to me when we were introduced." Kim was impressed by the friendly relationship between Gatewood and Susan. "Their love for each other, their support for each other was so obvious to me in my first meeting with them."

Kim and Gatewood enjoyed spending time with one another and bonded over their numerous road trips. Gatewood did not like to fly, so he and Kim would drive all over the country for speaking engagements at pro-marijuana marches and rallies. They would drive, talk, march, and grow in love on the road. Their relationship was pure fun; they truly valued each other's intellects, and they could make a good time out of any situation.

Kim was in all ways Gatewood's partner in life and in his campaigns for office and for marijuana. When he was preparing for the Science & Truth Hearings, Kim ferried the participants from the airport to the Hyatt. She stepped in to do whatever was necessary. She loved the man, but she also believed in the mission herself.

Sometimes it was hard to keep their privacy. Gatewood was so magnetic, and knew so many, that it was relatively impossible to go anywhere that they wouldn't be chatted up or interrupted. "Always when you were with Gatewood," said Kim, "it was never me and Gatewood. We had to go pretty far away if we wanted Kim-Gatewood time."[23]

Kim worked for a local law firm in Lexington, so she also had some understanding of Gatewood's law practice. She remembered how talented he was as a trial attorney. He could always get the jury on his side. Some of the financial difficulties Gatewood experienced during this time also spoke to his generosity. He did pro bono work, according to Kim, on a daily basis. Already splitting his time between his practice and the campaign, he truly couldn't afford doing this work for free. He did it anyway.

Kim would be one of the most important parts of Gatewood's life for the next decade, and they would remain friends. She had an important role to play in the rest of his story, and her partnership and love were clearly vital to Gatewood.

Back in early February, a one-line report appeared in the *Lexington Herald-Leader*, tucked into their weekly list of arrests, legal proceedings, and court cases: "Marc Graviss vs. Gatewood Galbraith for $70,000 etc., claimed due on a note."[24] Mistakes made during his first gubernatorial campaign continued to haunt Gatewood as he planned his next one. In the years following his bankruptcy filing in early 1993, Gatewood's missteps and debts came into even starker relief. At the time of his filing, he owed the Internal Revenue Service $65,000, local Lexington lawyer Terry McBrayer $16,000, his children's school more than $6,000 for tuition, and the city of Lexington $1,000 for 125 unpaid parking tickets.

Most devastatingly, Gatewood's run for public office didn't even spare his family and friends. Marc Graviss was a Lexington realtor and lifelong friend. He had lent money to Gatewood in the past, noting that he had been repaid nearly $30,000 on a prior loan. In this case, Gatewood had borrowed more than $80,000 from Graviss and considered his Chapter 7 bankruptcy proceeding as freeing him of this debt. Graviss disagreed, and sued Gatewood for repayment. "He kept saying he was going to get a big hit on a case he was working. That big hit never came. He would come up with a multitude of reasons why he couldn't pay me." When asked if he thought Gatewood would make a good governor, Graviss was unequivocally negative. "For one reason, the guy is as dishonest as he can be." This must have been heartbreaking for Gatewood. His desire to create change and to fight for his passions had a real cost. In this case, the payment was a friendship he'd had since he was a boy. By spending so much of his time campaigning instead of practicing law, he simply couldn't keep up with how quickly money flowed out of his coffers. Asked about these debts and the decisions he made, Gatewood didn't show remorse for trying to make his political dreams a reality. "It costs a lot," he said, "to run a revolution."[25]

With the next round of his revolution taking shape, Gatewood still had work to do before he could announce his campaign. He continued to practice law in Lexington, even as he planned as many fundraisers and public events as he possibly could to build momentum for the 1995 race.

In late 1993 he participated in a statewide protest of tuition increases for public universities. There were coordinated protests at the University of Kentucky, the University of Louisville, Murray State University, Northern Kentucky University, and Eastern Kentucky University. Gatewood spoke at the latter, holding court for over forty minutes amid a crowd of EKU students. Even after promising not to focus on marijuana legalization in his political campaign, Gatewood spoke about the need to legalize the plant, and how the growing cost of running and filling prisons in Kentucky was stealing funding from higher education.[26]

In another series of events that caught headlines, Gatewood hoped to take part in an environmental conference held in Louisville at the Convention Center. The event allowed exhibitors to display their products, technologies, and information related to the environmental movement. When NORML requested a booth to display hemp products, they were initially rebuffed by the conference organizers. The issue was a state law that had passed in 1992 that made all parts of the marijuana plant illegal. This included hemp, or even hemp-derived products like paper, fabric, rope, and canvas. The law was absurd. As Richard Cowan, the national director of NORML, pointed out, "It outlawed most of the old family Bibles in Kentucky because a lot of them have hemp in the paper."

To argue against the law, Gatewood showed up in court wearing a hemp suit, which had become something of a signature outfit for his public appearances, and asked the judge to force the conference organizers to allow hemp products to be displayed. Gatewood argued that this was a case of violating First Amendment rights, saying that showing people hemp products "is as expressive as any written word."[27]

Gatewood and NORML were vindicated when Judge Roger Crittenden ruled that they could display some hemp-derived products at the conference. The judge did stop short of overturning the broader law regarding the classification of hemp, against which Gatewood had filed a lawsuit months before.[28] The booth was a success, with conference attendees lining up to touch Gatewood's off-white suit or to see the plethora of hemp products that he brought to display. The event featured Vice President Al Gore, who opened the conference with a speech regarding environmental protections. As one attendee noted of Gatewood's booth, "They don't want us to see the truth. Hemp is coming back. The war is over."[29]

Throughout his work on the campaign and in the public eye, Gatewood continued to specialize in defending those arrested and accused of marijuana possession or trafficking. While he was perhaps not the most by-the-book attorney, his ability to connect with juries and to argue in court did sometimes pay dividends. In one case, Gatewood represented a man named Steven Edward Robey who was arrested and accused of marijuana trafficking in Hardin County. Robey was thirty-three, but during his arrest his eighty-five-year-old grandfather, Albert Hartsell Sr., was also arrested. Hartsell was hard of hearing and nearly blind. Robey faced a felony charge of trafficking in marijuana, but Gatewood was able to work with the Commonwealth's Attorney to have the charges reduced to a misdemeanor. Hartsell's charges were dismissed, as Gatewood pointed out the injustice of charging this poor grandfather, as well as how extreme a felony charge would be for a young man in possession of only cannabis.[30]

While Gatewood continued in his law practice during these years, he always had an eager eye turned toward his next race. The 1995 race was quickly approaching, and Gatewood needed a winning strategy. This took the form of recruiting new supporters, decrying controversial trends in the federal government, and courting a vital new running mate.

In 1991, televangelist Pat Robertson wrote a book called *The New World Order*, which laid out one of the wildest conspiracy theories of the twentieth century. According to Robertson, a dark and shady cabal made up of wealthy investors and corporations, the Federal Reserve banking system, and international politicians was responsible for promoting a world government. All of this was done to benefit themselves, but also to make way for the ascendency of the Antichrist.

The idea of a New World Order was nothing new, with conspiracy theories about a unilateral world government going back to the eighteenth century. These were usually related to Christian fundamentalism or religious ideas about the "end times," and were variously linked to dire warnings about Freemasonry, the "Illuminati," Zionism, alien abductions, UFOs, mind control, and more.

While many of these movements were tied to Christian fundamentalism, as Robertson's was, some attracted a new crowd: antigovernment and antiestablishment activists who promoted militancy in pushing back against this perceived threat. In his first run for governor, Gatewood had dabbled in ideas about a New World Order as they connected to his theories about corporations and what he called "synthetic subversion," and as he approached the 1995 election, these beliefs became even more prominent in his mind.

Gatewood did not accept the fanatical religious theories, but he did see proof of the outsize influence that corporations and financial institutions had on governments around the world. Most prominently, he saw many of the international trade agreements of the 1990s as proof of this influence. The General Agreement on Tariffs and Trade (GATT), which Gatewood had derided on the campaign trail leading up to the 1991 election, was formally ratified by the United States Senate in 1994. This renewed Gatewood's rhetoric against the deal and against the businesses that stood to benefit from free trade agreements that lowered prices for consumers but drove many production and manufacturing jobs overseas.

Gatewood had a keen eye for recruiting interest groups that aligned with his beliefs. His inability to raise adequate funds for campaigning, or to make a bigger splash in vote totals in previous elections, also led him to court groups that might provide a boost in fundraising, or in the polls. One such group was the growing "militia" movement. Members of this group agreed with Gatewood's assessments about the New World Order and specifically hoped to cement their freedoms by advocating for their right to bear arms.

This was a strange marriage of supporters. Gatewood, a self-proclaimed "hippie," sought the votes and support of militia groups across the commonwealth. As his memoir put it, "It was time to merge the efforts of all those citizens in danger from their own government. It was time to marry up Marijuana and the Militia."[31]

It's worth questioning this strategic move on Gatewood's part. Most of his family did not recall any major interest in guns or deeply held beliefs about the right to bear arms. Granted, Gatewood was a strong believer in the Constitution, and as such pointed to the Second Amendment as one of the bedrocks of American democracy. But he didn't focus on this much until he set his sights on Kentucky militias and gun activists as a possible voting bloc in the 1995 election. Gatewood had organized, marched, and protested against the Vietnam War in the 1960s and 1970s, and allied himself mainly with left-wing political supporters in previous runs for office. This courting of militia groups indicated an interesting turn in his political philosophy, one marked by a more vehement antigovernment rhetoric.

One of the main political organizers affiliated with militia groups in Kentucky was Norm Davis. Davis resided in western Kentucky and started an organization called Kentuckians for the Right to Bear Arms (KRBA), which represented citizens in many Kentucky counties. In preparing for the 1995 race, Gatewood courted Davis's support and spoke to as many KRBA chapters as he could. The argument, at least in Gatewood's mind, was simple. As he wrote, "I would explain my view of the New World Order and global economy and how it had been engineered by the synthetic manufacturers, who had displaced the farmers from producing the necessities of society: fiber, fuel, medicine and food." He would tell them, "Look, I know that you and I don't agree on everything. . . . But we can't let our disagreements on two or three issues divide us and keep us from coming together on the 10 or 12 bedrock issues which bind us together as Americans."[32]

It seemed that Gatewood did win over Davis to this cause, as Davis lent the KRBA's mailing list and digital operation to Gatewood's campaign, with somewhat mixed results. Gatewood admired Davis, saying, "I like Norman Davis. Hell, I love Norman Davis, warts and all. He is the orneriest, savviest, don't-give-an-inch unpaid citizen watchdog I have ever met."[33]

Davis was a constant presence in Kentucky politics throughout the 1990s and the first decade of the new century. The KRBA spawned other Second Amendment rights groups, including Take Back Kentucky, a right-wing political organization that focuses on gun rights and endorses political candidates in the commonwealth. The group is known for various protests, usually involving the displaying of firearms and assault rifles. Davis died in 2013, but he left a legacy as a tireless and controversial advocate for Second Amendment rights and antigovernment beliefs in Kentucky.

The marrying of Gatewood's political fortunes and militia groups also never made much sense to Jack Brammer, the lead political reporter for the *Lexington Herald-Leader*. "If I could mention one issue that surprised me, all these issues that he spoke out on seemed consistent with his beliefs, I never understood his advocacy for gun rights." Brammer referenced the cover of Gatewood's autobiography, published in 2004, on which he is pictured holding a large assault rifle, with rounds of ammunition crisscrossing his chest. "But I'm always surprised because I think Gatewood at one time seemed like a liberal Democrat and then his position on guns did not seem to align with some of the liberal policies that he stood for. And I never did understand that."[34]

Did Gatewood really agree with Norm Davis and other Second Amendment activists? Or could you explain this alliance as purely a political strategy, meant to take advantage of a strong voting bloc and to make his future candidacy more effective? While opinions are mixed on what Gatewood truly believed in, he certainly continued this advocacy for the rest of his public life and made many fans in the process. It also muddied his legacy and led many to question the finer points of his political philosophy.

As Gatewood tried to court support for the 1995 race, he faced a major decision: who he would choose for a running mate. Since the new state law made governor-and-lieutenant-governor tickets a requirement, Gatewood had to choose carefully someone who he thought could propel him to office.

By the spring of 1994, the time had finally arrived for Gatewood to make official what he had hinted at since the primary in 1991. Appearing on a local Lexington government news program, Gatewood announced his intent to run for the Democratic nomination for governor in the 1995 race. Alongside Gatewood was an unassuming, bespectacled older man he introduced as Jerry Hammond. As Gatewood stated on air, the announcement of his new running mate was a "historic moment."[35]

Originally from rural Shelby County, Jerry Hammond was already widely known throughout the commonwealth. He was employed as an ironworker, and quickly rose in the ranks of labor organizations related to skilled trades and construction. Hammond was a devout Christian and lived a life familiar to many Kentuckians: he memorized the Bible, attended church on Sundays, lived in humble circumstances, and learned to value the work of his own two hands and the country that he loved. He demonstrated this by serving in the air force, following in the footsteps of his father, who had served during World War II. He was trained in Air Force Intelligence, which led him to a lifelong fascination with computers and the emerging realm of digital technology.

As he continued his career and raised a family, Hammond became known throughout Kentucky as a particularly skillful and engaging union representative. He spent a fair amount of time in the state capital, working as a liaison between organized labor and the state government, through the Kentucky Department of Labor. Hammond was also outspoken about the relationship between government and organized labor, particularly pertaining to fiscal decisions made by the governor and state legislature.

In his memoir, Gatewood laid out Jerry's role in one particular case: the building of the Toyota production facility in Georgetown, Kentucky. In order to land the facility, Governor Martha Layne Collins and the state legislature agreed to hundreds of millions of dollars' worth of tax incentives to the Japan-based automaker. Incensed by the special treatment given to a foreign company and the lack of union workers included in their construction plan, Hammond spearheaded a lawsuit contending that the deal violated the state constitution. The case made its way to the Kentucky Supreme Court, which narrowly rejected it, 4–3.

As part of his battle against what he saw as irresponsible fiscal decision making, Hammond was able to secure more than ten million combined hours of union labor for the future construction of the facility in a victory for unions and workers in Kentucky.[36]

After Gatewood successfully recruited Hammond to join his ticket, the blowback from other organized labor leaders in Kentucky came swiftly. Many saw Hammond's willingness to join Gatewood as making a mockery of the serious work of organized labor. Gatewood was still seen as "the marijuana candidate," even though Gatewood maintained that this wouldn't be a part of his 1995 platform.

In a joint statement, Kentucky labor leaders Paul Barrick and Gene Marksberry decried Hammond's decision as a betrayal of the principles of union workers: "We wish to state for the record that the Kentucky Laborers and Operating Engineers resent the portrayal of organized labor in general as an ally to Mr. Galbraith's objectives. Mr. Hammond's participation on this slate as a representative of organized labor flies in the face of the values held most highly by the working men and women of this commonwealth." Gatewood couldn't understand such a quick and decisive strike against his beliefs and the campaign, saying in response, "We are highly surprised that anyone could take a stand without seeing our platform. We anticipated some knee-jerk reaction, but this doesn't make sense."[37]

Gatewood became the first candidate to officially file for the election in the summer of 1994 and—referencing the new campaign law providing that candidates able to raise $600,000 would receive a 2-to-1 match from the state government—claimed that he and Jerry Hammond would "have our six hundred thousand several months prior to the election."

Even as he pushed back against the image of being a one-issue candidate, the media couldn't stop asking him about his personal stance on marijuana. As he repeated his views on individual freedom and cannabis, he tried to refocus the campaign on broader ideas and principles that both he and Hammond endorsed: fighting against government corruption, defending personal liberty, and putting government back in the "little box where it belonged." Gatewood declared that he and Hammond were going to "make believers out of cynics," and criticized other candidates who were toying with running for the Democratic nod. "The other people eyeing the race are all officeholders, but they have not used their positions to try to stop the erosion of personal freedom by big government. They are a part of the problem. They are not a part of the solution."[38]

Gatewood and Hammond were soon joined in a crowded primary field. Their most prominent challenger was political veteran and coal company operator Paul E. Patton, who had served the previous four years as Governor Brereton Jones's lieutenant governor. A native son of eastern Kentucky, Patton had long set his sights on the Governor's Mansion. Recalling the 1995 race, he said he never considered Gatewood a serious challenger: "Gatewood was pleasant. He wasn't adversarial. He was friendly. I don't ever remember having any issue with him. I didn't take him too seriously, and I never figured out whether he took himself seriously or whether he just enjoyed the publicity and promoting the cause of marijuana and hemp. . . . And I don't know whether that was just his motive or whether he really thought he had a chance to become a viable political figure. I don't ever remember him getting a lot of votes."[39]

Even though Patton remembered having a happy personal relationship with him, Gatewood blistered Patton on the campaign trail and in his personal recollections. When the Building and Trades Council, an organization that Hammond had served up until the announcement of his candidacy, endorsed Patton, Gatewood wrote of Jerry, "He was so very disappointed with the rest of the union leadership, especially those who had been persuaded to back Patton because of God knows what. Here was a scab coal operator who had fought strikes at his coal mines with armed guards and scab labor, yet the other union leaders organized for him and supported him."[40]

Also throwing their hats into the ring were Kentucky Senate president John "Eck" Rose and Secretary of State Bob Babbage. Democrats were still dominating statewide races, even though the Kentucky Republican Party was increasingly making headway in local and regional elections. The Kentucky GOP ended up nominating Larry Forgy, a longtime party operative and Board of Trustees member at the University of Kentucky.

Gatewood kept his focus on the primary and took every opportunity to appear with the other candidates and to speak his piece. He documented one such speech in his autobiography, from when he spoke to the Kentucky Association of Counties meeting in Paducah. In this speech, apparently given off the cuff, Gatewood made an immediate splash. He followed both Babbage and Patton, and began with the line "Well, I haven't appeared in front of a crowd this large since they called a meeting of the creditors in my bankruptcy."

Throughout the speech, Gatewood used his usual animated style to poke fun at the other candidates and the state of the Kentucky Democratic Party, specifically mentioning their recent losses and implicitly admitting that they were losing their hold on the commonwealth. He also referenced what he saw as government overreach, specifically regarding tax breaks to corporations and the militaristic tendencies that resulted in the death of Gary Shepherd and the imprisonment of thousands of Kentuckians: "Well, I have a novel solution for many of Kentucky's problems. Instead of bringing dogs into our schools to sniff our children, instead of having helicopters hover over our fields and gardens like we are in an occupied territory instead of the Land of the Brave and the Home of the Free, instead of trying to regulate everybody's lives from cradle to grave, let's try the solution of more freedom to the people, not less!"[41]

Aligning with Gatewood and Hammond's campaign theme, Gatewood attacked the other Democratic candidates for their history of supporting the status quo in Frankfort, most particularly what he saw as rampant corruption in the state legislature. Much of his criticism focused on a 1992 federal corruption investigation into a joint House and Senate Business Organizations and Professions Committee, codename BOPTROT, BOP being an acronym for the name of the committee, and TROT referring to harness racing, since the investigation covered the handling of a horse racing facility in Henderson, Kentucky.

A complicated series of events, the investigation was prompted by the processes and payoffs involved in deciding certain racing and wager dates for horse racing sites in Kentucky, specifically a facility called Riverside Downs in western Kentucky. The FBI instigated a sting, in which government officials in Frankfort took bribes from Riverside Downs administrators for preferential treatment.[42] While many of these bribes and behind-the-scenes payoffs were for small amounts, the investigation brought corruption to the forefront of the political conversation in Kentucky, as it involved a number of business and government personalities. The most prominent name implicated in the case was Don Blandford, the Democratic Speaker of the House, who was videotaped and recorded by the FBI as he accepted a $500 bribe from a former Kentucky House of Representatives member. Blandford was convicted on federal corruption charges and resigned his seat in 1993.[43] Gatewood used this as fuel for his campaign against corruption, and made it a centerpiece of the Galbraith-Hammond platform.

Gatewood's speeches became so raucous and so well performed that Babbage and Rose stopped appearing at the many forums and events that Gatewood attended. In the meantime, Gatewood and Hammond were being quickly outpaced in fundraising, especially compared to Patton, who had the wider support of the Democratic Party and wealthy donors at his beck and call. Even though he had promised to easily raise the $600,000 to secure matching funds from the new state law, Gatewood came out in August 1994 to declare that he and Jerry weren't interested in public financing. As he put it, the new law created "a greed trap we don't want to be caught in."[44]

While this about-face was likely due to the fact that he and Hammond were not able to raise the kind of money they anticipated, they played it off in classic Gatewood fashion. Gatewood claimed that the new law was a violation of First Amendment rights, and that it simply underscored what was wrong with public elections. It's worth noting, however, that when Gatewood came out against the law, his campaign had raised only $3,052 in the preceding month, putting them well off pace to hit the $600,000 benchmark. Ever the entertainer, Gatewood talked the *Lexington Herald-Leader* into including in a 1995 article a "Top 10" list of why he and Hammond were not taking part in the new fundraising process:

> 10. We've never been able to reconcile the morality of turning over taxpayers' money to politicians for politicking when so many unmet public needs exist.
> 9. We don't believe it should cost $1.8 million to tell the truth.
> 8. We don't want our contributors' names and detailed personal information loaded in some big ol' government computer.
> 7. We want folks to feel free to support our campaign without having to fear losing their jobs or businesses.
> 6. Our original goal was to remove politicians' hands from the public treasury—not stick ours in.
> 5. Of the legislators who sponsored public campaign finance, one (former Majority Leader Joe Wright, D-Harned) abandoned plans to run for governor because he couldn't make the laws he sponsored work for him. The other (former House Speaker Don Blandford, D-Philpot) went to jail because he could.
> 4. If Paul Patton calling Larry Forgy "yellow" is typical of '95 campaigning, we don't want taxpayers to think we expect them to pay for some low-grade name-calling contest.
> 3. We're reluctant to agree with anything Bob Babbage says because we support democracy—not hypocrisy.

2. Millionaire Wally Wilkinson may try to make public financing an issue and we wouldn't want to give any Kentuckian any reason to vote him back into public office.
1. Our mothers are against it, and we want their votes.[45]

Gatewood was quick to maintain the violation of constitutional rights related to marijuana and hemp in Kentucky, but he mostly made good on his promise to keep it out of the campaign. He had new ideas. Some were conventional and some not so much. One idea was to create a new manmade lake in central Kentucky in order to spur hospitality revenues. Another was what he called The Commonwealth Incentive, an idea that would guarantee any high school graduate or GED holder in Kentucky a $5,000 voucher to be used on tuition, books, supplies, or vocational training.

Gatewood continued to show up at any venue that would have him, and he campaigned tirelessly across the state in order to get out his message. As the May 1995 primary approached, Gatewood and Hammond got one more boost from an old friend. After discussing the race with him, Willie Nelson agreed to play a fundraising concert for the Galbraith-Hammond ticket at the Kentucky Theatre in downtown Lexington on April 17. Gatewood came straight from the Kentucky Educational Television debate to the concert. Willie was late but arrived at 10 p.m. to a chorus of applause and played for over two hours straight. In photographs of the event, Gatewood is all smiles in a dapper suit, standing next to his friend and cheering with the crowd.

A candidate profile published about Gatewood shortly before the primary showed that much of the public had noticed his more serious tone. A Bluegrass State Poll included in the column showed that Gatewood had impressive name recognition, with 50 percent of Kentuckians knowing who he was. Many did still view him as "the marijuana candidate," which led to a 65 percent unfavorable rating in the poll. Western Kentucky University government professor John Parker noted the change, saying, "My impression is he's taking himself more seriously now. If my recollection is right, he tried to do that four years ago and insists that he was about more than just marijuana. But he's still carrying that label."

The article's interviewees credited Gatewood for being an outstanding and charismatic speaker, noting his ability to turn a phrase. He was quick to use this skill in his stump speech, often starting with "Did my father's generation hit the beaches of Normandy and Iwo Jima so that I'd have to pee in a cup to hold a job in America?" Once he had the crowd in his palm, he would often use alliteration to his advantage: "We're going to take the government out of your bedroom, your bloodstream, your brain, your bladder, your business, your billfold, your back pockets, your bingo halls, and your Internet bulletin boards."[46]

Even with a more serious tone and the support of old and new friends alike, Gatewood came up well short in the May 23 primary. Patton, the presumptive favorite and leading fundraiser, scored a historic victory with 45 percent of the vote, the largest margin in twenty years of primary elections. Babbage finished second with 24 percent, and Rose was third with 21 percent. Gatewood netted only 9 percent across the state. While a disappointing outcome, this was nearly double the support he had received in 1991. When asked about the result, Gatewood lamented the state of political fundraising, saying, "You cannot win an election when you spend $20,000 and these other guys spend a couple million. We thought the public would appreciate that, but apparently the public couldn't see past the advertising on TV."[47]

With Paul Patton set to run against the Republican nominee, Larry Forgy, that November, Gatewood had some decisions to make. He was disappointed, but he had run a better campaign, which he owed mainly to Hammond, who had lent some professionalism and planning to the process. But a loss was a loss. Gatewood had poured his heart and soul into the campaign, and in the process had become even more of a household name throughout Kentucky. To his everlasting frustration, his popularity and his penchant for colorful speech did not result in success at the ballot box. It did, however, lead to other opportunities.

While campaigning in 1995, Gatewood continued to practice law, including defending a client charged with setting fire to an apartment building where he lived with his wife and their three young children, who all died in the fire. The accused was apparently disliked in their small Jessamine County community. At trial, two expert witnesses claimed that the fire had been the product of arson. With the case looking hopeless, Gatewood at the last minute discovered two eyewitnesses who both testified that the man was telling the truth and was trying to save his family from the blaze. He was acquitted of all charges, marking another notable legal victory for Gatewood amid a hectic campaign.[48]

In addition to his ongoing practice, Gatewood tried to capitalize on his renewed popularity with a new way to spread his voice and views throughout the state he loved. He joined a new talk radio show on a local AM station called WVLK. The host, Tom Martin, invited Gatewood on as a regular contributor, where he would guest host and appear one hour a week to discuss some of what he had elucidated on the campaign trail: personal freedoms, Second Amendment rights, ideas about governance, and more.

As Gatewood recalled, it was on one of these occasions that he heard about a story that gripped his attention. The upcoming 1995 Fourth of July parade in downtown Lexington had decided on a theme: "Independence Day: The U.S. and the U.N. for a Better World." In addition to celebrating the traditional holiday, it was the organizers' intent that the parade also celebrate the founding of the United Nations in the spirit of international cooperation. This set Gatewood's teeth on edge.

In accordance with his mistrust of large international ruling bodies, and because he felt that it was an insult to this particular American tradition, Gatewood vowed to protest the UN float that was set to lead the parade. Gatewood also felt that this decision slighted others who had a better claim to leading the parade: "Besides, I was aware of both a 101-year-old WWI veteran and a Bataan Death March survivor who would be honored to lead the parade."[49]

What transpired was perhaps the most memorable moment in Gatewood's public life. On the day of the parade, he made his way past the police protections blocking off the official parade route and stood right in the middle of Main Street in downtown Lexington and halted the progress of the giant UN float that heralded the beginning of the parade. Just before blocking the float, Gatewood spoke from the steps of the Fayette County Courthouse. "This misuse of Independence Day is yet another attack on U.S. pride and sovereignty promoted by globalists and internationalists who apparently believe that the concepts of national sovereignty and state independence are obsolete." The parade theme, he said, "demeans the sacrifices of generations of American patriots who risked everything they had to create this free nation."[50]

In a video clip of the protest, Gatewood can be seen in his signature business suit and fedora, handcuffed, being led away from the parade route. As he put it, "By God, I was leading the parade! It was true. I got to lead the 4th of July parade in 1995 in Lexington, Kentucky. It was a two-mile-long parade and had more than 75,000 spectators and never mind that I was under arrest, wearing handcuffs, and being led off to jail."[51]

Jerry Hammond quickly bailed Gatewood out, and he defended himself and another protestor in the weeks following the incident. The charges were eventually dropped, and Gatewood had succeeded, once again, in making headlines. This public demonstration cemented Gatewood's new antigovernment, paranoid turn in political thinking. It aligned him even further with some of the fringe political groups in Kentucky, including the militia movements and die-hard conservatives he had courted during the campaign.

Future Lexington mayor Teresa Isaac remembered the protest as something completely in line with Gatewood's beliefs. "Oh, he was always antiestablishment. Yeah. As long as I've known him, he was antiestablishment. No matter what the establishment was like, no matter what the establishment was."[52]

Another future Lexington mayor, as well as United States Senate candidate and Kentucky secretary of transportation, Jim Gray, also remembered the event. "Yeah, yeah. And he was very against kind of multinational or global trade agreements, things like that. . . . Gatewood was really hard to peg on, you know, traditional political lines of demarcation."[53]

Even Gatewood's youngest daughter, Molly, who was just eleven years old when it happened, recalled speaking with her dad about the public event. "So I remember talking to him on the phone and I said, 'What are you doing tomorrow?' Daddy said, 'Getting arrested, baby, what are you doing?'"[54]

Following this public spectacle, Gatewood and Hammond started a write-in campaign in the lead-up to the 1995 general election, which Patton won over Forgy by a slim margin of 21,560 votes. Gatewood and Hammond received 3,965 votes for all of their trouble.[55]

Gatewood had renewed his popularity in the quick four years following the 1991 race, and had matured as a politician and a public figure. He had continued his outspoken advocacy for marijuana and hemp, while choosing a political strategy that put other issues at the forefront of his campaign. He organized, protested, exhibited, and advocated, both for victims of criminal marijuana policy and for the benefits and promise of medicinal marijuana. Poor financial decisions and an inability to raise money for the race once again doomed his chances of attaining public office. Gatewood had found new love, and continued to navigate life as a divorced father and an ex-husband. The turn in political strategy, away from his more liberal, Democratic leanings, and toward a starker view of antigovernment sentiment and Second Amendment rights changed his public identity, if not the results of his campaign. Just as he had in 1991, Gatewood immediately started thinking about the next race. This wasn't the last time he would seek the governor's seat, and the election of 1999 loomed as the biggest political success of his career.

6

"Lean, Mean, Vote-Gettin' Machine"

After the chaotic campaign and events of 1995, Gatewood turned his attention to the national cannabis movement before jumping into his next race. Since the mid-1970s, rogue doctors and activists had been highlighting the medical benefits of cannabis. Whether for cancer patients, those experiencing chronic pain, or for nausea and other minor illnesses, the access campaign was growing in size and momentum. The epicenter of the medical marijuana movement was in California.

As the AIDS epidemic raged in the 1980s, an activist named Dennis Peron became the king of San Francisco's underground cannabis trade. Peron, a veteran of Vietnam and a gay man, had started selling cannabis in the 1970s. As he and others realized the plant's ability to treat the debilitating symptoms of AIDS, his business grew. Part activist, part businessman, Peron became a major figure in the fight for access to medical marijuana. Cannabis helped to fend off the loss of appetite and extreme weight loss in AIDS patients, which would further harm their already weakened immune systems. "These therapeutic effects have been discovered and at least partially confirmed by modern studies largely because of the brave efforts of AIDS patients and others in the Bay Area during the 1980's, whom no number of police raids could silence. They were determined to tell the rest of the nation and world how cannabis made their lives better," writes Nick Johnson in *Grass Roots*, his study of cannabis in the western United States.[1]

Dr. Tod Mikuriya, who had spoken at the Science & Truth Hearings that Gatewood had convened in 1993, also continued his work in pushing for medical cannabis. In the 1990s Mikuriya began treating veterans of the Gulf War who had post-traumatic stress disorder with marijuana, and endorsed its value for mental and emotional illness as well as for physical ailments.[2]

Thanks to activists like Peron and Mikuriya, opinions about medical marijuana in California had hit a turning point by the mid-1990s. Peron's thriving business had also begun to attract increased scrutiny from the authorities. Gatewood mentions in his memoir that Peron was incensed when his partner was targeted by police. “In the early 90's, Dennis' partner contracted AIDS and was in very bad shape. One night the police busted down the door, arrested Dennis, dragged his friend from his deathbed and threw him down the stairs.”[3]

His passion renewed by his work and the outrage of being targeted by California police, Peron began drafting a referendum by which California voters could approve medical marijuana via ballot initiative. Peron harnessed the changing tide of public opinion and led a statewide campaign for Proposition 215, which would legalize medical cannabis in the country's most populous state. Gatewood followed the initiative with interest, remaining in contact with Peron and eventually flying to California to be in San Francisco on November 5, 1996, the day of the vote.

In his autobiography Gatewood recounts this visit, where he toured one of Peron's main operations, the San Francisco Buyer's Club. Gatewood was blown away by the operation. “When I first got to the Club, I was amazed. It took up three floors of an old warehouse and had two health bars, hundreds of chairs and sofas and thousands of paper doves hanging from strings tied to the rafters. They were made of every color imaginable and each had the name of one of the Club members on it. Twelve thousand in all!”[4]

Gatewood, Peron, Jack Herer, and other activists all gathered at the initiative's headquarters and waited for the vote to come in. Gatewood was there to witness history, and to experience something that he longed for in his home state. For Peron and the other activists gathered, this was an end to an emotional and arduous journey. They had seen their friends and loved ones beleaguered by disease and pestered by authorities because they sought relief with cannabis. When the votes were tallied, Peron was vindicated. The measure passed with 56 percent of the vote, drawing broad support from across the political spectrum. California became the first state to legalize medical marijuana. In series of photos from that November, Gatewood is filled with excitement, beaming and posing with Peron, Herer, and others. Gatewood was floored. “At last, We, the People, had spoken. And in the language I had been listening for during the last 20 years.”[5]

Energized by what he witnessed in California, Gatewood turned with renewed interest to his work in Kentucky. This coincided with a major spectacle in eastern Kentucky, led by another major celebrity with an interest in cannabis legalization.

In late May and early June of 1996, actor Woody Harrelson visited Kentucky for a whirlwind publicity tour where he tried to spread the gospel of hemp and marijuana and the benefits they could provide to the commonwealth. Harrelson appeared at the Kentucky Industrial Fiber Hemp Conference in Lexington, where he expounded on the benefits of the crop. As part of his tour, he visited a fifth-grade classroom in Shelby County, where he explained the benefits of hemp to students. He wore an entire outfit made from hemp—surely something that Gatewood appreciated—and introduced hemp farmers from around the world who had traveled to Kentucky for the conference.[6] After speaking with the students, he continued on his tour of the state.

The actor was at a new height of fame, recently starring in the Oliver Stone box office hit *Natural Born Killers* and still enjoying fame from his longtime role on television's *Cheers* as well as other projects like *White Men Can't Jump*. As the tour garnered interest from news reporters and local television stations, Harrelson took a trip to rural Beattyville, Kentucky.

Harrelson had planned out his next publicity stunt, meant as an act to protest and challenge Kentucky laws that prohibited the cultivation of hemp. With the press gathered, and in clear view of a Lee County law enforcement officer, Harrelson used a hoe to till up a strip of soil and planted four hemp seeds in the ground. The sheriff arrested Harrelson immediately and transported him to the Lee County jail, where he quickly bailed himself out. After receiving instructions for a later court date, Harrelson addressed the crowd outside. "Kentucky used to be the number one hemp grower in the nation. I've talked to farmers around here and they would love to have something like this."[7] Harrelson would stay involved in a long, yet largely ineffectual, legal battle regarding his arrest. Donna Cockrel, the Shelby County schoolteacher who had invited him to speak to her students that spring—and again in a return trip the next January—became a public target of parents who disagreed with Harrelson's views. Cockrel was an outspoken advocate for hemp and did not fear public retribution. She was questioned and investigated following the visits, and was eventually fired in July 1997, allegedly for violations unrelated to her hemp advocacy.[8]

Gatewood followed these developments eagerly, as he continued to practice law and advocate for hemp and marijuana. Earlier in 1996 he had offered to represent Richard Evans, who ran a marijuana "buying club" in Covington, to provide the plant to the terminally ill. Covington police raided his operation on February 15, 1996. Gatewood looked forward to representing him—"I have been waiting, as had he, for any charges to be filed"[9]—but charges never materialized.

Even though Gatewood had been advocating for hemp since his run for agriculture commissioner in 1983, some hemp activists saw his involvement in the cause as a detriment because he also supported the legalization of cannabis. Gale Glenn, a Clark County farmer and wife of a doctor, said that Gatewood's image as "the marijuana candidate" in recurring elections hurt the cause for legal hemp. "Marijuana is our worst enemy. If not for marijuana, we would have this country covered with hemp."[10]

These words must have stung Gatewood. After all, he was one of the original voices for the hemp movement, even though he did originally set his sights higher. His public perception did sometimes turn more mainstream voters and Kentucky residents off the possibilities of hemp as an industrial crop, but he had also done more to advocate for it than perhaps anyone in modern Kentucky history. He had given up stable income, political viability, and immeasurable time with his family to pursue his beliefs. This was often the criticism directed at Gatewood while he was politically active: that he asked for too much, pushed too far, and found far too much enjoyment in the sound of his own voice. Gatewood had been on the leading edge of this movement for twenty years, yet he garnered far more criticism than praise. This was a sign of the cultural and political times. Today it is far easier to see his advocacy in a kinder light, as industrial hemp and medical or recreational cannabis have transitioned into a social norm.

In early 1997 Gatewood once again put his money where his mouth was. It started with a desperate legal plea from a woman in western Kentucky, and would define much of Gatewood's life and work for the next five years.

"So at that point, I just told him the truth, you know, that I was a disabled mother, a single parent who was struggling to raise her child and to stay off narcotics and away from addictive medicines, who was dealing with several different debilitating illnesses and chronic pain. That I had been raised an addict, because I grew up in abuse and had, you know, been taught by the government to medicate myself: 'here, little girl, take this pill.'"[11]

By June of 1997, Mary L. Thomas, more commonly known as the Reverend Mary Thomas-Spears, was in a bind. She had long suffered from glaucoma, fibromyalgia, and multiple sclerosis. Marijuana had made it possible for her to live and function. It reduced the pressure in her eyes from glaucoma, which caused massive migraine headaches. She kept most lights off and windows covered in her Bowling Green home to deal with the symptoms. She found that marijuana naturally relaxed her muscles, helping with the symptoms of fibromyalgia, which causes muscle tissue to "draw up and harden." Her multiple sclerosis made it difficult to swallow and caused nausea, insomnia, and lack of appetite. When she first started treating herself around 1988, she found relief. Marked by a past of abuse and drug addiction, Thomas-Spears saw marijuana as a path to living naturally and finding health in awful circumstances.

She became such a believer in the health benefits of cannabis that she began to see herself as a "healer." She introduced marijuana to others who were looking for healing and peace. She said that she would only sell it to adults "who were using it in a healthy manner as I was," rather than children or whoever showed up on her doorstep. The authorities saw it differently.[12]

She was arrested in 1997 for selling marijuana to an undercover policeman, who had discussed the sale with her several weeks before the bust. Originally charged with six felony counts of trafficking marijuana, Thomas-Spears was desperate for a suitable lawyer. A friend whose mother had worked with Gatewood on his 1995 campaign encouraged her to reach out to him. The only problem? The work would have to be pro bono. Thomas-Spears was not a rich woman and was staring a lengthy legal battle in the face.

> So at some point I called information and asked for Lexington and asked for Gatewood Galbraith and they gave me a number. And at that point, I tell myself I was going to have some secretary answer the phone and then you're going to have to convince her that he needs to call you back or whatever. But to my surprise, he answered the phone, which just really shocked me. Then I'm telling myself, oh, you've got maybe five or ten minutes to convince this man he has to represent you in court pro bono with no money, when he's got to drive from Lexington to Bowling Green.[13]

Thomas-Spears explained the situation to Gatewood, baring her soul in hopes that he would take her on as a client. She was in a desperate spot and had nearly convinced herself that she was crazy for trying to land Gatewood as her attorney. After she finished, she took a breath and waited for his reply.

"You know, I've been waiting for a case like this."

Gatewood had sat on the sidelines over the past few years as he witnessed the passage of Proposition 215 in California and dreamed of medical marijuana's potential in Kentucky. He had witnessed the public spectacle of Woody Harrelson, and while he valued the attention that the movie star directed to the benefits of industrial hemp, he was yearning for his own place in the movement he had championed for so long. This case was it. Thomas-Spears had her attorney.

Why was Gatewood especially interested in this case? The main reason was that it was not a simple case of marijuana possession but involved trafficking charges with serious legal consequences. Thomas-Spears was facing five years in prison as well as losing custody of her son—much of this due to the fact that three of the charges included trafficking within one thousand yards of a school, which carried harsher penalties.[14]

Not only was Gatewood representing Thomas-Spears pro bono, but he committed to a lengthy trial process that would likely be measured in years instead of months. Gatewood willfully sacrificed his time, his ability to generate badly needed income, and, perhaps most of all, traveling constantly to represent Thomas-Spears. Bowling Green is 155 miles from Lexington, and driving from Gatewood's home to the Warren County Courthouse took nearly three hours. Gatewood was already familiar with traversing the state both for work and to campaign, but this was a major commitment as he contemplated another run for office.

Much as Harrelson had hoped in his own legal episode, Gatewood saw this case and pending trial as a potential test case of marijuana prohibition in Kentucky. While the result would not necessarily change the Kentucky state constitution, he felt that Thomas-Spears showcased exactly why access to medical marijuana was needed. Here was a woman who had fought through a tough childhood and was specifically seeking alternatives to the opioids and painkillers that were beginning to spawn a spiral of abuse throughout Kentucky.

Thomas-Spears never denied breaking the law. As the *Bowling Green Daily News* reported in 1999, "Even with all the good that she said the drug does her, Thomas doesn't deny she broke the law. She admits to selling marijuana to an undercover officer, but she believed he was also using it for medicinal purposes after they discussed it for several weeks before the sale."[15]

With Gatewood's help, Thomas-Spears pled guilty to a single charge of trafficking marijuana within one thousand yards of a school and had her five-year prison sentenced reduced to probation. As part of her probation, she was required to submit to drug testing and was explicitly prohibited from using drugs or alcohol.

While the case seemed to be resolved, this was just the beginning of Thomas-Spear's legal troubles. They would soak up much of Gatewood's time over the next five years. Meanwhile, he still had work and family to care for in Lexington, and he still felt the pull of politics.

Following the disappointment of the 1995 race and during his involvement in the Thomas-Spears case, Gatewood continued to make a name for himself in Lexington. Long a source of entertainment, Gatewood cemented his

Gatewood loved and admired his mother, Dollie. She was a fixture in Lexington, devoting her time to various charitable causes and service well into her nineties.

legacy as one of Lexington's most famous sons through his acts of generosity—augmented, improbably, by his mother.

Dollie Galbraith had retired from her teaching job at Mary Queen of the Holy Rosary School in 1983 and proceeded to throw herself into volunteer work in her adopted city. She became a local celebrity, with neighbors and reporters alike marveling at both her dedication to good works and her endless well of energy.

Her prowess at walking long distances became a local legend. During her teaching career she had walked the four miles to school, and she continued the habit even following her retirement. She also began to compete in Lexington's Bluegrass 10k race, in which much of downtown and Main Street are cordoned off for a walk/run race on Fourth of July weekend. When asked about her recent first-place finish in the 80+ age category, she quipped, "I don't think there was anyone else in it."[16]

While Gatewood and his siblings drew energy and inspiration from their mother, their father, H.C., was in increasingly dire health at a local nursing home. He had long suffered from dementia and other ailments related to his lifelong battle with alcoholism, and in 1997 he passed away in Lexington.

As Gatewood recalled, "Dad was a fine man, kind and gentle until the very end, but he, like many of us, couldn't beat the bottle."[17]

Gatewood's big brother, Hank, remembered this time vividly, and even constructed a mental exercise to get some of the weight of the strained relationship off his shoulders. Hank said, "I wrote him a letter and did thank him for everything he'd done for me in terms of being a good role model, hard worker, honest, good to my mother, good to the kids. . . . He treated my mother with love and respect." Hank went on to say that he was also thankful for the difficult experiences that the family had endured with their father as his alcohol abuse worsened, as he separated from Dollie, and as he eventually required around-the-clock care in a Lexington facility. "I appreciate all these good things you did for me. And then I also appreciate you showing me how I didn't want to be in terms of letting alcohol be something that controlled my life."[18]

Gatewood had two distinct examples of how his personal choices could affect his future. He had already turned away from alcohol in the 1970s, partially due to the experiences of his father, and to deny his own predilections. He also had the example of his mother, who remained active and quick-witted, and was a local hero. From both, he learned generosity and kindness. One story, in particular, shows Gatewood's generous spirit, and his penchant for representing those who couldn't pay for his services.

When a woman came to Hank for his counseling and therapy services, he mentioned that his brother was an attorney named Gatewood. She told Hank that when she was a student at the University of Kentucky, her parents had saved up and bought her a car to use at school. During a meeting with classmates to work on a project, this woman had parked her car in the lot of her friend's apartment complex. When she came outside after they had wrapped up their work, her car was missing. She found out it had been towed, and she worked through the night to locate and free her car from the impound lot where it had been taken. Not only did she have to pay exorbitant fees, but they had damaged her new car in the process.

When she went back the next day to investigate, she found no No Parking signs posted. Determined, she walked up and down Main Street until she found a sign for an attorney's office. It happened to be Gatewood's. Upset and exhausted, she recounted the story to Gatewood and made her way through most of a box of tissues as he lent her a sympathetic ear. Gatewood promised to pursue recompense for the fees she paid, for the damage done to her car, and some extra so that the woman could pay her friend for carting her around town.

A week or so later Gatewood gave her a call and told her to come to his office when she had a moment. She did, and there waiting for her was a check bigger than she had imagined. She nearly wept with joy. She asked how much she owed him. Gatewood replied, "Honey, you don't owe me anything. I was glad to help you. I have three daughters in college and know that they, or you, don't have much money, so my services are free of charge."[19]

From the time that they were kids, the values of generosity, kindness, and love had been imprinted on Gatewood and his siblings. Gatewood spent a lot of time and energy helping others, but it was becoming increasingly apparent that he needed to care for himself in a more holistic way.

While Gatewood was in California in 1996, he had Dr. Mikuriya give him a full examination. He was diagnosed with emphysema, something that came as no surprise. Gatewood had been a heavy smoker through much of his twenties and had taken up the habit again during the stressful events of the 1995 campaign. Emphysema is a progressive disease that attacks the lungs, causing the tiny air sacs in the lung walls to become enlarged. It leads to breathlessness and coughing fits and has no cure. Gatewood had noticed the symptoms while on the campaign trail, as his speeches became more difficult to get through. Mikuriya prescribed marijuana for his ailment, even though Gatewood was already self-treating on a regular basis. The diagnosis, however, did encourage Gatewood to seek out new ways to improve his health.

He quit smoking cigarettes once and for all and began an exercise regimen of push-ups and daily walks, which began to grow in length and intensity. He became an advocate for the benefits of exercise, and even started to compete in the Bluegrass 10k race each year, inspired by his mother.[20]

His legal crusade for the Reverend Mary Thomas-Spears and his newfound focus on healthy living impelled Gatewood to begin thinking about his next move. In looking forward to the 1999 race, Gatewood hoped to take advantage of the changing tides in Kentucky politics to finally make his way to the Governor's Mansion.

With a renewed sense of energy and optimism, Gatewood turned his attention to the 1999 election. He stayed busy with his various legal cases, and became even better known in Kentucky popular culture. All the while, Kentucky's Democratic governor, Paul E. Patton, had shown himself to be a masterful politician during his first term.

Patton, governing while overseeing one of the strongest economic periods of the twentieth century, flexed his muscle in Frankfort. After taking office, he experienced a number of political victories during regular and special sessions of the Kentucky legislature in 1996, 1997, and 1998.

During these sessions, Patton pursued some of the major political issues he had discussed during the campaign. He sought to make Kentucky more "business friendly," which included reducing workers' compensation benefits, especially those for Kentucky miners who experienced the debilitating effects of silicosis, more commonly referred to as "black lung." This disease progressively destroyed the miner's capacity to breathe, and was directly caused by working in eastern Kentucky coal mines. A native son of Appalachia, Patton quickly became unpopular in that area of the state. Nonetheless, he succeeded in the reforms.

He experienced many victories related to higher education in Kentucky. Up until this time, the University of Kentucky oversaw the community college system throughout the state. Patton sought to reorganize the university and to remove the community college system from its control. In his eyes, this freed the University of Kentucky to pursue the status of a top-tier research university, on par with the country's other major public universities. Even with some resistance from administrators, Patton was able to win influence in the state legislature and make these changes a reality.

Finally, he found success in a variety of other initiatives. He pursued a more extensive crime package, trying to deter crime in Kentucky, in line with national story lines during the Clinton administration. He also sought and won reforms to Medicaid, business incentives, economic development, and more changes to higher education.[21]

Patton's first term was seen as a universal success, and his status as head of the Democratic Party in Kentucky was unchallenged. He had proved himself to be a persuasive and powerful politician, which left little hope for Kentucky Republicans to challenge him in 1999.

In 1997, Gatewood saw the writing on the wall. No way could he beat Patton in a Democratic primary. Rather than challenging a powerful incumbent, he changed his voter registration from "Democrat" to "Independent." This also kept his options open so that he could run in 1999, even if he hadn't completely made up his mind. As he wrote, "It was quite apparent that neither party held the answers to reforming the corruption that had institutionalized itself in Frankfort over the past 30 years. Both major parties had been bought out, both on the Federal and State level, from the top down. 'They' were moving to take control of our political apparatus to forestall any citizen's revolt against their coup."

Here Gatewood amplified the antigovernment sentiment he had been building for years and had been publicly on display during the Lexington's

1995 Fourth of July parade. Whether because of his disillusionment with the two-party system, the seeming invincibility of Patton in the Democratic primary, or other political considerations, Gatewood broke from the traditional party scheme. This had another benefit which Gatewood welcomed: he would no longer need to compete in May primary elections but, with five thousand signatures, could focus solely on the general election in the fall. "The day I registered as an Independent was a red-letter day for me. I actually felt physically relieved. No more Party bullshit! No more 'Our guy may be a S.O.B. but at least he's our S.O.B. so we've got to elect him' crap. And, no more May Primaries! Hot Dog! No more Primaries!"[22]

In the summer of 1997, Gatewood saw glimpses of progress in hemp legislation. Circuit court judge William Trude, reviewing a lower court's January ruling in Harrelson's trial, affirmed that a state law that treated industrial hemp and marijuana without distinction was so broad as to be unconstitutional. This did not legalize hemp, but it did begin to show cracks in how the Kentucky legislature dealt with the crop.

Emboldened by this progress, Galbraith made a splash across Kentucky by filing suits related to marijuana offenses in five different Kentucky counties. The motions in criminal cases in Allen, Butler, Clark, Rowan, and Trimble Counties constituted a strategic blitz to try to get judges to recognize the medical benefit of cannabis. In Gatewood's words, he wanted them to see the plant for what it was: "the safest therapeutic substance known to man."[23]

One of the cases, that of Rowan County resident Joseph D. Lewis, brought renewed attention as Gatewood attempted to appeal the nine-month prison term Lewis had been given for raising fifty-odd marijuana plants in his home. Lewis was the survivor of a catastrophic 1982 automobile accident, which left him partially paralyzed and caused a wide range of other symptoms, including numbness, dizziness, nausea, and back pain. Gatewood was not directly attacking the prohibition of cannabis but was arguing, as he did in the other four cases, that Lewis's use of marijuana privately, in his own home, was not grounds for arrest. Gatewood compared it to possessing alcohol in your own home in "dry" Kentucky counties, where the sale of alcohol was legally prohibited. These judges did not see the cases the same way, and they didn't lead to any major changes in how marijuana was policed in Kentucky.[24]

By early 1999 it was time for Gatewood to make his decision. Patton was running unopposed in the upcoming primary, and his reelection looked all but assured.[25] As Patton began campaigning in early 1999, his campaign was clearly wary of Gatewood's lingering presence in the race. This was due less to internal Kentucky politics than to a recent electoral upset some seven hundred miles away.

In Minnesota's 1998 gubernatorial election, navy veteran and former professional wrestler Jesse Ventura ran as the third-party candidate under the banner of the Reform Party, which had risen in fame during the presidential campaign of billionaire H. Ross Perot in 1992. Running a low-budget campaign that focused on grassroots organizing and clever advertising, Ventura shocked the country by defeating the Republican and Democratic candidates to become the governor of Minnesota.[26]

Governor Patton's deputy campaign manager and brother-in-law Paul Erickson brought up the risk of a third-party run as their campaign kicked off in eastern Kentucky. "We're reminding people of Minnesota. It's the Jesse factor. The Ventura effect. You never know what kind of independent is going to come out of the woodwork."[27]

Before Gatewood could officially announce his intent to run, he needed to find a new running mate. He approached Jerry Hammond, but Hammond begged off, saying that he was done with politics. This left Gatewood exploring other options, and he scoured Kentucky to find someone who was like-minded and willing to participate in the grueling process of campaigning. "I looked high and low around the Commonwealth for the right person. They had to be a registered Independent already and able to handle their own in public. They had to have a thick skin and a sense of humor. And we had to be in agreement on various issues."[28]

His search took him across Kentucky, and he met and recruited partners at a variety of events and public gatherings. During this time Gatewood also had to decide if he would carry any party banner in the governor's race. He had declared himself an independent, and could have run that way, but alignment with even a minor party provides benefits related to fundraising, media awareness, and popular support. Gatewood remembered evaluating all of the most prominent third parties, including the Libertarians, the Green Party, the Constitutional Party, and the Patriot Party. He couldn't see himself finding a home in any of those, so he stuck to his Independent label, at least for the time being.

Eventually he heard of a woman from Murray, Kentucky, named Kathy Lyons, and he drove out to meet her. While they didn't share perfectly symmetrical political beliefs, they agreed on the major planks of Gatewood's political philosophy: constitutional law, the Second Amendment, environmental protections, small government, and, perhaps most important, medicinal marijuana. Lyons had most recently worked as a technician on

Gatewood Galbraith with running mate Kathy Lyons. Running on the Reform Party ticket in 1999, Gatewood recruited Lyons as a candidate for lieutenant governor. Although Paul E. Patton won in a landslide, the 1999 campaign was Gatewood's most successful effort, drawing more than 15 percent of the vote.

archaeological digs for Murray State University, and lived on a farm with her husband, Wallace. Much of her political focus up to that point had been on environmental protections, where she led initiatives against large-scale hog and chicken farm operations in her native Calloway County. The couple greeted Gatewood on their front porch.

As Gatewood put it, "Hot damn, she had it all. A female, from Western Kentucky, who had never been arrested. She brought real balance to the ticket!"[29]

By the time Gatewood left their meeting, he felt confident that Kathy would join him. He was right. She agreed to be the candidate for lieutenant governor in early 1999. Since Gatewood didn't have to prepare for the May primary, he announced their run for office later than usual.[30] In a February 23 press conference in the Capitol rotunda in Frankfort, Gatewood and Kathy made it official. They would seek office in the 1999 general election. "The people of Kentucky need a choice in November."

Gatewood was coy about his platform, because there were additional hurdles to clear before he could make it onto the ballot. As independent candidates, he and Kathy had to collect at least five thousand petition signatures by August 10, 1999, in order to qualify.

They embarked on a tour of the state to drum up support and to collect as many signatures as possible. With Jerry Hammond assisting with campaign operations, they had already collected more than six thousand by early summer. That was when a representative of the Reform Party got in touch with Hammond to gauge Gatewood's interest in affiliating with the organization that had helped spur Ventura to victory in Minnesota.[31] This must have been a relief for Gatewood, who, even as early as his campaign announcement, had hoped to draw from Ventura's example and to gain the support of the Reform Party.[32]

In the May primaries, Patton ran unopposed, while a publicist from Hart County, Peppy Martin, won the Republican primary election by a mere thousand votes over a relatively unknown and unfunded utility contractor named David L. Williams. This was a further sign of the Kentucky GOP's weakness. They were basically conceding the 1999 election to Patton in light of his popularity and legislative victories.

"I interpret that to be that Martin was such a poor candidate," Patton said, reflecting on the election. "The Republican establishment made no effort to recruit a serious candidate against me. I think they made a mistake. I think they could have run a much more competitive race against me."[33]

In July 1999, Gatewood and Kathy Lyons made the announcement: they would run under the Reform Party banner. Gatewood didn't have to contort his beliefs to fit their platform. When their most popular candidate to date, H. Ross Perot, had run in the 1992 and 1996 elections, he had opposed the same free trade agreements that Gatewood so vehemently condemned as part of his argument against globalism and the evils he saw in multinational agreements that benefited corporations over the people.

Conveniently, because Perot had garnered 6 percent of the vote in the most recent presidential election in Kentucky, the Reform Party qualified for ballot access in Kentucky in the upcoming 1999 election, meaning that the petition and signatures were now a moot point.

While hopes of beating Patton were still farfetched, Gatewood felt emboldened by his new third-party identity, and by the relative weakness of the Kentucky GOP. He and Lyons embarked on his usual cross-commonwealth pre-election tour, appearing anywhere that would have him. Gatewood could also feel the effects of his new exercise and health regimen. He was a constant public presence in Lexington, where he was known for jogging in short running shorts and would pop up all over town, always with a wave and a grin.

"Especially as he got older, it [health] became increasingly important to him. He always walked . . . usually with his shirt off and his little bitty shorts on around Woodland Park. He would do yoga in the park. He would do push-ups and chin-ups," recalled his youngest daughter, Molly, who would go on to build a career around fitness and empowerment for women.[34]

As the *Lexington Herald-Leader* reported, "If you haven't seen Gatewood recently, I can report the man is buff. He runs; he snaps a quick set of pull-ups on overhead bars at Woodland Park. Gatewood is tanned up, bulked up and darn near hairless—a lean, mean, vote-gettin' machine. Doesn't mean Gatewood is going to win any election. But, for goodness sake, don't even think about arm wrestling the dude."[35]

Gatewood was soon to enjoy the most successful political campaign of his life, and things finally seemed to be going his way. This was possible not only because of the political realities of the 1999 election, but also because he got a little help from an old friend.

As the 1999 campaign progressed, it became increasingly apparent that the Republican nominee, Peppy Martin, was in big trouble. It was already a foregone conclusion that she and her running mate, Wanda Cornelius, would lose to Governor Patton, and now a new fear emerged: that they might finish third, behind Gatewood and Kathy Lyons. This fear was expressed not only by Kentucky Republicans but even by Governor Patton himself. In statewide elections, the party that finishes second place receives minority representations on a variety of boards and commissions. If Gatewood were to outpoll Martin, those seats would belong to the Reform Party, an organization that counted a minuscule number of Kentuckians as members.[36]

"If that situation occurred in November," Governor Patton said in a June 1999 interview, "I would suspect that the laws would be changed. I would suspect that would be what the Republicans would want, and I would support that. Because the Reform Party is not a major party in Kentucky."

The Patton campaign had a deeper worry. As successful as the governor had been over the past four years, and with a seemingly easy path to reelection, the threat of a small voter turnout loomed. "What does concern Patton," the *Herald-Leader* reported, "is the possibility that overall voter turnout will be so small that it could skew the results. Patton said that if only 10 percent of the eligible voters actually vote, he could very well lose. And a 20 percent turnout leaves his chances for a second term in doubt."[37]

Patton, and other members of the conventional two-party system, may have been alert to recent political developments in Kentucky. Yes, Governor Patton had been successful and had basically ruled Frankfort with an iron first, imposing his legislative priorities over the past four years. However, voter registration trends actually favored Gatewood's approach. While they had begun to tilt somewhat in the Republican direction, foreshadowing developments of the next two decades, Democrats still enjoyed a healthy majority of registered voters. But since Patton had taken office, the majority of newly registered Kentucky voters had actually chosen not to be aligned with either party, and were independent.[38]

This must have been music to Gatewood's ears, as he and Kathy officially declared themselves Reform Party candidates in July of 1999. With his place on the ballot secure, Gatewood used this coming-out press conference to lob insults at the other two candidates, citing Martin's nonviability and Patton's penchant for old-school tit-for-tat governing during his time in Frankfort. He hailed his new status as the Reform Party candidate, saying he was sick of the "donkey-elephant patty-cake game" in state politics. Alluding to his own financial troubles, he had Kathy present the $500 check for the election filing fee because, speaking to the secretary of state, he said, "I didn't know if you'd take mine."

Most of all Gatewood was determined to prove that this was not just another publicity stunt. It was certainly a marriage of political convenience, but it also made sense. Thanks to Ventura's successful campaign and recent trends, third-party candidates were getting more attention and more respect. Gatewood brought a transparent, if controversial, background in Kentucky politics, and he had great name recognition across the commonwealth. He said that Ventura "proved a vote for a third party is not a wasted vote."[39]

At the press conference, Gatewood made a second announcement: his friend Willie Nelson would be playing another event in support of his campaign that September at the Red Mile racetrack in Lexington. When he first approached Willie with the idea, Gatewood was nervous that he was asking too much of the country music star. But Nelson happily obliged and, probably mindful of the financial and legal difficulties of past shows, suggested that they make this one free, while encouraging donations to Gatewood's campaign.[40]

Gatewood received another major contribution from a friend: the offer of an old touring bus for his campaign events across Kentucky. He had "Gatewood for Governor" painted on the sides, and it became part of his folk-hero image in Kentucky. He could fit twenty-some volunteers in the bus, and he and Lyons used it both to campaign and as a place to convene, to party, and to bond with the volunteers who made his campaigns so special and memorable. At the very least, it was always easy to tell when Gatewood rolled into town.[41]

At that August's Fancy Farm Picnic, Gatewood once again commanded the stage. After Patton and Martin traded barbs, Gatewood laid into both.

After meeting Willie Nelson during his 1991 campaign, Gatewood maintained a lifelong friendship with the country music star, who regularly performed in benefit concerts to support Gatewood's campaigns.

Molly Galbraith, Gatewood Galbraith, and Abby Sears. Even in defeat, Gatewood's daughters and family always supported his campaigns and often joined him on election nights. ("Election Night '99" by Danny Pigman)

He claimed that Republicans had fallen victim to the same misdeeds that had plagued Democratic politics in Kentucky, and that they had turned away from the small-government brand of conservatism they had long heralded. He lambasted Patton and the Democrats for abandoning Kentucky farmers and workers, especially by neutering the state's workers' compensation benefits during the 1996 general session in Frankfort, and declared, "I claim that abandoned territory for the Reform Party."[42]

During one of the individual interviews following his speech, a television news reporter named Mark Herbert asked Gatewood a question he had heard too many times throughout his years in the public spotlight: "Gatewood, when was the last time you smoked marijuana?"

He answered, "Mark, when was the last time you took Viagra?"

When Herbert said that he didn't take the drug, Gatewood said, "Then how come you're such a big prick all the time, Mark?"[43]

Herbert was tickled by the response, and it got a fair amount of play in the coverage of the event. Gatewood was, as always, unabashedly himself, never afraid to speak his mind or to go toe-to-toe with the press.

On September 2, Gatewood opened the festivities at Red Mile with his stump speech and exhortation to the assembled concert crowd to vote for

Gatewood eventually acquired a bus to use for campaign appearances in the late 1990s and early 2000s.

him in November and to reject the traditional two-party status quo. The concert was free to attend, and Gatewood reached an agreement with Red Mile to use their property as long as he could ensure a minimum of 2,500 attendees who would purchase their concessions. Gatewood and Willie delivered. Nearly 9,000 attendees packed the grounds for the two-hour concert.

"The crowd was an eclectic mix—part Grateful Dead concert, part country-western bar, part AARP convention. Many came for the music, some for the politics, some for both," read a report from the *Lexington Herald-Leader.*[44]

As Gatewood remembered, "By the time he was finished, both he and the crowd were worn out. It was perfect from start to finish and one of the most exciting days of my life."[45]

After a crowded few weeks of campaign events and a final debate (in which Governor Patton refused to participate), Gatewood and Lyons felt good about their prospects going into the November general election.

Louisville Courier-Journal reporter Al Cross, who covered the race closely, remembered the strengths that Gatewood brought to his unconventional run. "First, he was entertaining. . . . he said things that had a degree of resonance with people. And as he went along, he became more skilled at communicating that and, in some of these governor's races, he was the most effective communicator of anybody."[46]

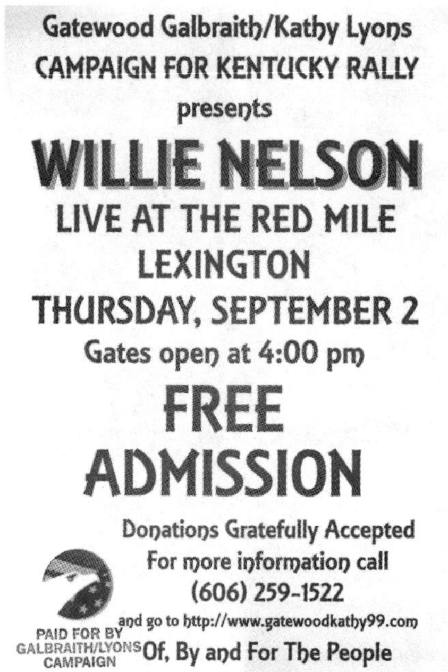

Willie Nelson continued to host benefit concerts for Gatewood's campaigns. In 1999 he played a free concert at Lexington's Red Mile racetrack to garner donations in support of Gatewood and his running mate, Kathy Lyons.

When the votes were counted, Governor Patton cruised to an easy electoral victory, scoring 61 percent of the vote. Peppy Martin finished with an embarrassing 23 percent, and Gatewood garnered 15 percent of the vote in what would be the most successful political campaign of his career.[47]

In his concession speech, Gatewood lamented the role of money in politics. Governor Patton had spent more than $1.3 million in a race with little competition, while Gatewood had raised just over $30,000 for his own run. "Big money won this," Gatewood claimed.

He was also introspective on what turned out to be one of the most successful third-party candidacies in modern American history, and the only one to top 10 percent in a Kentucky governor's race.

"I will never be satisfied with losing. But sometimes real change comes about in increments," Gatewood said. Fifteen percent, he thought, was very creditable.

A news report titled "Galbraith Sends Message" cemented the success of the 1999 campaign. It also addressed Gatewood's political evolution: "Reform Party nominee Gatewood Galbraith, who entered politics as an advocate of legalized marijuana but recast himself with a range of populist and conservative positions, finished with a bigger share of the vote in the governor's race than any previous third-party candidate."[48]

Gatewood had blazed his own trail and had made history running as a candidate separate from the political establishment. He would have no shortage of campaigning in the years to come, but the 1999 general election may have been the high-water mark of Gatewood's political success. He sent shock waves through the status-quo politics of the modern era and served as a wake-up call to Kentucky Republicans, who had reached the nadir of their political influence and would go on to claim a new path to dominance in Kentucky politics over the next twenty years.

Following the 1999 election with its breakneck pace, Gatewood took some time to rest and recover. His candidacy was historic, and he was riding high on a new wave of name recognition and public appeal. As he plotted his next move, Kentucky state politics rolled on in dramatic fashion.

Even with Patton's commanding win in the governor's race, the Kentucky legislature was beginning to show signs of the shift from traditional Democratic domination to increasing association with the Republican Party. In the summer leading up to the 1999 election, Kentucky Democrats held on to a narrow majority in the State Senate, but it didn't last long. Shortly after the election, two Democratic senators, Bob Leeper of Paducah and Dan Seum of Louisville, changed their party affiliation to become Republicans. This gave Kentucky Republicans a majority in the State Senate for the first time in the commonwealth's history. Preceding this party switch, a group of moderate Democrats and Republicans had already effectively wrested control away from the Kentucky Democratic Party, holding votes hostage. With a slim 20–18 majority, Kentucky Republicans now installed a fiery new Senate president in David Williams.[49]

Greg Stumbo (D, Prestonsburg), then majority leader of the House, blamed Kentucky's senior U.S. senator, Republican Mitch McConnell, for inciting this rebellion. "He can't do his job in Washington. He's got no business coming here and interfering with ours."[50]

As Gatewood put it, "I don't know what Mitch offered them to switch but it was worth it just to see the reaction of the Democrats. They were foaming at the mouth, especially when David Williams took over as President of the Senate and began treating the Democrats in the same fashion as they had treated the Republicans all those years. The Dems couldn't stand a taste of their own medicine."[51]

While the five criminal cases that Gatewood had pursued in trying to open up access to medicinal marijuana did not materialize into any substantial progress, he continued to commute to Bowling Green to represent the Reverend Mary Thomas-Spears in her ongoing legal battle. As part of the terms of her probation, Thomas-Spears was required to appear for regular drug testing and to abstain completely from drugs and alcohol. She agreed to the testing, but she and Gatewood argued that it should not include marijuana because of the drug's palliative effects on her health, and she told her probation officer, "if nothing else was working—if the medications didn't ease the pain and I wasn't able to function—that I would go back to using marijuana."

She failed a drug test in March of 1999, causing her probation to be revoked in June. She made the argument to the circuit court judge that cannabis was vital to her well-being. "I had stated to [Judge John D. Minton Jr.] that it was a medication I needed—and if they were going to lock me up for trying to remain healthy, they needed to go ahead and do so."[52]

Gatewood appealed the probation revocation to the Kentucky Court of Appeals, but that appeal was also rejected. Thomas-Spears prepared to serve her time in prison and made arrangements for the care of her young son. She was understandably despondent when leaving home to turn herself in. "I kiss my son goodbye and I walk out, climb in the car in the driveway . . . and I'm pulling out of the driveway to go turn myself in and before I can get out of the driveway my son comes running out of the house and he's holding the phone and going, 'Momma, Gatewood is on the phone,' and I said, 'Tell Gatewood I'm on my way to turn myself in now.'"

She finally got out of the car and heard the good news from Gatewood himself: Judge Minton had issued a stay in the case and had reinstated her probation rather than making her report to prison. Whether he had changed his mind on his own or been swayed by Gatewood's latest arguments on her behalf, Thomas-Spears could stay home with her son.

As she remembered, Gatewood practiced what he preached. "Yeah I mean, he always preached at events or whenever he was speaking to the public, he would tell you that if you were ever busted for possession or for your personal use, he would represent you for free. And hell, I was busted for trafficking!"[53]

As some of these legal battles wrapped up, a new jewel caught Gatewood's eye: the Sixth Congressional District, home to his native Lexington and up for grabs in the 2000 election. The Sixth District had passed between Democrats and Republicans for a number of years, being represented by former Lexington mayor Scotty Baesler from 1992 to 1998 and then by a young Republican, Dr. Ernie Fletcher. In the contentious political climate of 2000, the Democrats planned on helping Baesler reclaim his old district, while Republicans pumped Fletcher's campaign with funding to run a constant slew of attack ads on local television stations.

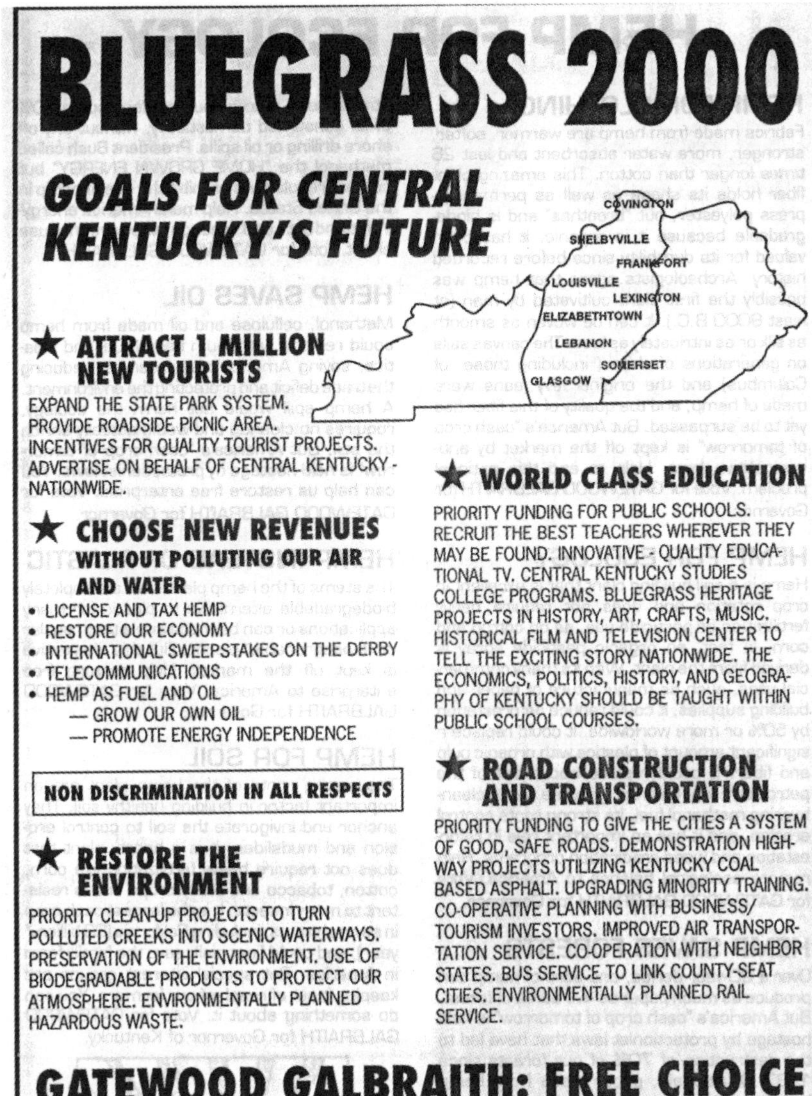

During his first run for Congress in 2000, Gatewood laid out his platform on fliers and posters, promising a new kind of candidate for his Sixth Congressional District.

Congressional campaign bumper sticker, 2002. Gatewood's red and yellow congressional campaign bumper stickers are still displayed throughout Kentucky.

Gatewood got interested in the race and decided to throw his hat into the ring. Running again with the support of the Reform Party, Gatewood hoped to capitalize on his recent surge in popularity. He had little funding, but he did still have the campaign bus. He had it repainted to read "Gatewood for Congress" and entered the race in late June 2000.

He made "big money" the center of his campaign, saying, "For every voter in the 6th District, this is the central question: 'Are you for sale?' Is your vote for sale? These other guys in this race think it is."[54]

Negative ads filled television screens and radio dials throughout the year, and Gatewood lacked the money to compete in traditional media. So he decided to try something different. He had massive signs printed and stood at busy intersections around Lexington to ask for votes.

"The response was immediate and gratifying. I started out by standing at Nicholasville Road and Man o' War and then moved to a different busy corner each morning and afternoon during rush hour."[55]

Both Baesler and Fletcher mostly ignored Gatewood's presence, but they still appreciated his wit and dedication to the race. During one of the debates the three candidates participated in, Fletcher remembered, Gatewood made the entire audience crack up.

"So they ask a question to Scotty . . . I had to come up and say Scotty was not good, why he was not a good candidate, why he was not the right candidate for this race," said Fletcher. Baesler followed the same line of attack, pointing out all of Fletcher's faults and insisting that he was not qualified to serve the people of the Sixth District. Finally, when it was Gatewood's turn, he stood up and said, "Ladies and gentlemen, I want you to know that I know these two gentlemen, they're honorable individuals and you can believe everything they just said about one another."

The crowd was left in stitches. Twenty years later Fletcher remarked, "You couldn't help but like him, he had a wonderful personality. . . . He was just as witty as anybody you'll find."[56]

Gatewood Galbraith onstage in 2002. Gatewood was made for appearances under the bright lights. A passionate and engaging speaker, he always made headlines.

When the dust settled, neither Gatewood's wit nor his public campaign advertising helped him make much of a dent in the heated and well-funded race. Nearly $8 million was spent, mostly by Fletcher and Baesler. Ernie Fletcher won the race with 53 percent of the vote, while Baesler finished second with 35 percent. Gatewood's showing was strong for how little money he spent on the campaign, claiming 12 percent of the vote with an especially strong showing in his hometown of Lexington.[57]

Gatewood once again lamented the role of money in politics, saying, "I thought the voice of the people would rise above the noise of big money. Once again, big money wins out."

When asked if he was planning to run in future races, Gatewood demurred. He reportedly claimed that he wasn't planning on running in future races since he couldn't compete with the massive electoral spending of twenty-first-century politics. "Last night," the *Herald-Leader* reported, "he said he has no immediate plans to run for office again and that he wouldn't consider another campaign unless he has better financial backing."[58]

In reality, Gatewood was in the middle of a punishing series of campaigns, which would come in frequent succession throughout the coming decade. He had spent much of his adult life fighting for relevancy on the campaign trail. The 1999 election and the subsequent double-digit percentage showing in the 2000 congressional race inspired him to pick up his yoke and to keep going.

Gatewood was now at the height of his popularity and influence. He reveled in his folk hero status, recognized throughout the state and loved in Lexington, where he became a community fixture and spectacle, even as politics became ever more corporate and divisive. He had spent the late 1990s probing the courts for legal challenges to harsh marijuana prohibition laws and made a national impact in these two most recent races. A new decade of challenges and difficulties beckoned. He was nowhere near done.

7

The Last Free Man

Gatewood claimed that he wasn't interested in any future runs for office, but the lure of politics won out. After the 2000 election he focused more on his law practice but also found a new creative outlet: as host of his own radio show. Broadcast on WVLK in Lexington on Saturday afternoons, Gatewood's call-in show covered any topic under the sun. He dedicated much of this time to echoing his well-worn campaign pillars, especially touting the benefits of medical marijuana and criticizing the federal war on drugs.

In his memoir, he noted one phone call that actually led to him representing a young man who had been convicted of drug charges through a police sting. "Entrapment, pure and simple," Gatewood called it. He was able to have his client's charges reduced when the state couldn't produce various witnesses, but the case gave him another example of the hurtful effects of the war on drugs and the injustice done to minor offenders who increasingly wound up in jail cells because of outdated federal policies.

He coined a term for this sharp uptick in incarceration over the past twenty years: the People Processing Industry, or "PPI." By the year 2000, the United States led the world in locking up its citizens. The incarceration rate was 699 inmates per 100,000 residents. One in every 143 U.S. residents was incarcerated.[1]

This renewed Gatewood's focus on social justice. He saw, firsthand, the deleterious effects of failed policy on his clients, many of whom were guilty only of consuming cannabis in their own homes and not exposing anyone else to harm.

"The PPI is designed solely to force-process people through a system that strips them of their liberty and dignity by making criminals of them for an increasingly wide scope of basic behaviors. Processing more people has become the aim of large corporations who now control the operations of prison systems in the U.S. and the more prisoners they can fill their beds with, the more dividends they earn," he wrote.

By the year 2000, according to the nonprofit Sentencing Project, Kentucky had 1,268 prisoners in private prisons, under the control of corporate entities. By 2012 the private prison population in the United States ballooned to 137,220 people.[2] Gatewood was a leading voice in censuring the country he loved, which he now often described as a "prison state": "The money earned by private interests, by forcing more and more people through the penal system, is blood money, based on the pain and suffering of literally millions of citizens. They are involved in a modern version of slavery and the private prisons they own should be shut down or they should be locked up in them themselves. Now that would be an appropriate use for that space."[3]

Gatewood's radio show allowed him to focus even more on local issues. On every show he heard from callers in Lexington and came to see what concerned them. When, in late 2001, he began to show interest in running for mayor of Lexington in the upcoming May 2002 election, some callers urged him on.

The idea, as alluring as all of the other political pursuits in Gatewood's past, was intriguing. As his family and friends had been telling him since 1983, he really should have focused on local politics from the start, as a springboard to the statewide offices he so coveted. The mayoral election in Lexington was, and continues to be, nonpartisan: candidates do not declare their party affiliations or run under any party banners. But Gatewood was concerned with the creeping influence of big-money politics in the race.

"I don't think Paul Patton or Mitch McConnell should be running Lexington," he said. "That scares me more than anything else."[4]

Gatewood eventually settled on not running, partially because he didn't want to give up his radio show or slow down his law practice. Instead he threw his support to Teresa Isaac, one of the candidates in a four-person race that would be whittled down to two candidates after the May primary. Isaac had first met Gatewood at the University of Kentucky Law School, and she had served as vice mayor of Lexington through much of the 1990s.

Gatewood frequently promoted Isaac on his radio show, and admired her principled approach to governing. "When you talk with Teresa, you will be talking with the Mayor. She won't have to run across the street and ask a group of businessmen in a corporate boardroom what their position of the Mayor is on the matter. She is her own person, un-beholden to the party machines."[5]

Reflecting on the race nearly twenty years later, Isaac was convinced that Gatewood's support really did make a difference in what would turn out to be an extremely close race. "I'm sure that it did. I think at that time he had a radio show and endorsed me on his radio show. So if there were . . . people that were undecided, I'm sure that helped. . . . He put out yard signs for me and he, you know, would talk to his friends about me. And, yeah, I definitely think that he helped with some of the undecideds."

One particular issue in the race really irked Gatewood. Leading up to the May 2002 primary, the local Lexington water utility, owned and operated by Kentucky-American Water, began negotiations with a large German conglomerate called RWE. This would remove local control, and it set off alarm bells for Gatewood. Always wary of large multinational corporations, Gatewood saw this as a major issue in the race. Isaac agreed with him that the company should stay under local control, and promoted the idea that the city of Lexington should purchase it themselves. Both Gatewood and Isaac feared a foreign corporation raising rates to drive up profits at home.

"We took the position that local government and local people should control the water resource and that it shouldn't be controlled by . . . a lot of shareholders in Germany," Isaac said. "And so Gatewood, of course, felt that the local community should control its own water resource."[6]

Gatewood and Isaac weren't alone in this belief. Former Kentucky governor Edward T. Breathitt penned an op-ed in the *Lexington Herald-Leader* in the lead-up to the race, supporting the local purchase choice. "Lexington, Louisville and the state are rapidly becoming colonies of companies out of the state and even out of the country," he wrote. "The Urban County Government and the leadership of this community must seize this opportunity, for it may never come again."[7]

As returns rolled in, Isaac had done the unthinkable. Even when being massively outspent by the other candidates, she won the primary election with 32 percent of the vote. She edged Lexington City Council member Scott Crosbie (31 percent), and businessman Jim Gray, who finished third and out of the general election ballot with 30 percent.[8] Isaac would go on to face Crosbie in the November general election, winning with 51.2 percent of the vote, again while massively outspent.[9]

His fringe involvement in local politics got Gatewood thinking about his own political future. He enjoyed his time as a radio host and local voice, but the bigger stage always beckoned. This desire, and a new drama unfolding in Frankfort, drove Gatewood back into the spotlight.

David Fitts and his wife, Sue McKaig, met Gatewood in the early 1990s at a party thrown by David's brother, who had volunteered for Gatewood's 1991 campaign for governor. Impressed by Gatewood, David donated to his campaigns and voted for him when he could. David had been a marijuana user since the 1970s and had seen its benefits firsthand. When his brother, who suffered from leukemia, was in the hospital for chemotherapy treatments and was miserable, unable to eat or sleep, he finally asked David to bring him some marijuana. They smoked it in his room (the doctors asked them to kindly bring it baked in brownies next time) and it made an immediate difference. His brother ate a burger and fries and a milkshake, and David was convinced of the medicinal value of cannabis. His brother passed away in 1984, just after Gatewood hit the political scene.

David Fitts was also deeply interested in politics and spent much of his time volunteering for various campaigns and working on issue advocacy. "Mainly I was really concerned after 9/11 and with things like the Patriot Act and what they were doing to the Constitution, the Bill of Rights, and Gatewood was, too."[10]

Fitts and McKaig had an avid interest in politics and local issues and were partly responsible for Gatewood considering running against Congressman Ernie Fletcher again in the November 2002 midterm election. Other events in Kentucky state politics brought a whole new level of drama and intrigue to the upcoming elections, as well as looking forward to the 2003 gubernatorial race.

Part of Gatewood's public and political profile now included his strong belief in the Second Amendment and his alignment with guns rights and militia groups throughout Kentucky. He had used this as a major campaign plank in his 2000 run for Congress. Gatewood had befriended a man named Charlie Puckett, who was deeply involved in the militia movement in Kentucky, and who sought Gatewood's legal advice about his ability to possess firearms.

Puckett had been convicted of a criminal offense as a nineteen-year-old in West Virginia, and wanted to know if his felony conviction prohibited him from owning a weapon. Gatewood confirmed that it did, but he encouraged Puckett to try, as any violation would likely be caught before he was issued a license. "I told him that, if he was a felon, he wasn't supposed to own a weapon. But if the FBI, after a mandatory background check, cleared him for a permit, it must be all right."[11]

Puckett received a license through official channels, and began to amass a stockpile of weapons and ammunition. As his involvement in the militia scene increased his public persona, Kentucky authorities began to investigate and found that they disagreed with Puckett's and Gatewood's conclusions.

Following a media appearance in Lexington, the Bureau of Alcohol, Tobacco, and Firearms arrested Puckett after finding various guns, pipe bombs, and nearly 35,000 rounds of ammunition in his home and office. He pled not guilty, but much of Gatewood's legal strategy proved to be ineffective, and Puckett faced a lengthy prison sentence. During the trial, Puckett claimed he found a note that contained a threat on his life at his home, so Puckett disappeared into the wind, in clear violation of his bail agreement.[12]

An intense multistate manhunt followed Puckett's posting a last message on an Internet forum: "It is my last testament that I have NOT committed ANY criminal acts, nor will I donate years of my life for something that I have NOT done."[13]

Gatewood produced the supposed note, and even suggested that perhaps Puckett had been abducted by other nefarious actors. Gatewood feared that Puckett's reputation would allow law enforcement to shoot first and ask questions later if they tracked Puckett down. Worse, other militia members or groups might take up arms against law enforcement in order to protect Charlie. "Yes I am [worried]. Yes I am. I invite all the people I know in the militia or who attended any training sessions or who know Charlie personally—I'm asking them to be calm about this and let's find out what's going on. Certainly I hope when Charlie is located that cooler heads will prevail and that there be no violence in his apprehension."[14]

Finally, nearly three weeks after disappearing, Charlie Puckett turned himself in for arrest. Luckily the situation ended with no bullets fired, but the entire legal spectacle further cemented Gatewood's place in the public eye as a fierce supporter of guns rights and militia groups, for better or worse. His suggestion that Puckett had been abducted, or that authorities were responsible for the threatening note, signaled his shift to a more paranoid and conspiracy-theorist status in Kentucky.[15]

While Gatewood was engrossed in the Puckett case, allegations arose that rocked the Kentucky political landscape. A woman named Tina Conner claimed that during Governor Patton's first term, they had engaged in an extramarital affair. Conner owned a bankrupt nursing home in western Kentucky, and she claimed that Patton had given her business preferential regulatory treatment, but then began a state investigation into her facility once she broke the affair off. Patton initially denied the affair, but then admitted to it during a live address from Frankfort. Patton denied he had done anything illegal, while finally owning his personal shortcomings: "I apologize to the people of Kentucky for my failure as a person. I have already apologized to Judi and my family. I'm also sorry that I initially denied mistakes I made in my private life."[16]

Following this scandal, multiple investigations were opened against Patton, and his remaining political influence and power evaporated overnight. The new Republican majority in the State Senate was already flexing its muscle, as the House and Senate budget committees couldn't come to an agreement on a biennial budget during the regular session in 2002.

Gatewood enjoyed poking fun at the inadequacy of the Kentucky political system, but finally decided to get involved in a new campaign for Lexington's congressional seat. The incumbent in the Sixth District, Republican Ernie Fletcher, was running unopposed. With the Democrats failing to field a candidate, Gatewood saw an opportunity.

He depended on David Fitts and Sue McKaig to run his campaign, and they both worked diligently for very little money. They believed in Gatewood and his message, and they counted him as a close friend. They were also convinced of Gatewood's genuine charitable nature, which they witnessed firsthand. As David recalled, "Yeah, he was just somebody it was really easy to talk to and he was very generous and I remember one time when we met at Sam's hot dogs and then we ate across the street and he saw some homeless people. And I just saw him reaching into his wallet and [he] got twenty dollars out to go over and put his hand on his brother and say, 'Here, you look like you might need this.'"[17]

Gatewood announced his intent to run in August, following the petition procedure he had endured in previous campaigns. Since the Kentucky Democrats had recruited no one to run in what had been a competitive congressional race, Gatewood criticized their lack of commitment. He also attacked Fletcher for having one foot out the door, as he looked ahead to running for governor in the 2003 statewide elections the next year: "I believe the Democratic Party really let people down by not posting competition for Ernie Fletcher. If there was a Democrat in this race I wouldn't be in it, but the people of the Sixth District deserve a race."

Following the collapse of the Reform Party from its prominence just a few years earlier, Gatewood ran in the 2002 congressional race as a true independent, without the backing of any political party. Gatewood made Fletcher's interest in the governor's mansion a common line of attack during the campaign. "We need a full-time congressman; we don't need a transient person in this office," Gatewood said. "It appears he will be running two campaigns at the same time. While he's in Paducah, I'll be campaigning in Bourbon County."[18]

Gatewood continued his strategy of a district-wide bus tour, as well as printing out large signs and standing on busy intersections to ask voters for support. The hours standing on the side of the road began to take their toll on Gatewood. While he was still in great shape, he began to slow down in 2002, no doubt feeling the long-term effects of his chronic emphysema and a punishing campaign schedule.

He didn't pull any punches against Fletcher, whom he saw as a puppet of U.S. Senator Mitch McConnell. Critical of Fletcher's penchant for changing

Gatewood Galbraith on a street corner in 2002. In response to lagging fundraising, Gatewood took an unorthodox approach to campaigning—he became a regular sight at busy Lexington intersections, working for votes.

careers, Gatewood quipped, "I know that my opponent has been a Baptist preacher, an engineer, a pilot, a doctor, and now a Congressman. That only means he is highly trainable. But so is my parakeet."[19]

As an added stressor, Gatewood received horrible news just a few weeks before the election. His longtime friend and advisor, Jerry Hammond, died of a massive heart attack in October 2002.[20]

Even with David and Sue working around the clock and Gatewood pouring himself into the campaign, the results weren't what Gatewood wanted. He finished with 27 percent of the vote to Fletcher's 71 percent. As was his nature, he found a silver lining in the disappointment. When asked for comment on the night of the election, Gatewood said, "We had very little money and no party, but we got about 40,000 votes and I think that's a significant bloc of voices that had a chance to be heard."[21]

For a few months, the disappointing result in the 2002 congressional race dissuaded Gatewood from exploring a run for office in the 2003 statewide elections. Apart from the breakneck campaigning schedule of the past few years, he wasn't interested in running for governor because the Democrats looked likely to nominate someone whom he respected, deeply, for the office.

Ben Chandler began his life in Kentucky politics by serving as state auditor from 1991 to 1995. Chandler was Kentucky political royalty: his paternal grandfather, Albert Benjamin "Happy" Chandler had served as governor of Kentucky, commissioner of Major League Baseball, and a United States senator in a political career that spanned thirty years.[22] Ben Chandler had gone on to win the 1995 race for attorney general. Chandler impressed Gatewood with his stellar record, even investigating Governor Paul E. Patton, the highest-ranking member of his own party, during Patton's second term in office. As Gatewood wrote, "Simply put, Ben Chandler could not be bought."[23]

Chandler defeated Kentucky House Speaker Jody Richards and businessman Bruce Lunsford in the May primary, setting up a showdown with Congressman Ernie Fletcher in the November 2003 state election. As predicted throughout his 2002 run, Fletcher had indeed been deeply interested in running for governor. Gatewood's respect for Chandler was apparent in the races he chose to sit out, in the recent past, in 2003, and in the future.

"He had quite a number of opportunities to run against me and never did," Chandler remembered. "And I, of course, always appreciated that. I think he and I had a nice sort of mutual friendship and consideration for each other."[24]

The governor's race was heated from the moment it started, as both parties poured money into advertising to try to give their candidate a leg up. Chandler faced an uphill battle, mostly due to the actions of Governor Patton. The Tina Conner scandal and investigations left Patton essentially a pariah in Kentucky, and Fletcher did all he could to paint Chandler as part of a corrupt and soulless party.

Since Gatewood had no interest in running for governor while there was hope that Chandler would defeat Fletcher, he turned his eye to another race. In the May 2003 primary, Kentucky Democrats had nominated the majority floor leader of the Kentucky House of Representatives, Greg Stumbo, for the office of attorney general. Gatewood didn't have kind words for either Stumbo or the Republican nominee, Jack Wood. "In the primary for Attorney General, both Parties had a tight three-way race which ended with the nominations in the hands of a couple of scalawags whose track record qualified them for jail time more than their Party's nomination."[25]

According to Gatewood, he had multiple members of both parties encourage him to run for the office as an independent. While he doesn't name any names in his memoir, it's fair to assume that this may have been because they wanted Gatewood to split votes in a way that would benefit their party's nominee, rather than actually thinking that he could win the race. Nevertheless, Gatewood used this as motivation to get involved. This was the first and only time he would run for attorney general.

He made it official in July, announcing that he was collecting signatures in order to put his name on the ballot. He also changed his campaign message. While he referenced the fact that he supported medical marijuana, he promised to not make it a main message in his campaign. Instead he wanted to focus on corruption and the prosecution of illegal drugs, mainly heroin and the opioids that were beginning to ravage Kentucky citizens.

In his introductory press conference he chided both the Democratic and Republican nominees, saying, "Relativity is a wonderful thing, you know. I look good against these two guys."[26]

Stumbo had known Gatewood since the mid-1980s, when they had met through mutual friends when the eastern Kentucky attorney first joined the House of Representatives. Stumbo remembered Gatewood always discussing politics and the latest goings-on in Frankfort on those occasions when their group would visit a bar or restaurant together. Even with Gatewood's harsh words for him in public, Stumbo enjoyed a friendly relationship with Gatewood and admired his dedication to the legal and medicinal cannabis movement. He didn't agree with Gatewood's views on marijuana but remembered respecting his knowledge and dedication.

"Gatewood was a guy who believed in what he said, and, you know, that's a rarity sometimes in politics these days. . . . He was willing to suffer the slings and arrows of outrageous fortune, if you will, to promote his cause," Stumbo said. "He was willing to stand up. And even though he knew it wasn't the most popular thing to do or knew that . . . he may be criticized for it, he had the fortitude to get out in front on the issue that he believed in. And you have to admire people like that."[27]

Gatewood's friends David Fitts and Sue McKaig also worked on the 2003 campaign, where they and Gatewood could be seen out in Lexington asking for votes at the usual places: busy intersections, farmers' markets, or any public event. By this time it was pretty apparent to David that Gatewood stood little chance of breaking through in any election. "If you run for office and lose two or three times, you're probably not going anywhere," David said. "And very consistently when I would be out talking to people about him, they would say, 'I really like him, but he can't win.'"[28]

But it certainly didn't stop Gatewood from pouring his time, attention, and money into the race. Whether for a Don Quixote–like personal odyssey or as a practice in political principle, Gatewood always ran to win and was committed to each race he entered.

The day before the filing deadline, Gatewood arrived at the State Capitol in Frankfort along with his daughters Abby and Molly and delivered the required signatures and $500 check to qualify for the November ballot. He was optimistic about this race, as he was for each one he entered, saying, "The chemistry of this race is just phenomenal. I could not pass it up."[29]

When Stumbo, in a televised debate between the candidates for attorney general, detailed his plans to crack down on illegal drugs in Kentucky, he mentioned that Galbraith might not support it because it would probably catch some "friends" of Gatewood. Gatewood "resented" Stumbo's comment. He was not running on the legalization of cannabis and mentioned his emphysema for why he used marijuana. As Gatewood had in many court cases over the past decade, he explained that his private use of cannabis in his home was similar to Kentucky residents who lived in "dry" counties but consumed alcohol at home. "Isn't it refreshing to have some honesty out here in politics, folks?" Gatewood asked.

Once again proving his insight into future issues, Gatewood explained that police should prioritize going after hard drugs, like methamphetamine or heroin, rather than wasting time and money on cannabis. It was no threat to society, while hard drugs were eating away at rural communities throughout the state. Foreshadowing the legal battles of the 2020s, Gatewood said that the state should "seek $2 billion from pharmaceutical companies to expand education and treatment, rather than criminalizing addicts."[30]

Gatewood did receive support from one powerful source: Lexington mayor Teresa Isaac, for whom he had campaigned the previous year. She said, "Gatewood has a reputation as an excellent attorney, and I believe he will make a fine attorney general." Isaac even hosted a fundraiser for Gatewood's campaign in the lead-up to the November election.

Published on the same day as the fundraiser, a *Lexington Herald-Leader* article blasted Gatewood for his "ludicrous" stance on constitutionality regarding private cannabis use and dragged him over the coals for more financial hardship. Speaking to Kenton Smith, president of the Kentucky Commonwealth's Attorneys Association, the *Herald-Leader* reported that Gatewood's theory regarding marijuana use did not stand up to serious scrutiny. "Under Galbraith's theory, people could commit other supposed 'victimless' crimes in their homes, such as gambling and shooting up heroin."

This "profile" also reported Gatewood's own understanding of himself as a true conservative. He opposed abortion, perhaps in part because of his Catholic upbringing, and believed strongly in Second Amendment rights.

It also mentioned a new lien filed against Gatewood in December 2002 by the Internal Revenue Service, which claimed that he owed $110,734 in unpaid income taxes from the previous four years of work. Gatewood played this off as he always did, saying, "They'll get paid like they always do," and pointing to his divorce and frequent campaigns as reasons for being short. In fact, Bill Estep, the *Herald-Leader* reporter who wrote the pre-election profile, found that "Court and county records in Fayette County show more than two dozen lawsuits or liens filed against Galbraith—some before his 1993 bankruptcy and some since—by vendors, local government and the school board, and state and federal taxing authorities claiming he failed to pay bills and taxes."[31]

When the dust settled on election night, Gatewood came up short again. Stumbo won comfortably with 47.7 percent of the vote, after spending more than $300,000 on the race. Wood polled 41.6 percent, while Gatewood finished a distant third, drawing only 10.6 percent of votes. His local popularity was on display once again, as he drew nearly a third of the votes in Fayette County, home to Lexington.

Outspent and out-attacked, Chandler lost to Fletcher, marking the first time since 1967 that a Republican would be in the Kentucky Governor's Mansion. Helped by President George W. Bush and the growing political machine of Senator Mitch McConnell, Fletcher nabbed over 55 percent of the vote. Long showing signs of a shift from Democratic to Republican power, Kentucky's politics were clearly going through a major realignment.[32]

The 2003 elections wrapped up the most dizzying stretch of politics in Gatewood's life. He had run four campaigns in a short five years, and the strain was beginning to show. He was fifty-seven years old and had poured his life into these political pursuits. His chronic health issues and lack of solid financial footing became clearer and clearer. Whether he actually believed he could win these races or not, the consistent theme of rejection on the major stage also surely took a toll.

Gatewood showed no signs of planning for any imminent campaigns. Instead he focused much of his time over the next few years on his practice in Lexington, and on continuing to advocate for the issues close to his heart.

This included a new tradition he had started in 2003, namely a rally and march dedicated to legalizing marijuana that occurred on the first Saturday of May. Interestingly enough, this always coincided with another Kentucky tradition: the world-famous Kentucky Derby. On May 2, 2004, Gatewood and around seventy supporters rallied in downtown Lexington, just across the street from the courthouse where Gatewood both argued cases and, thirty years ago, had protested as a student at the University of Kentucky.[33]

Gatewood constantly felt a sense of guilt about the lack of progress he was making on reforming cannabis laws in Kentucky, even though he went so far as to step back from his firm stance on legalization in his recent campaigns, trying to make himself more politically palatable. It didn't have much effect, partly because he still admitted to using cannabis personally, and partly because this was the issue that got him constant media attention. He could talk all he wanted about fighting against political corruption, for Second Amendment rights, for environmental protections, or for vocational education, but ever since his first race in 1983, he had been stamped as "the marijuana candidate." It turned out that voters in Kentucky, and the news reporters who followed the campaigns, had a long memory.

Gatewood was growing older, and his daughters had grown into smart, accomplished young women. Gatewood's ex-wife, Susan, had put herself through law school in the years following their divorce and was a successful attorney. She had also remarried to a Lexington attorney, William Rambicure.

Gatewood's relationship with Kim had also ended in the late 1990s, mainly a casualty of the financial instability he brought to the table. As she remembered, "I've seen Gatewood Galbraith with ten thousand dollars, right in front of him, cash, and, you know, thirty minutes later have a hundred dollars . . . [and he would ask,] 'Where do you want to go have dinner?'" Gatewood could never learn a healthy approach to money, even after he had been burnt time and time again by his own inattention and carelessness. "He just lived on a different planet when it came to financial responsibilities."[34]

One idea had been growing in Gatewood's mind ever since his first run for governor in 1991: writing a book. He had collected some writings, speeches, letters, and other recollections here and there, but began to formally plan an autobiography only in the early 2000s. Gatewood was a talented writer, and his trademark quick wit and storytelling abilities encouraged him to record his experiences. He also hoped that it would ease some of his financial difficulties or would help him pay off his looming bill to the IRS.

A mainstay of Gatewood's life in Lexington was the Perkins Restaurant and Bakery, a diner located just off Richmond Road. You would often find Gatewood and various friends there in the morning, drinking cups of coffee and discussing politics, or Gatewood's latest campaign, or anything else that came up. The owner, Mark Perkins, was a member of the family that in 1958 had started the original Perkins Restaurant, which grew into a nationwide chain of restaurant franchises. Mark opened his own location in Lexington in 1991.

Mark had originally met Gatewood in the early 1990s when his wife was helping Gatewood with filing his taxes. Gatewood began to visit Mark's

In 2004, with the help of Mark Perkins, Gatewood published *The Last Free Man in America: Meets the Synthetic Subversion*. He hoped sales of his autobiography, bursting with his trademark wit, would fund future campaigns. This portrait was made to promote the book.

restaurant, and a friendship bloomed. When Gatewood had the tour bus for his campaigns, Perkins offered the Perkins Restaurant parking lot for storage.

One day Gatewood came to Perkins with an outrageous idea. Perkins remembered walking up to Gatewood as he sat in his usual booth. Gatewood took off his fedora and said, "Mark, I need you to publish my book."

Mark replied, "Well, I'm not a book publisher."

Gatewood saw Perkins as an intrepid businessman, and as someone he could trust. Gatewood had shopped the book around traditional publishers and had exhausted all of his connections. He was desperate for help.

"I said, 'Gatewood, there's no way in the world I could ever publish a book. I'll make you an omelet," Perkins said.

But once Perkins dug into an idea, he became immersed in it. He did research over the weekend, and when he presented his findings to Gatewood the next Monday, he thought his response would be bleak.

"I knew I wasn't going to publish the book, but I knew I had to communicate it to Gatewood in a way that he would understand in less than forty-five seconds. So, you know, I studied all weekend long and I came up with the most fantastic answer to tell him no," Perkins remembered. "I said, in 2001, did you realize there were one hundred and eighty thousand books published? Only four percent sold more than two thousand copies. We need to sell two thousand copies to break even, so we have a ninety-six percent chance of failure."

Thinking that this would immediately talk Gatewood out of the idea, Perkins was shocked when Gatewood jumped out of the booth and said, "Great! Four percent!!"[35]

They scraped together the funds to have the book printed, after working together to compile, edit, and produce it from Gatewood's notes and writings. The book was published in 2004, and Gatewood set out on a publicity tour trying to sell it. Holding a machine gun on the cover, Gatewood had no problem coming up with a title: *Gatewood Galbraith: The Last Free Man in America.*

It did garner a mostly positive review from the *Lexington Herald-Leader*, a newspaper that often shows up in its pages as a source of scorn. "Galbraith writes like he talks," reported book critic Steve Flairty, "in a straightforward, often rambling but entertaining style with a strong tone of conviction. He loads his prose with engaging, often humorous anecdotes and salty language, and blows no smoke in his highly negative analysis of such luminaries as Paul Patton, Bill Lear, Bob Babbage, Ernie Fletcher, David Williams, and Greg Stumbo."[36]

While it never amounted to the financial success Gatewood envisioned, it does provide insight into Gatewood's life and serves as a valuable artifact that embodies his wit, guile, and uncompromising pursuit of political office and cultural popularity.

If Kentuckians hoped that the political dysfunction of the Patton administration had been left in the rearview, they were sorely mistaken. After taking office, and with Republicans in four of the seven elected statewide offices, Fletcher followed through on his campaign promise of not raising taxes. This meant severe spending cuts on a multitude of government programs. Fletcher was also frequently at odds with Attorney General Greg Stumbo.

In 2005 their conflict reached a heightened pitch, as Stumbo opened an investigation into the hiring practices of the Fletcher administration. More specifically, he accused Fletcher and top aides of violating the state merit system and improperly hiring friends of the administration to fill key government roles.

Stumbo announced the investigation in May of 2005, saying, "It appears to be a pattern of conduct that is designed—intentionally designed—to thwart the protection of the merit system of state employees. It does appear that there are some potential areas where some criminal conduct did occur."[37]

Stumbo's office raided the offices of Fletcher's staff and removed troves of documents that showed violations in the hiring of nearly four hundred positions in state government. After the initial announcement, other anonymous tips of patronage hiring filtered into the attorney general's office, and the investigation loomed over Fletcher's administration for the next two years in office.[38]

In 2006, after a disastrous string of headlines and deep into his reelection push for the 2007 race, Governor Fletcher was indicted on three misdemeanor charges tied to his hiring practices, as were multiple aides in his office. Fletcher used his pardon power to forgive the transgressions of his staff but did not pardon himself in the investigation. Following the charges, Fletcher and Stumbo settled the legal case. Fletcher admitted to the violations of the merit process while skirting personal guilt. Although Fletcher was now free of prosecution for the offenses, his political future was doomed.[39]

With the corruption and dysfunction in Frankfort now obvious to nearly every Kentucky voter, Gatewood once again saw an opportunity in the upcoming governor's race. In January 2007 he announced his intention to run for governor that November.

Now sixty years old, and understanding the political realities of elections in Kentucky, Gatewood focused on a campaign message separate from marijuana. Perhaps the most reserved he ever was on the subject, he said that medical cannabis should be available to the "sick and dying. That's as far as I go." Instead Gatewood tried to turn attention to the corruption in Frankfort, the failings of the two major parties, and legislative ideas about economic development and environmental protections.

Partly as a result of the major budget cuts of the Fletcher administration, college tuition in Kentucky began rising dramatically in the mid-2000s. Gatewood said the rising rates were "casting off a lot of middle-income families from being able to" afford college. He detailed his proposal to give every Kentucky high school graduate a $5,000 voucher to use for college, vocational school, or training in response to the growing prices.

He colored himself the "most conservative candidate," in that year's race, saying, "I'm for limited government. That's what the Constitution was set up to do."[40]

Condemning Democrats both for their recent transgressions and for their inability to hold on to control in state government, and Republicans for Fletcher's more recent difficulties, Gatewood said, "Both parties have been architects of decline in Kentucky."

Galbraith denied attacks framing him as a perennial candidate, instead saying that the state had "perennial problems." He could offer "vision and hope. We need new blood."

When asked about the fundraising that had doomed his past campaigns, Gatewood referenced his autobiography, saying that he would ask "each of the 15,000 people who have read his book to contribute $100 to his campaign."

He also said he was going to try to sell another 10,000 to 30,000 copies during the campaign. "If you're a Democrat, you get it for free. If you're a Republican, it costs you $10."[41]

This time around, Gatewood would once again participate as a member of the Democratic Party, competing in the May primary in hopes of earning a matchup with the likely Republican candidate, Governor Fletcher. Gatewood chose Mark Wireman, a retired state employee and native of Jackson, Kentucky, as his running mate.

Gatewood campaigned on a variety of new ideas, further showcasing his political evolution. He focused much more on issues of funding and business development. He encouraged Kentucky legislators to reconsider expanded gaming and casinos, in part to raise money for other initiatives. Gatewood urged voters to endorse his position of cutting down on government spending and waste, to fund ideas like his voucher system.

As rates of opioid and heroin abuse skyrocketed in Kentucky, he once again called for pharmaceutical companies to pay for their misdeeds. Gatewood said that he would file suit against drug companies in an

Gatewood was known for his hemp and marijuana advocacy but his true political purpose was protecting freedom, truth, and the common Kentuckian against corporate and political interests.

effort to get them to pay $1 billion to construct drug treatment centers in Kentucky.

"How many billion-dollar ideas do I have to come up with before I'm elected governor?" he asked.[42]

As part of a series of questions posed to all the candidates in the *Lexington Herald-Leader*, Gatewood also responded to a question related to restoring voting rights to felons, an issue that would gain steam over the next fifteen years. Gatewood was always committed to social justice and believed in giving people second chances—especially those who had served time or been convicted of crimes related to marijuana possession, whom he frequently defended in court.

Before qualifying that there were certain crimes that should preclude felons from ever voting, Gatewood explained, "It is important to give people hope and a stake in our political process, and many felons have learned their lesson. These may well be the most motivated of all voters, grateful to have another chance."[43]

On the problem of drug addiction, Gatewood detailed ideas that he first brought up in his 1991 campaign: "Kentucky's hospitals, courts, and prisons are overtaxed because of addiction to prescription drugs. After prescribed pain management ends, many will become hooked and look to the streets because we have given them nowhere else to turn. Treatment must become part of the solution for those addicted or we will never solve this crisis."[44]

Big money loomed over the race. Just a few weeks shy of the primary, Gatewood had only raised $18,000. By the same time, Governor Fletcher had raised $3 million. Gatewood defended his figure, saying, "I haven't made the first phone call to ask for money. And I will not make a phone call to ask for money. That is the root of what's wrong with politics in Kentucky today."[45]

In an unusual April snowstorm, with snow blowing sideways during the morning Lexington commute, Gatewood stood at the intersection of Versailles and Huntertown Roads, holding his campaign sign, waving to voters. His old high school classmate, television reporter Ferrell Wellman, said, "Here's a guy who's been running in statewide and congressional races since the eighties, but it doesn't bother Gatewood at all to stand out on a road with his sign in damn near unbearable weather to get his name out."

Defending his lifelong quest, Gatewood said, "I want to be governor because I don't think it's a foregone conclusion that Kentucky's got to remain poor and illiterate throughout my lifetime."

Ever the political outsider, Gatewood had a new identity in the twenty-first century: a small-government conservative with liberal ideas; an anticorruption crusader without two dimes to rub together. As the *Lexington Herald-Leader* profile put it, "Galbraith is an agrarian populist, who believes the small farmer is king. He is a nationalist."[46]

Would this transformation affect his chances in the 2007 primary? The answer was a clear and emphatic "no." Longtime Kentucky politician Steve Beshear won the Democratic primary handily, with 41 percent of the vote, setting up a November matchup with Governor Ernie Fletcher, who prevailed in the Republican primary despite his problems while in office. Gatewood finished with just shy of 21,000 votes, tallying only 5.9 percent and placing fifth out of the six Democratic candidates.[47]

Another election, another resounding defeat, but it didn't discourage Gatewood from seeking office in the future. For now, he settled into his busy law practice, and served as a Lexington social figure and political critic. In the 2007 race, Steve Beshear used Fletcher's weakness to trounce him in the November general election, securing 58.7 percent of the vote and returning the Democrats to the Governor's Mansion.[48]

In the years following the 2007 election, the legal and medical cannabis movement was spreading like wildfire across the country. By the fall of 2009, fourteen states had legalized access to marijuana for medicinal purposes. In an October 2009 memorandum, the U.S. Justice Department directed federal prosecutors not to pursue patients or distributors in those states, as long as they were in agreement with state law. Basically, the federal government announced that medical marijuana rules would be up to the states that had made it available: Alaska, California, Colorado, Hawaii, Maine, Maryland, Michigan, Montana, Nevada, New Mexico, Oregon, Rhode Island, Vermont, and Washington.

Attorney General Eric Holder made this clear in an accompanying statement: "It will not be a priority to use federal resources to prosecute patients with serious illnesses or their caregivers who are complying with state laws on medical marijuana, but we will not tolerate drug traffickers who hide behind claims of competence with state law to ask activities that are clearly illegal."[49]

Gatewood celebrated these developments, urging Kentuckians to find ways to provide access to cannabis while profiting from its taxation. In a *Herald-Leader* op-ed, Gatewood wrote, "For 38 years, I have tried to position Kentucky to take advantage of this transition which I knew would come eventually. It had to. So while other states might consider this proposition like 'hogs staring at a wristwatch,' Kentucky's lawmakers should be educated and motivated to act in nonpartisan unison to take advantage of this epic opportunity. Time is of the essence."[50]

In June of 2009, Gatewood and his family lost their mother, Dollie, at the age of ninety-six. She had long been a hero and inspiration to Gatewood and supported his advocacy and attempts for public office. She was a gracious and tenacious force for good in Lexington, and was mourned by her children and, by then, fourteen grandchildren.

Just a month after this loss, Gatewood got an early start on the 2011 Kentucky governor's election. On July 8 he announced his intent to run and secured Dea Riley, a Frankfort political consultant, as his running mate. Energized by Riley's political bona fides and her ability to fundraise, Gatewood came out with big promises. "I believe we can raise over a million dollars and win this race." Ever mindful of making splashy headlines, Gatewood said he was running "to combat Kentucky's electile dysfunction. Nothing has happened in this state for years, and it's the fault of both major political parties. I want to help the electorate change that."[51]

Gatewood would run again as an Independent candidate, meaning he could have a long runway leading up to the November general election without having to survive a primary race.

From the outset, Gatewood's 2011 campaign lamented the sorry state of Kentucky, as it frequently found itself ranked last in many measures of

Gatewood retained his mischievous streak throughout his life. He was often the center of attention and was widely known for his off-the-cuff one-liners and turns of phrase.

well-being, and as it continued to experience the economic doldrums radiating from the 2008 financial crisis and recession.

Communities in eastern Kentucky were also increasingly feeling the environmental effects of mountaintop removal mining (MTR), where coal companies leveled hills and mined coal from the surface of coal deposits, effectively destroying vast swaths of Appalachian terrain. This also caused more pollution and especially flooding, as MTR removed trees and soil that helped with retaining water. While Beshear, who won the May primary running unopposed, and David Williams, the longtime Kentucky state senator and Republican nominee, favored coal businesses over environmental regulation, Gatewood took a stand against both candidates. He said that the practice caused "unsurpassed environmental damage" and should be outlawed. Always a candidate of contradictions, he paired his small-government conservatism with an insistence on increasing government regulation of the coal industry.[52]

Gatewood took the stage for a final time at one of his favorite scenes, the Fancy Farm Picnic, in August 2011, delivering a blistering condemnation of Governor Beshear and of the Kentucky Republicans. Gatewood campaigned with all of the energy he could muster, as his health and energy continued to decline under the rigors of a statewide campaign. It was seen as Gatewood's most traditional and poised campaign, with others crediting Riley with a newfound organization and focus.[53]

In the weeks leading up to the election, Gatewood sounded at peace, and curiously retrospective, about his life in politics. "Win or lose," he said, "I feel confident; I'm following my path."[54]

As expected, Governor Steve Beshear won a second term on November 8, 2011, after raising more than $10 million for the race. Gatewood, aided by Riley's organization, raised just less than $200,000, eclipsing the total he had raised in all of his past political campaigns combined. Beshear carried 55.7 percent of the vote to Williams's 35.3 percent. Gatewood finished a distant third, with 9.0 percent.[55]

Struggling with chronic emphysema and exhaustion from the campaign, Gatewood retreated into private life with no future plans announced. Neither he nor his close circle of friends and family truly understood the seriousness of his condition, and just how close he had pushed himself to the brink over the past two years.

Just a few weeks after the 2011 election, Susan Sears, Gatewood's ex-wife but lifelong friend and coparent, had their entire family over for a Christmas celebration. Of course, this included Gatewood. Susan and Gatewood had

Shown here at the Courtyard Deli in 2009, Gatewood frequented local businesses and made friends everywhere he went. Gatewood was a fixture in Lexington until his untimely death in 2012.

made good on their promises and had maintained a loving and healthy relationship as they navigated life after divorce. Susan remembered Gatewood vividly on that day, soaking in the joy of his family and his grandson, Connor.

"He was with us before the Christmas of 2011," she said. "And I remember it, it's just emblazoned in my brain. I remember he was wearing a yellow sweater and he sat in a rocking chair near where Connor and Abby . . . And I remember him watching Connor open his presents and I remember his laughter. You know, this deep moving laughter and the look in his eye when he would watch this little two-and-a-half-year-old open his Christmas gifts."

Gatewood's declining health and physical weakness were apparent to the entire family. Susan remembered, "He wasn't well. He was slow, it was taking him longer to get up the steps. . . . He did have a shortness of breath and it was increasingly obvious during the last year of his life."[56]

Following the holidays, Susan, Abby, and Molly grew increasingly concerned about Gatewood's health. (His daughter Summer lived overseas during this period, but stayed in close touch with her father and family.) They took turns staying with him as his breathing and cough grew worse. Finally, on January 1, 2012, Susan and her husband, Bill, called Susan's stepson, Ben, who was a physician in Lexington, to come to Gatewood's house for an examination. Ben listened to Gatewood's breathing and prescribed a strong antibiotic for the pneumonia Gatewood was suffering from. He encouraged the family to make sure that he stayed hydrated and rested and made plans to check back in after a couple of days to decide if there was progress or if Gatewood needed to be hospitalized.

The past five or six years had been particularly taxing on Gatewood, as his long-term health problems resurfaced. Gatewood was also never stable financially, often joking that his retirement plan was to live in his daughter Molly's pool house. He did not have health insurance, and despised hospitals, so he often self-medicated and avoided the healthcare system, both out of preference and for financial reasons. His siblings, who had all gone on to productive careers and had stable financial lives, worried about Gatewood's health, and stayed close over the last years of his life.

Since Abby and Molly had been caring for him over the holidays, Susan took over nursing Gatewood, caring for him and helping him to drink water so the girls could get back to work. At one point they reminisced together and looked at scrapbooks of family pictures that their middle daughter, Abby, had made. Susan reports that this time with Gatewood was extraordinary, especially in retrospect. At the time, she wasn't sure why—but recalls they both felt grateful and introspective. She remembers Gatewood specifically

With daughters Abby (*left*) and Molly. Nothing brought Gatewood more joy throughout his life than his children.

saying, "Well, Susie, we did pretty well, didn't we? We did a damned good job with these girls. They're pretty cool young women. And they can make their way in this world, can't they?"[57]

On January 3, Susan called Kim Eisner, who had planned to see Gatewood on Wednesday, and urged her to visit him on Tuesday night instead. Kim sat with Gatewood, Abby, and Molly, and massaged Gatewood's feet and visited with him. Abby stayed the night to care for her dad and to make sure he had anything he needed.

Early on January 4, Susan called to see how Gatewood was doing, and Abby told her they both were still sleeping, which Susan knew they both needed. Within just moments, Abby called back, screaming. Louis Gatewood Galbraith, age sixty-four, had passed away peacefully in the night, at rest and without pain.

His final days were a reminder of what he valued most in his life. After having spent forty years pursuing political power and recognition, he retreated to the love of family. He spent time with his siblings, with Susan, with his daughters, with his friends. He looked back on a long and eventful life, and decided that what was most important was not the love of the voters, but of those close to him. A testament to love, dedication, strength, and optimism, Gatewood's parents, siblings, partners, children, and grandchildren imbued his own life with value. He had much to celebrate.

One of the last voicemail messages that Molly had on her phone from Gatewood was left on her birthday. Molly still had the recording years after her father's death. In his iconic Kentucky baritone, he exuded warmth and love. "One of the great days of my life was watching you being born. I just can't tell you how much pleasure went with that. I love you. You're a remarkable young lady, and I couldn't be prouder of you."[58]

8

A Splendid Torch

Word of Gatewood's passing spread quickly, and triggered an immediate outpouring of recognition and support. A lengthy obituary published in the *Lexington Herald-Leader* recognized Gatewood's contributions to politics in Kentucky, and how his personality and generosity made a lasting impact. Kentucky political leaders, including those that he had chided and argued with on the campaign trail, had glowing things to say about Gatewood's life.

Governor Steve Beshear, who had just beaten Gatewood handily in the 2011 race, said, "He was a gutsy, articulate and passionate advocate who never shied away from a challenge or potential controversy. His runs for office prove he was willing to do more than just argue about the best direction for the state—he was willing to serve and was keenly interested in discussing issues directly with our citizens. He will be missed."

Greg Stumbo, who enjoyed a friendly private relationship with Gatewood, led a moment of silence in the Kentucky House of Representatives in memory of Gatewood. In a floor speech before the memorial, Stumbo said, "One of the most admirable things that could ever be said about someone is that they had the courage to stand up for what they believe. Whether you agreed with Gatewood or you didn't agree with him, I think we can all say we admire the courage that he had advocating his convictions."

Even Senate minority leader Mitch McConnell, a common target of Gatewood's attacks, released a statement saying that Gatewood was "a truly memorable character who loved our state and its people."

Wood Simpson, a close friend of Gatewood's and cofounder of Wrigley Media Group, remembered his friend's generosity more than his political acumen. Wood and Gatewood played chess a few times a week, and Simpson would often witness his generous spirit firsthand. "Despite the fact that he never had much money, he used to go downtown on Sunday mornings and hand out dollar bills to the homeless and leave them with a few words of encouragement. So he taught me to be more compassionate and to help the less fortunate. Gate's enormous heart and his beautiful soul are now everywhere in Kentucky, in the great mountains, in the small towns and in all the good people, everywhere."[1]

Joel Pett, the *Herald-Leader* political cartoonist, also weighed in. Pett had depicted Gatewood in cartoons multiple times throughout his life, usually emphasizing Gatewood's marijuana use and hippie background in a way that the family felt denigrated his attempts at public office. Susan had met and become friends with Pett over the ensuing years, and hoped that he would memorialize Gatewood with his art. She was not disappointed.

"He did this amazing political cartoon for the editorial page," Susan said. "It was a picture of Gatewood's hat on a black sky with stars. It had a halo around it. It was called 'Hat in the Ring' and it had the dates of his birth and death years."

Gatewood was known for his signature fedora, and it became a meaningful memorial of his life and work. The family took this a step further. During a memorial service for Gatewood put on by the city at Lexington's Carnegie Center, they set up a hemp rope in a circle and encouraged attendees to bring scarves, hats, mittens, and gloves to "throw in" to the ring, which they then donated to the local Salvation Army.[2]

At the memorial service, Gatewood's cadre of friends, supporters, fans, and admirers paid tribute to his life. Those included Ben Chandler, Judge Lewis Paisley, Jim Gray, and others. They remembered his kindness and his passion for social justice; his care for the environment, and for his fellow man; his passion for the law, for youth, and for those left behind in the status-quo politics of his life. Perhaps most important, they remembered how he made them feel. That they were important, and loved, and worthy of friendship.

Gatewood left a lasting legacy in Kentucky politics. But he also deeply affected a number of other movements that were in motion during his life: for Lexington, his family, hemp and marijuana, the opioid crisis, the war on drugs, and more.

The outpouring of support in his home city showed the cultural and political folk hero that Gatewood was. Yes, he had fallen short on many occasions. By the time of his death, he had run for governor five times, as well as for Congress twice, attorney general once, and agriculture commissioner once. While these political failures did garner some space in his obituary, they did not define Gatewood to those he knew and loved. He was Lexington's adopted son, and his presence became synonymous with the Lexington and Fayette County community. Whether standing on the side of busy intersections with his trademark yellow and red campaign sign, doing pull-ups in Woodland Park, occupying his usual booth at Perkins, or leading

Gatewood was known for his fiery speaking style, but he also got some attention for wearing hemp fiber suits and his signature fedora.

a protest on the steps of the courthouse, Gatewood was a community fixture and a beloved spirit.

Congressman Andy Barr (R), who would go on to win the first of a succession of Sixth District races in 2012 against Ben Chandler, grew up in Lexington and remembered Gatewood as a "fixture" of life in Central Kentucky. He would often see Gatewood on the news or in newspapers, and grew up understanding that Gatewood was part of Lexington's culture. "He was someone who I think people understood really loved Kentucky and our history," Barr said. "Whether you agreed or disagreed with some of his views, whether you thought he was eccentric or whether you fully embraced his political agenda, one thing everybody knew about Gatewood is that he loved Kentucky. And we all loved him for loving Kentucky."[3]

Former Lexington mayor, Senate candidate, and now Kentucky transportation secretary Jim Gray knew Gatewood and saw him as an integral part of Lexington's culture. He remembered, "He was just wicked smart, just a very very smart guy with a . . . real wit. . . . He was a giving, generous person."[4]

Jack Brammer, the longtime *Lexington Herald-Leader* political reporter, thought that part of Gatewood's appeal was his ability to connect with anyone he met. "He was able to talk people's language, either if they were elite or not elite. And the elite admired him because he was straightforward and honest . . . and the people . . . appreciated him for his sincerity and frankness."[5]

The shy, mischievous kid from Carlisle, who showed up in Lexington with rotten teeth and a love of fighting, grew into a local legend. Gatewood's ability to communicate, along with his penchant for generosity and his imposing and impressive appearance, endeared him to the people of Lexington and surrounding communities. His innate ability to show up constantly in the media also made him a fixture of life in Lexington.

Many who lived in Lexington during Gatewood's life will always remember him. Whether for his laugh, his kind nature, his flamboyant political personality, or his wit in the courtroom, Gatewood's memory lives on.

While Gatewood's image as a cultural figure in Lexington was how most knew him and now remember him, his family had a deeper personal understanding of Gatewood. Things weren't always rosy. Gatewood's siblings navigated the difficulty of often helping Gatewood with his money problems. Those same financial issues often strained his relations with Susan and Kim. Gatewood's three daughters loved him and valued him, but their relationship was sometimes complicated by their parents' divorce, and by Gatewood's constant pursuit of political office and recognition.

Gatewood's brother Mike remembers the power of his example and memory. When asked about the legacy Gatewood left behind, Mike said, "Love and respect for one another, certainly in the family, to be a champion for the underrepresented. To always be wary of too much control and authority. To always stand up for yourself and others. To have some integrity as an individual. . . . being a fighter for whatever cause you decide to take up. . . . He was my big brother, you know, that's always first and foremost."[6]

Gatewood's sister Liz echoed the sentiment. "Well, Gatewood was a good man. He believed in humanity, he believed in the Constitution and he believed everyone should on the same equal basis: black, white, Native American. . . . I think he should be remembered as a very intelligent, kind-hearted human being."[7]

Even when his family didn't always understand the financial or political decisions that Gatewood made, they always supported and loved him. Gatewood's sister Edna nodded to this complicated legacy, but said that Gatewood's legacy came down to one thing. "You know, I truly believe that in my heart, he wanted everyone to have had the opportunity to be successful and to follow their dreams. He was a good man."[8]

Gatewood, and all of his siblings, credit their parents, Henry Clay and Dollie, with instilling the values of love, charity, and respect in them from an early age. Even as their parents experienced their own hardships, the love of the Galbraith children remained in constant effect through the thick and thin of life. Gatewood had only kind words to say about his brothers and sisters. As he wrote in his memoir, "All of my brothers and sisters are well-balanced, successful human beings, hard-working and practical. I know they have to put up with hearing 'Say, are you related to that fellow Gatewood?' every time they give the name Galbraith. But they do so with humor and patience. Ain't I the luckiest guy around?"[9]

Gatewood's oldest daughter, Summer, remembered her father with love, but also with frustration. As the oldest sibling, she was more attuned to what was going on leading up to and following her parents' divorce, as well as how the decisions Gatewood made impacted her family and her mother. But she also remembered the lesson of Gatewood's life. "I guess the general philosophy was, do what your passion is and also to stand up for other people."

Summer remembered a consistent line of reasoning her father would provide if any of the girls were complaining about the many difficulties of life: "Baby, is anyone you know sick or dying? No. Are you sick or dying? No. Then you have nothing to worry about."[10]

She also found some frustration in the outpouring of memories and support following her father's death. For every politician who chimed in after he passed away, Summer wondered where they were before he died. Where were their words of support and admiration for his political pursuits when he was still alive? When they could have actually helped?

Abby, after navigating some anger and resentment for her father's work, developed a close relationship with Gatewood as she got older. Having entered the legal field herself, she remembered her father's innate sense of fairness. "Looking back now, I see that I witnessed time and again, and what I grew to understand was that my dad had an intrinsic sense of justice. It was just there. It was fundamentally part of him. It was not to be compromised, nor was it to be denied. To sum it up, my dad had a bedrock sense of calm and confidence in the righteousness of his cause. His sense of justice . . . He taught me that the power of respect lies not in the word itself, but in the deed."[11]

Molly sometimes had trouble understanding why Gatewood sacrificed so much for his political campaigns, but later understood his conviction. "The way I look at it is . . . he loved us so much that he felt like the best thing that he could do for us was to be true to himself and to try to change the world in the ways that he believed it needed to be changed," she said. "I know there were times he wasn't there for us, especially when we were younger, whether that was financially or time-wise or whatever. But I mean, I don't feel any anger or resentment towards him because I know what it's like to have a mission that feels bigger than everything else in your life and everybody else in your life, because it ultimately feels like the thing that you can do that's going to benefit everyone that you love the most."[12]

Even after their romantic relationship ended, Kim Eisner and Gatewood remained close friends throughout the rest of his life. She cherished the few short moments she had with him before his death, where she was able to comfort him as he struggled with pneumonia. Aside from their loving relationship, Kim remembered Gatewood as a crusader for truth and justice, especially as regards cannabis. "It's medicine. And people should not be in jail for it. And Gatewood fought [for that] every morning when he woke up. That's what he was fighting for. He was fighting for people who are in jail for it, and he was fighting for people that needed it medically."[13]

Susan was the glue that held their family together, through her and Gatewood's divorce, through the ensuing years of financial difficulty, and as she took on the main role of raising their daughters. Susan is a powerful example of empowerment and accomplishment. She put herself through law school following the divorce, and became an extremely successful and accomplished attorney in Louisville and Lexington. She has also been a civic leader, dedicating her time and money to various charitable causes in support of the Lexington community.

The difficulties of their relationship speak to the inherent goodness in both Susan and Gatewood. Even as Gatewood continually failed in his child support obligations and Susan tried to keep their heads above water, she never spoke ill of him. She would often sneak out early in the morning and hide the local newspaper to be sure her girls were not reading or seeing negative things about Gatewood. Their relationship was amicable and positive, and they prioritized family and peace over everything else.

Susan echoed Molly's words about piecing together the decisions Gatewood made about running for office. "Gatewood made . . . what some people thought was a selfish decision. I really think it was a selfless decision, because he made a decision for what he believed to be the greater good. He was going to give up what I think was most individually important and the thing that was most personally paramount in his life and his heart and soul, and that was his three children."

Gatewood and Susan remained lifelong partners, bonded by the love of family and for their children. Through years of toil, sacrifice, controversy, and strife, they prioritized the lives of their three daughters. When others may have fallen to finger pointing or criticism, Gatewood and Susan remained steadfast partners through the difficulty of life after divorce.

More than anything in his life, whether political campaigns, activism, celebrity, or professional accomplishment, the most powerful example of Gatewood's legacy is his family and the relationships he cherished.

Just a couple of years after Gatewood passed away, one of his dreams came to fruition. In the debate over the 2014 federal Farm Bill, which dictates a vast and complicated number of programs related to agriculture in the United States, Mitch McConnell, then Senate minority leader, finally saw the light. He led the push for including Kentucky as one of the nine states outlined in the bill that would be eligible to grow hemp for research and academic purposes. This was a major turning point in the fight for industrial hemp as an economic force, and signaled the resurgence of the hemp industry in Kentucky.

The Kentucky agriculture commissioner in 2014, James Comer, was deeply involved in the movement for hemp. Comer didn't remember engaging Gatewood in this pursuit, mainly because of his public association with marijuana, something that Comer worked hard to keep away from the efforts related to hemp. Even if he thought that Gatewood's past muddied the waters of hemp, he did give Gatewood credit for his advocacy. "I think it did help with issue awareness. . . . the problem with Gatewood, he was probably right on hemp, and he was probably right on marijuana, but he always mixed both in the conversation. And I don't think a lot of people understood the difference between hemp and marijuana."[14]

Comer claimed that when he pushed for hemp once he took office, he only framed it as a crop that would help farmers, while Gatewood took a more radical tack. Comer was mistaken. While Gatewood did often advocate for recreational and medicinal marijuana, many of his campaigns framed industrial hemp as a pathway to stability and profit for Kentucky farmers. In later years, while Gatewood did stand by his support of medical marijuana, he mainly discussed hemp as a sustainable and profitable crop for the struggling agricultural industry in Kentucky. Comer's association between these issues probably had more to do with Gatewood's depiction in the media than it did with his actual campaign messaging.

The 2014 pilot program allowed hemp crops to be grown in Kentucky for purposes of research, and to evaluate whether it would be a viable commercial or industrial crop. Multiple farmers took advantage of the opportunity, and by 2018 it had the backing of many of Kentucky's residents and politicians.

Seeing the political and commercial benefits of hemp, Mitch McConnell, by then Senate majority leader, made it a central tenet of the 2018 Farm Bill. The 2014 bill allowed for research on hemp, but the 2018 bill was much more expansive. It legalized the cultivation of hemp, as well as allowing the transportation and trade of hemp and hemp-based products across state lines.

Farmers and businesses still had to meet strict federal requirements for their hemp crops, including keeping the tetrahydrocannabinol (THC) content below 0.3 percent, which ensured that hemp would not provide the psychoactive "high" that its close cousin, marijuana, brought to users if smoked or ingested. Growers also had to obtain permission to grow the crop, open themselves up to frequent inspections, and institute safeguards.

Nevertheless, the 2018 Farm Bill effectively legalized the cultivation of hemp in the United States. Not only did this allow for hemp to be grown in Kentucky and the other forty-nine states, but it also made hemp-based products legal. For many years, Gatewood had worn hemp cloth, displayed hemp products, and advocated for the health benefits of hemp and hemp seeds. With its passage in 2018, the bill made it possible to found businesses based solely on hemp cultivation and production, for industrial products. Companies immediately sprung up to raise hemp, and many focused on one product: cannabidiol (CBD) oil.[15]

CBD does not provide a "high" to users and does not contain any THC. Most often it is sold as an oil, a capsule, an extract, or an additive in foods, drinks, or even beauty products. While it is not fully evaluated by the Food and Drug Administration, many companies, and users, claim that CBD oil and its derived products are a nonprescription alternative for treating many ailments, including insomnia, migraine headaches, chronic pain, anxiety, and more.

The hemp and CBD businesses in Kentucky boomed in the ensuing years. By 2020 the Kentucky Department of Agriculture oversaw 970 licensed growers and 178 processors. That year, over 5,000 acres of hemp were grown in Kentucky. In 2019, hemp processors, including those who produced and sold CBD oil, had gross sales of nearly $200 million.

The boom in the market eventually created a glut. The Kentucky Department of Agriculture, led by Agriculture Commissioner Ryan Quarles, gave out a large number of approvals for growers and processors, seeing hemp as a growth industry in a state desperately looking for new products to bolster agricultural production. With many new businesses trying to enter the industry, and given the somewhat burdensome regulations related to the crop, many businesses and growers failed in their first years. Most prominent among these failures was that of GenCanna Global, a hemp processor and CBD product manufacturer based in Winchester, Kentucky. Started as part of the 2014 hemp pilot program, GenCanna grew along with the hemp industry in Kentucky, overextending its reach and eventually filing for bankruptcy protection in 2020.[16]

With processors failing, many of the farmers who began growing the crop found themselves with nowhere to turn when it came time to sell. As the University of Kentucky College of Agriculture explained, "Many processors either folded or have tried to salvage what they can of their business by bankruptcy restructures as investors fled. We have witnessed the invisible hand play out in a novel market. Is hemp dead? No, but we have had a resetting of the market expectations."[17]

Agriculture Commissioner Ryan Quarles, first elected in 2015 and reelected in 2019, pointed the finger not at the policies of the Kentucky Department of Agriculture but at the Food and Drug Administration in Washington. By the time of this writing, the FDA still had not introduced a comprehensive plan for regulating or approving CBD products.

Quarles explained how this hampered the business: "The nation's hemp market continues to face supply chain issues and uncertainty given the Food and Drug Administration's inability to provide a regulatory framework for hemp-derived cannabidiol, or CBD, products. Despite the ongoing uncertainty, I continue to believe there will be a long-term hemp market in the United States and that Kentucky will remain the leader on the national stage after the dust settles."[18]

After losing the Republican primary election for Kentucky governor in 2015, former commissioner Comer was elected to the U.S. House of Representatives, representing Kentucky's First District. Having been integral to the revitalization of the hemp industry in Kentucky, Comer lamented Quarles's mismanagement in a 2021 interview. "He gave permits to all these quack companies that didn't have any money, and they were supposedly signing multimillion-dollar contracts with farmers, and they didn't have a market," Representative Comer said. "The whole hemp thing was so good for so many years, and Gatewood was a pioneer in it, and then for Quarles to come in and let this CBD thing take over . . . it's just real disappointing. . . . there are a lot of farmers who have lost a lot of money."[19]

While the hemp industry did resurface as a major player in Kentucky, these business-related and regulatory hurdles have hampered its progress. The hemp and CBD industries live on in Kentucky, but their success has been somewhat muted compared to initial expectations—none more elevated than those raised by Senator McConnell, who used the inclusion of hemp legalization in the 2018 Farm Bill as a major campaign plank in his successful 2020 reelection. As McConnell said, "My being in the majority leader position is a real advantage to Kentucky. It gives us a chance to kind of punch above our weight. This opportunity for Kentucky produces things like the legalization of industrial hemp."[20]

Both McConnell and pundits claimed that hemp would be one of the major legacies of the senator's time and contributions to his home state, an idea that made Gatewood's family bristle.

"I actually read somewhere the other day that Mitch McConnell thinks that hemp could be his legacy in Kentucky," said Molly Galbraith in 2016. "And I almost went through the [expletive] computer screen. He is sorely mistaken if he thinks that that can be his legacy in Kentucky. Credit's not going where it's due."[21]

Gatewood had spent much of his life, money, and health making the dream of hemp farming a reality in Kentucky. Did he always go about it in the most conventional or strategic way? No. But this does not take away from the passion and courage he showed supporting a cause that was a political taboo for decades.

When asked how Gatewood's work and advocacy influenced the Farm Bills or the hemp industry in Kentucky, Senator McConnell's office chose not to comment.

Gatewood's life and political career took place against a backdrop of dramatic political changes in Kentucky. During the 1980s and through much of the 1990s, the Kentucky Democratic Party had a viselike grip on the state's highest offices and majorities in the legislature. The BOPTROT scandals, as well as Paul E. Patton's sordid affair, damaged the party's standing in Kentucky, but they paled in comparison to the cultural and political shifts at play across the country.

Al Cross contends that the shift was not recent, but actually began as far back as the 1950s, when Republican candidates John Sherman Cooper and Thruston B. Morton won both U.S. Senate races in Kentucky.

"Liberal Democrats in Kentucky have always been in a minority. And as cultural issues came to dominate, people were driven by their culture and their backgrounds into the Republican Party," Cross said. "Republicans started eating away at the Democratic seats in the state senate . . . but it was a ten-year process and then it was a fifteen- or sixteen-years process to flip the House. It was Donald Trump who gave [Kentucky] a supermajority in the House in 2016. But fundamentally, the story is they appealed to culture. You know, Kentuckians are culturally conservative. And as the Republican Party embraced these issues of cultural conservatism, people in Kentucky found a more comfortable home in the Republican Party."[22]

These cultural issues that drove socially conservative voters away from the Democratic Party in Kentucky centered mostly on the political buzzwords of today: abortion, gun rights, and gay marriage.

In 2020, then-president Donald Trump carried Kentucky with more than 62 percent of the vote. This followed the 2019 statewide election, where Attorney General Andy Beshear, the son of former Kentucky governor Steve Beshear, eked out a 5,000-vote victory over Matt Bevin, a relatively unpopular and vulnerable incumbent, while every other statewide office in Kentucky was won handily by Republican candidates.[23]

In the 2020 election for the Kentucky House of Representatives and Senate, Kentucky Republicans further flexed their muscle. When Gatewood first ran for governor, in 1991, the Kentucky Democratic Party enjoyed comfortable majorities in both houses, holding 25 Senate seats to the Republicans' 13 and a 72-to-28 margin in the House. By 2020, in just under twenty years, the script had flipped dramatically. As the dust settled in November 2020, the Republicans now enjoyed a 75-to-25 advantage in the state House and an astounding 30–8 advantage in the Senate, clear supermajorities that eliminated Governor Andy Beshear's ability to veto legislation. It also allowed them to pass legislation and constitutional amendments without any support from Kentucky Democrats.[24]

Jack Brammer, the *Lexington Herald-Leader* political reporter who retired in 2021 after forty-three years of covering Kentucky politics, explained that

Republicans were able to strategically employ a few major issues in order to expand their reach and gain dominant control. "I think some social issues, some religious issues, especially abortion, gay rights, and gun rights, the Republicans have been able to use those issues and get people lined up to say, 'Oh, I'm a Republican, not a Democrat.'"

Greg Stumbo, who lost to Republican Daniel Cameron in the 2019 attorney general race, explained the shift that he witnessed in his decades of political experience. "It really is kind of like they want to buy apples, and you're selling oranges. You've got the wrong product."

When asked what Kentucky Democrats needed to do in order to wrest back some measure of control in the state, Stumbo said, "Well, the first thing they have to do is remember the old saying: 'The definition of insanity is doing the same thing over and over again and expecting to get a different result.' You can't run the same thing over and over and over again. . . . the state Democratic Party has to start recognizing the [moderate] branch of the Democratic Party, and it needs a name and its own identity."

Stumbo maintained that Democrats in Kentucky needed to break away from the national image of the Democratic Party, so that they could be pro-life, pro-gun candidates who did not necessarily buy in to the rest of the Republican platform or did not swear fealty to former President Trump. "Our diversity is our strength, and we're not playing to our strength. We're allowing them to use our strength as a weakness."[25]

Rather than having to align themselves on every single cultural issue, Stumbo believes that Kentucky Democrats need to be all right with being different. Some more liberal members will align very closely with the national Democratic Party platform, while others need to have a broader and more local appeal based on cultural and social issues important to many Kentuckians.

Some of this shift also mirrored the increasing political polarization and media climate in the United States. Al Cross pointed to Fox News and social media as forces of confirmation and conflict in the United States. On the impact of the conservative media empire on national political opinion Cross said, "We live in a media environment now where you have dozens of sources of information and most people really aren't looking for information. They're looking for confirmation. They don't want to be given information that's contrary to what they believe."[26]

In March 2020 the first cases of the SARS-COV-2 virus, or COVID-19, were found in Kentucky. Along with the rest of the country, and the world, the coronavirus crisis would define much of Governor Andy Beshear's time in office. Taking a largely successful and cautious approach, Governor

Beshear went on to closely follow Centers for Disease Control protocols, closing daycare centers, schools, sporting events, and nonessential businesses in an effort to drive down deaths in Kentucky from the novel virus. There followed a widespread social campaign to promote health and social civility: a community fund to assist those impacted financially, a drive to donate personal protective equipment and supplies to healthcare providers, an ongoing memorial for COVID-19 victims of green lights on people's homes and businesses, and daily addresses from Frankfort to keep Kentuckians informed about the disease and the steps that were taken.

Governor Beshear's trademark saying became synonymous with the crisis in Kentucky: "We will get through this. We will get through this, together."

Even in this, there was divisiveness and conflict. Many groups, mostly conservatives, business owners, and militias, spoke out against Beshear's actions, riding the wave of misinformation and conspiracy theories propagated on social media and elsewhere about the virus.

On Memorial Day weekend of 2020, protestors gathered in front of the Kentucky Governor's Mansion and State Capitol building for what they called a Patriot Day 2nd Amendment Rally. Many of the protestors were armed with assault rifles and in full body armor, and some even ignored barriers set up in advance of the event, to yell from the porch of the governor's residence, just feet from where his family remained inside.

One of the protestors "strung a noose around an effigy of the governor and raised it from a tree branch beside the mansion. Underneath, they had printed the words John Wilkes Booth claimed to yell after shooting President Abraham Lincoln: 'Sic semper tyrannis,' Latin for 'thus always to tyrants.'"

When the event began, multiple Republican members of the Kentucky House and Senate spoke to and took pictures with the gathered protestors. In response, Governor Beshear said, "Standing in front of a radical militia group, these elected officials claim that people including me aren't Christian and even told them that people wanted babies to be murdered. What do you think was going to happen after throwing out these types of claims to this group? You cannot fan the flames and condemn the fire."[27]

In perhaps the most divisive political environment in the United States since the Civil War, how do we understand Gatewood's legacy in Kentucky politics? How would he be viewed today if he survived?

Gatewood borrowed from both political parties, while simultaneously criticizing them for their staid platforms and what he saw as rampant corruption. He saw himself as marrying the best components of both parties.

As explained in his 2011 election profile in the *Herald-Leader*, Gatewood "embraces views on gun and property rights espoused by Tea Party movement conservatives, and views on medical marijuana and environmental issues espoused by liberals."[28]

Gatewood was a staunch supporter of the Second Amendment, was against abortion, and for the death penalty. All standard conservative stances. He believed in small government, and often referenced the need for government to go back in the "small box where it belonged."

He also dedicated much of his life to the movements for industrial hemp, medical marijuana, and recreational marijuana access, and came to believe strongly in environmental protections. In light of the opioid epidemic that he had predicted as far back as the early 1990s, he believed in treatment over punishment, and lamented Kentucky's willingness to incarcerate its citizens. Gatewood believed in providing government subsidies for higher education and vocational training. All of these positions do not necessarily bespeak a small-government conservative.

As he had been first inspired, convalescing in Carlisle and reading about the fictional hero of *All the King's Men*, Willie Stark, Gatewood saw himself as a populist. A champion for the common man, someone who prioritized farmers over corporations, rural communities over conglomerates.

Through the 2010s, in the years immediately following Gatewood's death, recreational marijuana movements exploded in momentum. If he were alive in today's political climate, could it be that he would have been more successful? He was often credited with being "ahead of his time." Has Gatewood's time finally come, a decade too late?

"If he were still living, I think he would find this current political environment one in which he would enjoy operating, as we've got a lot of people pissed off at the way things are," Al Cross said. "There's lots of people who just think the whole system needs a shakeup, and that goes all the way from far left to far right. And Gatewood would appeal to people like that. He was an advocate of new ideas, different ideas, thinking out of the box."[29]

According to the United States Department of Health and Human Services, the opioid epidemic resulted in over 70,000 deaths from overdose in 2019. Some 1.6 million people had opioid use disorders, while nearly 750,000 were regular users of heroin, a cheaper and more accessible drug that many opioid addicts turned to when they couldn't find prescription painkillers.[30]

Perhaps more alarming was the sharp rise in illicit fentanyl, a synthetic opioid much more powerful and much more dangerous than the class of opioid painkillers developed and popularized in the 1990s. Often produced in Asia and entering the United States through Mexico, fentanyl was cheap and powerful, meaning it was often cut into other illicit drugs, such as heroin, cocaine, ecstasy, MDMA, and more. Often, drug users didn't even know that what they were ingesting contained fentanyl, which resulted in an even larger wave of overdose deaths.

The impact was felt strongly in Kentucky. According to the Kentucky Injury Prevention and Research Center, overdose deaths grew steadily from 2012 to 2017, when they reached 1,565 in a single year. Opioid use and abuse boomed during the COVID-19 pandemic, as much of Kentucky shut down for months at a time and residents had to face heightened anxiety, isolation, joblessness, and despair. In 2020 the opioid epidemic claimed 1,964 lives in Kentucky, marking a 49 percent increase from the year before. Fentanyl was found to be present in more than 70 percent of drug overdose deaths in Kentucky in that year.[31]

By 2016 the opioid epidemic was costing the United States as much as $500 billion per year. Far worse was what it was doing to the life expectancy of the developed world. The United States of America enjoyed the strongest and most powerful economy in the history of the modern world, yet saw its life expectancy falling due to an increase in what the CDC termed "Diseases of Despair," including depression, drug use, alcohol abuse, and suicide.[32]

As the opioid epidemic grew and raged in Kentucky, it became a major component of our state's political environment. Many politicians lamented the drug companies who produced the drugs and doctors who abused their professional licenses to shop them.

Following his time in office, former Kentucky governor Ernie Fletcher returned to his roots as a practicing physician, eventually founding an organization, the Fletcher Group, dedicated to building and running various institutions for recovery from substance abuse in Kentucky. Launched in 2017 in partnership with Kentucky real estate developers and philanthropists Don and Mira Ball, the Fletcher Group was an outgrowth of work started while Governor Fletcher was still in office, when he and the Balls, with the cooperation of various Kentucky state government agencies, began a model program called Recovery Kentucky.

"It really becomes a chronic disease.... It takes nine to twelve months to heal that. And so a lot of your treatments, there are thirty days or whatever, and you may get an individual on a track, but they relapse. This recovery program in Kentucky was a program that worked for people who can stay nine to twenty-four months, and it really had good outcomes," Fletcher explained. "Communities are just really responding very well because they see that there's no quick fixes here and they're trying to go in the community and develop what we call a recovery ecosystem, that you've got to bring all the parties of that community together and say we really need to change the way we're doing things and provide the support for these individuals."[33]

The Fletcher Group now runs eighteen recovery centers throughout the country, and is showing the way to fight back against the plague of opioid abuse in the United States.[34]

As a native son of eastern Kentucky, Greg Stumbo witnessed the impact of the opioid crisis firsthand. "The big tragedy that I've seen in my political career is the opioid epidemic, and it's touched home. It's taken people from my family. I don't hardly know a family that hasn't been affected by it, not just in eastern Kentucky—it's statewide." Stumbo made holding big pharmaceutical companies responsible for their impact on Kentucky communities a major component of his unsuccessful 2019 race for attorney general. Marking a change from the 2003 race when he accused Gatewood of being soft on crime for his support of medical marijuana, Stumbo now gives Gatewood credit for his forward-thinking approach: "Gatewood . . . He was on the right track. He didn't have the data, the guy was ahead of his time. . . . Let's give it to people who have an addiction or who, you know, who need it. And let's use this tool to help combat this illegal drug problem that we have. And now I think there's enough evidence and enough scientific data to back that up."[35]

Gatewood predicted this crisis as far back as his 1991 race for governor, and made the abuse of synthetic drugs a focus of his political campaigns. The argument he made was that opioids, along with many other synthetic products, were hollowing out rural communities. Kentucky spent millions of dollars raiding farms and arresting marijuana users, when they could have spent the time and money cracking down on drugs that actually did egregious harm. Gatewood was fond of saying that if it grew from "God's green earth," then it was safe. He despised the pharmaceutical companies that strategically preyed on Kentucky communities, and was constantly frustrated by the inability of the state and federal governments to ignore a potential alternative that was staring them in the face: access to medical cannabis.

The Overton Window is a concept in public policy that reflects how ideas in society and politics interact and change over time. The basic premise is that politicians are limited in what policy positions they can support to only those ideas that have broad public appeal and are accepted in society. These ideas are said to exist within the Overton Window. Policy ideas outside the Overton Window are generally seen as risking the loss of electoral appeal or support for candidates who choose to endorse them. These ideas are either too radical, too extreme, or too controversial, so if candidates choose to publicly support them or to make them part of their campaigns, they are less likely to win popular elections.

But the Overton Window constantly shifts and expands, as we have seen throughout United States history. Seventy years ago, opposing Jim Crow laws and segregation in the South was just outside the window. Twenty years ago, support for gay marriage was not seen as politically viable. The Overton Window depends on the slow, mysterious, and complex evolution of social norms and values.[36]

This is an appropriate lens for understanding Gatewood's approach to political campaigning. The issue that Gatewood dedicated much of his life to, access to medical marijuana and the possibilities of recreational marijuana, brought him renown and celebrity. It also made it nearly impossible for him to win elections or to raise money for his campaigns, even as he tried to moderate his stance in later years. For better or worse, this issue defined Gatewood's place in popular and political culture.

But the Overton Window has shifted, and at a dizzying pace. One of the great tragedies of Gatewood's passing was that in a just a few short months following his death, the dam holding back recreational access to marijuana in the United States would finally break. Following California's example, by the end of 2011 seventeen states offered access to medical marijuana. In 2012 both Colorado and Washington passed initiatives that fully legalized recreational marijuana. In Colorado, since seen as a model for its ability to tax the plant and use it as a booster for tourism, they dedicated the first $40 million in tax revenue from marijuana sales to building public schools. By 2020, Colorado boasted more than $2 billion in marijuana sales, generating hundreds of millions of dollars in tax revenue.

It is difficult to overstate how quickly the tide has turned on the legalization movement. Nearly every year, more ballot initiatives are put to voters, and they are usually passed by very comfortable margins, even in conservative states.

In a 2019 poll, the Foundation for a Healthy Kentucky—whose director, former congressman Ben Chandler, was interviewed for this project—found that 90 percent of Kentucky adults favored access to medical marijuana, while 59 percent supported its use under any circumstances. "Support for medical marijuana is very strong, but we also learned that it's well ahead of the science showing that marijuana is safe and effective for most of the medical conditions claimed by pro-legalization advocates," said Chandler. The foundation encouraged an intensive look at any potential problems of legalization, including ensuring accurate dosages, and investing in studies that provided data related to any negative health outcomes of marijuana use.[37]

With experts admitting that more research on the long-term impacts of marijuana use is necessary, it's now universally accepted that access to medical marijuana is far less dangerous, and cheaper, than using prescription painkillers. In a study released in 2022, researchers from Cornell University analyzed Medicare and Medicaid data from all fifty states, from 2011 to 2019, to try and see whether access to medical marijuana had an impact on pharmaceutical prescriptions. They found that in states that have legalized the use of marijuana, there was a credible decline in prescriptions targeting "pain, depression, anxiety, sleep, psychosis, and seizures."

The study, published in April 2022 in the *Journal of Health Economics*, has important implications for proving that access to marijuana saves money and allows patients a welcome alternative to prescription drugs. One of the principal investigators, Shyam Raman, said, "The reductions in drug utilization that we find could lead to significant cost savings for state Medicaid programs. The results also indicate an opportunity to reduce the harm that can come with the dangerous side effects associated with some prescription drugs."[38]

One of the state representatives who has led the charge for medicinal access is Jason Nemes, a Republican who represents portions of Jefferson and Oldham Counties. Nemes, an attorney, was initially against medical marijuana, but had his mind changed by testimony from his district's voters. "I never really thought of medical marijuana. . . . I had constituents who contacted me [about it]."

Nemes remembered meeting with them and hearing out their arguments. He listened to example after example of the steps that families took to provide medical marijuana to their family members who were suffering from debilitating health conditions. He decided that it was his responsibility to fully investigate the issue, so that's what he did. Over the ensuing months he spoke with doctors, nurses, and community members about the issue, and he came to a striking conclusion: "I was wrong. And so I changed my position."[39]

Nemes became the leading advocate for medical marijuana in the Kentucky state House. He had allies across the aisle, but with a Republican supermajority in Frankfort, Nemes knew that the charge for the issue had to come from a Republican. Since that time, Nemes has worked incessantly to pass bills that provide access to medical marijuana in the Kentucky legislature.

In the days before the COVID-19 pandemic derailed American life, it appeared possible that his medical marijuana bill, House Bill 136, would get its vote. Due to the realities of the pandemic, and the hesitancy of certain members of the Kentucky House and Senate, it never saw the light of day.

Things changed in 2022. A new version of House Bill 136, sponsored primarily by Nemes, passed the Kentucky House of Representatives by a 59–34 vote. In floor testimony before the vote, Nemes implored members to vote yes on this bill, which would still be one of the most restrictive medical marijuana measures in the country. Invoking his conversations with voters, Nemes gave an impassioned plea to his fellow lawmakers: "If your wife or husband's physician, or God forbid your child's physician, told you that this product works in other states and it would help your child, what would you do? If you would fight for your kid, hit the green button," he said.[40]

While successful in the House vote, the bill was never sent to committee in the Senate, dooming its passage. It didn't come up for a vote in the closing days of the 2022 legislative session, and Kentucky remained one of the few states without access to medical marijuana. Supporters immediately shifted focus to the next year's general session where they hoped it would fare better with a revised approach.

Senator Robert Stivers (R-Manchester), president of the Senate, remained a critic of the bill and wouldn't lend his approval to its passage. Likewise, the majority floor leader, Damon Thayer (R-Georgetown), publicly derided the medical marijuana movement. Thayer, who co-owns a Kentucky bourbon producer,[41] appeared on Kentucky Educational Television to preview the upcoming 2022 general legislative session. When asked about Nemes's efforts, he replied, "I've been hearing about it for years, I know my constituents are for it . . . but they elect us to go to Frankfort and make decisions on their behalf, and if they don't like it, they can take it out on me in the next election. . . . I think medical marijuana is a slippery slope for recreational marijuana, which I'm not for."[42]

Cannabis prohibition is also tied to social justice in Kentucky. As is true in most states, the majority of marijuana arrests in Kentucky are of racial minority groups. An April 2020 report by the American Civil Liberties Union showed that Black Kentuckians were 9.4 times more likely to be arrested for marijuana possession than white residents, the second worst disparity in the country. In 2018 there were 7,600 arrests for marijuana violations, constituting more than 20 percent of all drug-related arrests in the state. Kentucky continues to incarcerate its citizens for possessing marijuana, and the effects are disproportionally felt by African Americans.[43]

While Nemes tried to convince lawmakers to pass medical marijuana legislation in 2022, Kentucky Democrats filed a more expansive bill that would legalize the recreational use of marijuana, would expunge the records of those convicted of marijuana-related crimes, would provide funding for substance abuse treatment, and would create state revenue by taxing the sale of marijuana to fund local governments. They unveiled the legislation, titled the L.E.T.T.'s Grow Bill (Legalize, Expunge, Treat, and Tax), in February 2022. A predictably futile effort, the bill never received a reading or vote in the legislature. The sponsors emphasized the fact that Kentucky was far behind the times on access to cannabis, and was perfectly positioned to make marijuana a new Kentucky industry.

One of the bill's sponsors, State Representative Rachel Roberts (D-Newport), spoke about what she saw as the inevitability of legalization in the United States. "So why am I dedicating a ton of my year to building this bill? Well, the reason is because this is where the federal government is going, and I truly believe that in the next couple of years, cannabis will be decriminalized. It will be removed off the Schedule One [federal drug classification] list. And when that happens, I want the commonwealth to be ready to capitalize on whatever piece of this pie is left over," she explained. "And I always say, make no mistake, cannabis is being smoked and consumed in Kentucky, it's being grown in Kentucky, it's being sold in Kentucky. It's just not being regulated or taxed."[44]

This could very well have been Gatewood speaking about the destiny of marijuana, and the realities of its use, back in his first run for agriculture commissioner in 1983.

Representative James Comer in 2021 referenced the political shift toward medical marijuana that he saw as a member of Congress. "It's just a matter of time until it's legal in Kentucky. And I think from where I sit in Washington, representing a tobacco state . . . there's a lot more support in Washington for marijuana than there is for tobacco and even hemp." He had a bold prediction, one that seemed at odds with the leadership of his own party: "It's gonna be legal in all fifty states very soon . . . at least medical, and then recreational will eventually . . . follow suit."[45]

Ben Chandler reflected on Gatewood's role in shifting the political conversation regarding marijuana. "Yeah, I think he certainly deserves credit for bringing that issue to the fore. He was talking about it when nobody else would talk about it. And there were a lot of people who did not want to talk about it publicly, disagreed with it, and they were happy he was talking about it. So I think, yes, certainly he has played a role in lifting that issue up here in Kentucky."[46]

Working to pass medical marijuana legislation, Nemes gave Gatewood credit for his life's work. "But Kentucky wasn't ready for those arguments. And Kentucky is still not ready for a lot of his arguments, a lot of his positions

. . . but I think you need that guy yelling into the wind." Reflecting on whether, when marijuana legislation finally passed, Gatewood would get his due, Nemes said, "I don't know that he'll get the credit he deserves, but he does deserve credit for softening the ground . . . for making people's ears open up. . . . I think he deserves a lot of credit for that."[47]

Through years of campaigning, of self-funding campaigns, of "yelling into the wind," Gatewood was discouraged with the progress he made in working toward legalizing cannabis in Kentucky. But as is so often the case, his work went unrecognized during his life, only to start paying dividends after his death. The politicians who have been working toward changing marijuana laws in Kentucky pay homage to Gatewood's influence and sacrifices.

Today Kentucky ranks last, or close to last, in many measures of citizen well-being, including measures of public health, disease, and depression. Kentucky legislators have recently made cuts to the social safety net, including for medical coverage, unemployment insurance, and SNAP food access benefits. Our public education system is underfunded, and teacher pay ranks near the bottom of the country. Massive public pension obligations weigh down the Kentucky state budget.

Marijuana offers a new industry that would create a new and valuable agricultural product for Kentucky farmers, while offering a new tool to boost tourism, one of Kentucky's hallmark industries. Imagine adding cannabis tourism to a state that already offers some of the most beautiful outdoor recreational environments in the country, along with its two signature industries and economic drivers: horse racing and bourbon. The Kentucky legislature could regulate and tax cannabis, and use the profits to fix holes in the budget and to ensure a higher quality of life for Kentucky voters.

On this issue, Gatewood most certainly shifted the Overton Window. Support for medical and recreational access to cannabis has gone from a highly controversial idea, relegated to the radical fringes of society, to a popular campaign promise among members of both parties. One thing is certain: Gatewood did not receive enough credit for this.

Finally, during the spring 2023 legislative session, Gatewood's work, and the work of thousands of organizers, activists, and organizations, finally came to fruition. On Thursday, March 16, the Kentucky State Senate passed Senate Bill 47, sponsored by Senator Steve West (R), by a vote of 26–11. This bill legalized medical marijuana in Kentucky for a limited range of diseases and disorders, including cancer, multiple sclerosis, chronic pain, epilepsy, and post-traumatic stress disorder. It goes into effect in 2025, giving Kentucky time to create rules and procedures to govern its use.[48]

Although it will be one of the most restrictive medical marijuana laws in the country, its passage still marked a major transition in the state legislature. Even Senator Thayer, claiming he was moved by his support for "those who suffer," voted in favor.[49] Especially important to the bill's passage was the testimony of multiple Kentuckians who stood to benefit from access to medical marijuana. Longtime advocate Eric Crawford, a quadriplegic since suffering a vehicle accident over thirty years ago, spoke in the committee meeting in support of the bill: "We need your help to make us be safer, so we don't have to use all these pharmaceuticals and opioids. Help us not be criminals. Let's utilize this for sick people."

It quickly passed the Kentucky House of Representatives, and on March 30, 2023, Governor Andy Beshear signed it into law in the rotunda of the Kentucky State Capitol in Frankfort, making Kentucky the thirty-eighth state in the country to provide access to medical marijuana to its residents. Kentucky politicians on both sides of the aisle celebrated. Representative Jason Nemes, who had long fought for its passage, was emotional on the day of the signing, saying, "There are thousands and thousands of Kentuckians who just want to be and want to feel better, and this will help them with that."[50]

Gatewood's life had a profound impact on his friends, his family, on future developments related to hemp and marijuana, on recognition of the opioid crisis and environmental protections, and on the larger landscape of Kentucky politics. These ideas and developments allow us to place Gatewood within the historical context of Kentucky, but do they speak to his personal legacy? What will Gatewood be remembered for?

By the time of his death in 2012, he had participated in nine primary or general elections in Kentucky. In all of these elections, combined, he garnered 470,156 votes. Is this how we measure worth? Was Gatewood a failure because he never achieved public office?

Gatewood was a talented and busy attorney, who practiced in the commonwealth for over thirty years. He is remembered for his ability to connect with juries, for being able to read the room and to feel out which arguments or tacks would be most effective for each situation. He won cases and lost cases, and sometimes he found himself in court for his own mistakes. Does a legal scorecard tell us anything about his legacy?

Gatewood was a prolific activist, speaking at engagements across the country, working on ballot initiatives and publicity campaigns in states like Oregon and California, speaking at cannabis festivals and events in Michigan, Georgia, Washington, DC, and more. He was a talented and moving writer and speaker, who could express his thoughts with animation and deep emotion. He was quick-witted, clever, and intelligent. We have seen how many mainstream political candidates were blown away by his humor and ability to deliver a line. But does this prove anything about his success in life?

While this book has focused on Gatewood's political pursuits and on the things that brought him some measure of fame, far more important to understanding his legacy is gaining a deeper understanding of Gatewood's humanity.

As a child in Carlisle, Gatewood knew he was destined for bigger things. His daydreams made way for a reality where he was universally recognized and well liked. He became a cultural icon in Lexington and throughout Kentucky. While many disagreed with his stances, or his politics, they could not deny Gatewood's talents or his love for his state and community.

He was generous, and kind, and respectful. In a life full of difficulty and struggle, much of it self-inflicted, he was positive and optimistic, and never hesitated to give to others even when he couldn't afford it.

This was a man who, as he felt the pressure of sometimes hundreds of thousands of dollars of debt, would break a twenty-dollar bill in the morning to walk around downtown Lexington giving the homeless a couple bucks and a pat on the back.

He would represent people in court who could not afford to pay him. He gave his work and talent away because he felt it was the right thing to do, often with complicating consequences for his own life.

Gatewood was a husband, a partner, and, most importantly, a father and grandfather. When he and Susan divorced, they didn't fill their souls or their homes with animosity or spite. Gatewood never said a bad word about his ex-wife, and they remained close friends as they united in their shared goal of raising strong, powerful, and compassionate daughters. Likewise, Susan went to great lengths to protect her children from the negative things said or written about their father.

Gatewood was a brother and a son. When his father struggled with alcoholism, he wasn't ostracized, but cared for and forgiven. Even when Gatewood's relationships with his siblings were strained by money or disagreement, they maintained a deep and abiding love for one another. As Gatewood wrote, they were all talented and smart and successful, in a variety of fields, in a variety of settings. Dollie, Gatewood's mother, is perhaps the biggest hero of his story. Her steadfast love, for their family, for others, for her community, set a powerful example for her children and left its own important legacy in Lexington.

Following Gatewood's death, when Susan and others were clearing out his possessions, she came upon a printed quote that he had left in a dresser

At the Kentucky State Capitol, 1999. While Gatewood never won public office, his legacy in the history of Kentucky politics is secure.

drawer. Penned by George Bernard Shaw, it read, “I want to be thoroughly used up when I die, for the harder I work, the more I live. I rejoice in life for its own sake. Life is no ‘brief candle’ for me. It is sort of a splendid torch which I have got hold of for the moment, and I want to make it burn as brightly as possible before handing it on to future generations.”

Remember Gatewood as all of these things: an attorney, a politician, a candidate, an activist, a folk hero, a brother, a son, a father and grandfather, a champion for the persecuted, the downtrodden, and the common man.

More than that, remember Gatewood as a complicated, flawed, and admirable human being, who used his life to fight for what he believed in with unflinching determination.

Gatewood was a tireless worker, a crusader, a warrior for his beliefs: for freedom, dignity, justice, and compassion. This is the legacy of Louis Gatewood Galbraith. Not the perennial candidate, not the marijuana candidate. He was the Kentucky candidate.

Acknowledgments

This book exists because of the dedicated effort, help, and encouragement of many people. It would not have been possible without the trust and support of Gatewood's family, who have been part of this project from the very beginning. They participated in interviews, fact-checked my writing, provided guidance, and welcomed me into their lives. The lasting testament to Gatewood's life are those he loved and left behind. My deepest thanks to Susan Sears, Molly Galbraith, Abby Sears, Liz Whitehorn, Mike Galbraith, Tim Galbraith, Edna Hancock, and their families. While I never spoke personally with Summer Galbraith Sears, her oral history interviews provided the clearest glimpse of what life was like with Gatewood as a father. Tragically, she passed away suddenly and unexpectedly in 2022. Likewise Hank Galbraith, whose interview lent emotion and vulnerability to the project and who was also lost in 2022. To all of you, the rest of your family members, and your loved ones, thank you for sharing part of Gatewood with me.

My sincerest thanks to the University Press of Kentucky for believing in this project, and for taking a chance on a first-time author. To Patrick O'Dowd, who shepherded this project to ensure it was done well and (mostly) on time, thank you for your constant input and positivity, and for your steadfast patience most of all. The University Press of Kentucky is a vital part of the culture and history of Kentucky and deserves the highest measure of support from us all.

My colleagues at the University of Kentucky Libraries and the Special Collections Research Center are too many to name, but I consider myself extremely fortunate to work with such outstanding professionals. Thank you especially to Jay-Marie Bravent for your mentorship and leadership, not to mention your kindness and understanding. Thank you to Anu Kasarabada who put up with me talking about this book for two-plus years, always with humor and support. I appreciate the help of Shawn Livingston, Sarah Coblentz, Crystal Heis, Shell Dunn, and student workers in obtaining and using archival materials. Thank you as well to Deirdre Scaggs and Doug Way for your support of this project and your dedication to the scholarly life of librarians, archivists, and oral historians.

I'd like to especially thank the members of the Louie B. Nunn Center for Oral History at the University of Kentucky, without whom this book would not have been possible. My sincerest thanks to Doug Boyd, Kopana Terry, Jennifer Bartlett, and the rest of their staff who helped me to conduct oral history interviews, fielded constant requests, and were gracious the entire time. A special thanks to Jeff Suchanek, who provided crucial assistance and connection to many of the individuals interviewed. Finally, I'd like to note the contributions of Terry Birdwhistell, one of the preeminent scholars of oral history, whose impressive professional and academic contributions were outweighed by his compassion and friendship. Tragically, we lost Terry in January 2023. His memory and example will continue to guide my career.

Among my past colleagues at Emory University, who gave me a start in this field, my thanks to Courtney Chartier, Sara Logue, Kathy Shoemaker, Laura Starratt, and especially to Gabrielle Dudley, who is the clearest example of kindness, empathy, and excellence in our field, and whom I count as a very dear friend.

Thank you to the archivists and professionals who work, across the world, to make these stories possible. Often going unnoticed, archivists, records managers, librarians, museum professionals, and many others are preserving our histories and sharing our stories. We all owe them our gratitude and ongoing support, for a country or a people, to exist, must be able to access and understand its past. Likewise, I thank all the teachers, librarians, and colleagues from my past, especially those at Indiana University, Bloomington, and at Hanover College for welcoming me into this field and for encouraging and enabling my studies.

I'd like to thank the talented professionals that I've had the honor to work with as graduate students. Natalie Bishop introduced me to Gatewood and curated an outstanding exhibit that sparked my interest. Kaylee McMunn provided encouragement and help with this project. The future is in good hands.

I would also like to thank the journalists who made much of this book possible. Newspaper reports are quoted extensively throughout, and multiple journalists, particularly Al Cross, Jack Brammer, and Ferrell Wellman, provided valuable input via interview. Thank you specifically to the staff of the *Lexington Herald-Leader* and the *Louisville Courier-Journal*, whose political reporting is cited constantly. Thanks too to Kentucky Educational Television for help in securing video and audio resources.

Close friends who always lent humor and support are Kyle Bohnert, Clint Burney, Chris Cason, Jake Stawick, and Elliot Ward. Brad Newbold was a valuable sounding board and preliminary editor, and part of this project from the very beginning. Brad, thank you for your dedication and your suggestions, many of which have been incorporated in the final product. A heartfelt thank-you to these six, who make my days enjoyable. I'm lucky to know each of you and I love you all.

My father, Steven, provided valuable feedback and research help. Dad, thank you for sharing your love of history with us, and for always encouraging your kids to strive to do great things. I can't thank you enough for how you made this life possible for us. Thanks too to Katie, who is a talented educator, historian, and advocate; to Emily, who always evokes kindness and compassion, and Elliott, who is her perfect match; to Charlie and Carol for welcoming me into their family; to Charlie III, Sarah Faye, Tricia, and my beloved nieces and nephews.

I'd also like to thank my mother, Nancy Strandmark, whom we lost in 2016. If there are parts of me that are empathetic, funny, understanding, or gracious, they come from my mother. Her memory continues to inspire many of us. The same goes for Tim, Grandma B, Aunt Jean, Grandma Strandmark, Uncle Dale, and others who made me the person I am today and who I wish were still with us.

I will always treasure my time growing up in Madison, Indiana, a magical place filled with wonderful people, and my home in Lexington, Kentucky, one of the finest cities in the world.

To my children, Maddie and Miller, who fill my life with joy, I love you both more than you could ever imagine, and I am so proud to be your dad. Also, if your dad can write a book, you can do anything in life.

Finally, and most importantly, to my wife, Allie, thank you for your encouragement during this project and, on every day of our lives together, for your grace, care, humor, and sustaining love.

Notes

Many of the interviews that form the backbone of this book are part of the Gatewood Galbraith Oral History Project at the Louie B. Nunn Center for Oral History, University of Kentucky Libraries, Lexington, Kentucky. For concision, references to items in this collection will employ the shortened form "GGOHP, Nunn Center."

Prologue

1. "State of Well-Being: State, City & Congressional District Well-Being Report, Kentucky 2011," Gallup-Healthways Well-Being Index, 2011, https://kftc.org/sites/default/files/docs/resources/gallup-healthways_ky_2011report.pdf.

Introduction

1. Ted Van Green, "Americans Overwhelmingly Say Marijuana Should Be Legal for Medical or Recreational Use," Pew Research Center, November 22, 2022, www.pewresearch.org/fact-tank/2022/11/22/americans-overwhelmingly-say-marijuana-should-be-legal-for-medical-or-recreational-use/.

2. Interact for Health, Kentucky Health Issues Poll 2019, www.interactforhealth.org/whats-new/tag/kentucky-health-issues-poll-2019.

1. "Wild as a March Hare"

1. Gatewood Galbraith, *The Last Free Man in America: Meets the Synthetic Subversion* (Lexington, KY: Mark Perkins Press, 2004), 5–7.

2. Gatewood Galbraith, *The Last Free Man in America*, 8.

3. Hank Galbraith, "Three Boyhood Misadventures of Henry Clay and Gatewood: Thanks Dad for Loving Us Anyway," 2016, original story in the author's possession, 2–3.

4. Liz Whitehorn, interview by Matthew Strandmark, February 25, 2021, GGOHP, Nunn Center.

5. Gatewood Galbraith, *The Last Free Man in America*, 11.

6. Gatewood Galbraith, *The Last Free Man in America*, 13.

7. Liz Whitehorn interview.

8. Liz Whitehorn interview.

9. "Tetracycline," University of Michigan Health, January 6, 2017, www.uofmhealth.org/health-library/d00041a1.

10. Liz Whitehorn interview.

11. Gatewood Galbraith, *The Last Free Man in America*, 12.

12. Hank Galbraith, interview by Matthew Strandmark, February 25, 2021, GGOHP, Nunn Center.

13. Hank Galbraith interview.

14. "1990 Census of Population and Housing: Kentucky," U.S. Department of Commerce, Economics and Statistics Administration, Bureau of the Census, September 29, 1992, www2.census.gov/library/publications/decennial/1990/cp-2/cp-2-19.pdf.

15. Hank Galbraith interview.

16. Hank Galbraith interview.

17. Liz Whitehorn interview.

18. Edna Galbraith Hancock, interview by Matthew Strandmark, April 22, 2021, GGOHP, Nunn Center.

19. Hank Galbraith interview.

20. Edna Galbraith Hancock interview.

21. Edna Galbraith Hancock interview.

22. Tim Galbraith, interview by Matthew Strandmark, February 22, 2021, GGOHP, Nunn Center.

23. Ferrell Wellman, interview by Matthew Strandmark, December 1, 2020, GGOHP, Nunn Center.

24. "Candidate Close-up: Governor," Kentucky Educational Television, May 1991.

25. Ferrell Wellman interview.

26. Gatewood Galbraith, *The Last Free Man in America*, 25.

27. Gatewood Galbraith, *The Last Free Man in America*, 26.

28. Gatewood Galbraith, *The Last Free Man in America*, 26.

29. Mike Galbraith, interview by Matthew Strandmark, February 3, 2021, GGOHP, Nunn Center.

30. Gatewood Galbraith, *The Last Free Man in America*, 26.

31. Gatewood Galbraith, *The Last Free Man in America*, 27.

32. Gatewood Galbraith, *The Last Free Man in America*, 31.

33. Gatewood Galbraith, *The Last Free Man in America*, 33.

34. Gatewood Galbraith, *The Last Free Man in America*, 36.

35. Edna Galbraith Hancock interview.

36. Gatewood Galbraith, *The Last Free Man in America*, 47–74.

2. The Model Plan for Legal Marijuana

1. Gatewood Galbraith, *The Last Free Man in America*, 76.

2. Kevin D. Hill, interview by Matthew Strandmark, December 1, 2020, GGOHP, Nunn Center.

3. "SG to Replace 'Zoo' Services," *Kentucky Kernel*, April 19, 1971.

4. Don Edwards, "Angry Student Grabs Chandler, Gets Slugged by Ex-Governor," *Lexington Herald*, May 6, 1970.

5. 2018ua028: Terrence Fox University of Kentucky student protest film, May 5–7, 1970, University of Kentucky Special Collections Research Center.

6. Gatewood Galbraith, *The Last Free Man in America*, 77.

7. Mike Wines, "Rain Dampens Numbers at Crossen Rally: Students Protest 'Political' Trial," *Kentucky Kernel*, October 9, 1970.

8. Hank Galbraith, interview by Matthew Strandmark, February 25, 2021, Galbraith Oral History.

9. Gatewood Galbraith, *The Last Free Man in America*, 81.

10. "Bankruptcies," *Lexington Herald*, June 10, 1970.

11. Kevin D. Hill interview.

12. Kevin D. Hill interview.

13. Sally Denton, *The Bluegrass Conspiracy: An Inside Story of Power, Greed, Drugs & Murder* (New York: Doubleday, 1990).

14. "Former Aide Who Supplied Murder Weapon Freed," *Tampa Bay Times*, October 1, 2005.

15. "4 Students Arrested in All-Night Drug Raids," *Kentucky Kernel*, November 10, 1970.

16. Wendy L. Wright, "Students Plan Strike; Set April 21 as Date," *Kentucky Kernel*, April 7, 1971.

17. Bob Brown, "Prof Charges FBI Intrusion in Class," *Kentucky Kernel*, November 9, 1970.

18. Susan Elswick, "Bright Criticizes University Action in FBI Inquiry," *Kentucky Kernel*, November 12, 1970.

19. "Mason May Seek to Bar FBI Questioning Students," *Lexington Herald*, November 10, 1970.

20. "A Form on the Hiring & Firing of University Faculty," *Kentucky Kernel*, December 8, 1970.

21. Stephen B. Bright, interview by Matthew Strandmark, January 14, 2021, GGOHP, Nunn Center.

22. "Fayette Judge Convicts Ex UK Professor," *Kentucky Kernel*, July 27, 1972.

23. Kevin D. Hill interview.

24. Gatewood Galbraith, *The Last Free Man in America*, 82.

25. Kevin D. Hill interview.

26. Thomas McDowell, interview by Matthew Strandmark, December 15, 2020, GGOHP, Nunn Center.

27. Dean Drawford, "City Investigates Ex-Narc, Student Scuffle," *Kentucky Kernel*, March 31, 1972.

28. Gatewood Galbraith, *The Last Free Man in America*, 95.

29. Edna Galbraith Hancock, interview by Matthew Strandmark, April 22, 2021, GGOHP, Nunn Center.

30. Teresa Isaac, interview by Matthew Strandmark, January 27, 2021, GGOHP, Nunn Center.

31. Joshua Clark Davis, "The Long Marijuana-Rights Movement," *HuffPost*, December 6, 2017, www.huffpost.com/entry/the-long-marijuana-rights_b_6113894.

32. Gatewood Galbraith, *The Last Free Man in America*, 95.

33. James T. Wooten, "Carter Seeks to End Marijuana Penalty for Small Amounts," *New York Times* , August 3, 1977.

34. Gatewood Galbraith, "Marijuana: Laws, Views Must Change," *Kentucky Kernel*, August 25, 1976.

35. Gatewood Galbraith, "History of Marijuana Plagued with Attackers," *Kentucky Kernel*, August 26, 1976.

36. Gatewood Galbraith, "Marijuana's Future: Prospects for Big Business in Kentucky," *Kentucky Kernel*, August 27, 1976.

37. 2014ms0254: Articles of Incorporation, box 3, folder 9, Gatewood Galbraith papers, 1935–2013, 1976, University of Kentucky Special Collections Research Center.

38. Gatewood Galbraith, *The Last Free Man in America*, 105.

39. Liz Whitehorn, interview by Matthew Strandmark, February 25, 2021, GGOHP, Nunn Center.

40. Gatewood Galbraith, *The Last Free Man in America*, 106.

41. Susan Sears, interview by Josh Burczyk, April 20, 2016, GGOHP, Nunn Center.

42. Susan Sears interview.

43. Susan Sears interview.

44. Gatewood Galbraith, *The Last Free Man in America*, 116.

45. Will Rowan, "The Incredible Quadractor from Traction, Inc.," *Mother Earth News*, July/August 1979, 46–47.

46. Gatewood Galbraith, *The Last Free Man in America*, 117.

47. Susan Sears interview.

48. Gatewood Galbraith, *The Last Free Man in America*, 117.

49. "Here Is a List of the People Who Passed State Bar Exam," *Louisville Courier-Journal*, May 10, 1981.

50. Gatewood Galbraith, *The Last Free Man in America*, 118.

3. A True Pioneer in the Kentucky Spirit

1. "Call It a Stash Crop," *Lexington Herald-Leader*, June 8, 1981.

2. Thomas Tolliver, "Court Typist Says She Gave Away Carbons of Grand Jury Transcripts," *Lexington Herald-Leader*, April 17, 1984.

3. "Woman Acquitted of Prostitution," *Lexington Herald-Leader*, October 25, 1984.

4. Sue Wahlgren, "Music to Fill the Air at Kentucky Horse Park," *Lexington Herald-Leader*, August 4, 1987.

5. Gatewood Galbraith, *The Last Free Man in America*, 124.

6. Susan Sears, interview by Josh Burczyk, April 20, 2016, GGOHP, Nunn Center.

7. Gatewood Galbraith, *The Last Free Man in America*, 121.

8. "Up in Smoke," *Lexington Herald-Leader*, January 4, 1983.

9. "Up in Smoke," *Lexington Herald-Leader*, January 4, 1983.

10. Mary K. Bonsteel Tachau and Bruce L. McClure, "John Y. Brown Jr. (1979–1983)," in *Kentucky's Governors*, edited by Lowell H. Harrison (Lexington: University Press of Kentucky, 2004), 221–24.

11. Al Cross, interview by Matthew Strandmark, April 6, 2021, GGOHP, Nunn Center.

12. Al Cross interview.

13. Edna Galbraith Hancock, interview by Matthew Strandmark, April 22, 2021, GGOHP, Nunn Center.

14. Liz Whitehorn, interview by Matthew Strandmark, February 5, 2021, GGOHP, Nunn Center.

15. Liz Whitehorn interview.

16. Mike Galbraith, interview by Matthew Strandmark, February 3, 2021, GGOHP, Nunn Center.

17. Susan Sears, interview by Josh Burczyk, July 13, 2016, Gatewood Oral Project.

18. "Agriculture Commissioner Candidates Disagree on Milk Law," *Lexington Herald-Leader*, May 18, 1983.

19. "Commissioner of Agriculture Candidate Forum," Kentucky Educational Television, May 1983.

20. "Nominate David Boswell, Keep Harris Down on Farm," *Lexington Herald-Leader*, April 27, 1983.

21. Gatewood Galbraith, *The Last Free Man in America*, 127.

22. https://elect.ky.gov/SiteCollectionDocuments/Election%20Results/1980-1989/1983/83priagriculture.txt.

23. Gatewood Galbraith, *The Last Free Man in America*, 127.

24. Susan Sears interview, July 13, 2016.

25. Susan Sears interview, July 13, 2016.

26. Nick Johnson, *Grass Roots: A History of Cannabis in the American West* (Corvallis: Oregon State University Press, 2017), 121–22.

27. Jim Warren, "Kentucky Marijuana Considered for Spraying with Herbicide," *Lexington Herald-Leader*, August 16, 1983.

28. Warren, "Kentucky Marijuana Considered for Spraying."

29. This and the previous two quotes are from Art Jester, "Marijuana as a Cash Crop: Is It Saving Some Kentucky Farms?" *Lexington Herald-Leader*, August 26, 1984.

30. D. Paul Stanford, interview by Matthew Strandmark, March 11, 2021, GGOHP, Nunn Center.

31. Gatewood Galbraith, *The Last Free Man in America*, 109.

32. "Gatewood Galbraith & Jack Herer—Pharmaceutical Monopolies, Henry Ford's Hemp Car," Time 4 Hemp, https://www.youtube.com/watch?v=qK_vkgiofsM.

33. Thomas Tolliver, "Edgar Wallace Released from Jail," *Lexington Herald-Leader*, June 14, 1986.

34. Gatewood Galbraith, *The Last Free Man in America*, 128.

35. "Auctioneer Added to Suit over Marks Estate Bid," *Lexington Herald-Leader*, September 28,1987.

36. Kit Wagar, "Charges Dismissed Against Defendant in Garden Springs School Arson Case," *Lexington Herald-Leader*, May 6, 1989.

37. Ernesto Scorsone, interview by Matthew Strandmark, January 12, 2021, GGOHP, Nunn Center.

38. Kevin D. Hill, interview by Matthew Strandmark, December 1, 2020, GGOHP, Nunn Center.

39. Bob Treadway, interview by Matthew Strandmark, December 18, 2020, GGOHP, Nunn Center.

40. Gatewood Galbraith, *The Last Free Man in America*, 137.

41. Hank Galbraith, interview by Matthew Strandmark, February 25, 2021, GGOHP, Nunn Center.

42. Edna Galbraith Hancock interview.

43. Bob Geiger, "Lawyer Who Favors Legal Pot May Run for Governor," *Lexington Herald-Leader*, August 6, 1989.

44. William Hershey, "Legal Marijuana Could Finance War on Hard Drugs, Lobbyists Say," *Akron (OH) Beacon Journal*, September 7, 1989.

45. Susan Sears interview. July 13, 2016.

46. Edna Galbraith Hancock interview.

47. Mike Galbraith interview.

48. Gatewood Galbraith, *The Last Free Man in America*, 138.

4. Spectacular Bid

1. Bob Geiger, "Pro-Marijuana Lawyer Running for Governor," *Lexington Herald-Leader*, November 22, 1989.

2. Gatewood Galbraith, *The Last Free Man in America*, 139.

3. Roger C. Adams, "Wallace Glenn Wilkinson (1987–1991)," in Harrison, *Kentucky's Governors*, 238–43.

4. Penny M. Miller, "Brereton C. Jones (1991–1995)," in Harrison, *Kentucky's Governors*, 246.

5. This and the preceding three quotes are from Summer Sears, interview by Josh Burczyk, June 27, 2016, GGOHP, Nunn Center.

6. Susan Sears, interview by Josh Burczyk, April 20, 2016, GGOHP, Nunn Center.

7. Mark Chellgren, "Galbraith's Finances in Shambles," *Lexington Herald-Leader*, October 30, 1990.

8. Gatewood Galbraith, *The Last Free Man in America*, 128.

9. Chellgren, "Galbraith's Finances in Shambles."

10. Gatewood Galbraith, *The Last Free Man in America*, 142.

11. Stephen L. Betts, "Flashback: Willie Nelson Settles IRS Tax Debt," *Rolling Stone*, February 2, 2017.

12. Jack Brammer, interview by Matthew Strandmark, January 19, 2021, GGOHP, Nunn Center.

13. Al Cross, interview by Matthew Strandmark, April 6, 2021, GGOHP, Nunn Center.

14. Elizabeth Wade, "Rally Backs Legalizing of Marijuana," *Lexington Herald-Leader*, March 23, 1990.

15. Al Cross interview.

16. Kevin Nance, "An 'Old Hippie's' Uphill Battle," *Lexington Herald-Leader*, April 8, 1990.

17. Chris Iovenko, dir., *Gatewood* (Pan-Opticon Productions, 2013), film, 28 minutes, for Kentucky Educational Television, ket.org/program/gatewood.

18. Nance, "An 'Old Hippie's' Uphill Battle."

19. Bob Geiger, "Baesler Nets $601,681 for Gubernatorial Bid," *Lexington Herald-Leader*, April 3, 1990.

20. Bob Geiger, "Jones Fund-Raising Total Hits $1.1 Million in Governor's Race," *Lexington Herald-Leader*, April 4, 1990.

21. Chellgren, "Galbraith's Finances in Shambles."

22. The quotations in this and the preceding paragraphs are from Ferrell Wellman, "Candidate Close-up: Gatewood Galbraith," Kentucky Educational Television, May 1991.

23. Summer Sears interview.

24. "Country Star's Maysville Date on Hold after Galbraith Report," *Lexington Herald-Leader*, September 20, 1990.

25. Alex Williams, "High Times Wants to Be the Playboy of Pot," *New York Times*, April 2, 2016.

26. John Holmstrom, interview by Matthew Strandmark, March 31, 2021, GGOHP, Nunn Center.

27. This and the previous four quotes are from Joseph S. Stroud, "Galbraith Hits Campaign Trail with Help from Willie Nelson," *Lexington Herald-Leader*, October 15, 1990.

28. Stroud, "Galbraith Hits Campaign Trail."

29. John Holmstrom interview.

30. Gatewood Galbraith, *The Last Free Man in America*, 149.

31. Al Cross interview.

32. Al Cross interview.

33. Joseph S. Stroud and Eric Gregory, "Galbraith Says He Has Smoked Marijuana Regularly for 22 Years," *Lexington Herald-Leader*, October 16, 1990.

34. Susan Sears, interview by Josh Burczyk, July 13, 2016, GGOHP, Nunn Center.

35. "Galbraith Fails to Appear in Court," *Lexington Herald-Leader*, December 5, 1990.

36. David A. Hall, "Galbraith Pleads Guilty, Fined for Failing to Pay $4,300 in Taxes," *Lexington Herald-Leader*, February 1, 1991.

37. Bob Geiger, "Galbraith Says Phones for Campaign Tapped," *Lexington Herald-Leader*, March 28, 1991.

38. This and two previous quotes are from FBI investigative files supplied by the Lexington field office on November 30, 2020, following a Freedom of Information Act request by the author.

39. Joseph S. Stroud, "Galbraith Talks to Students about Marijuana Issue," *Lexington Herald-Leader*, March 30, 1991.

40. Gatewood Galbraith, *The Last Free Man in America*, 150.

41. Bobby King, "Three-Day Concert Set as Galbraith Fundraiser," *Lexington Herald-Leader*, April 24, 1991.

42. Joseph S. Stroud, "Gatewoodstock Opens Without Much Fanfare," *Lexington Herald-Leader*, April 27, 1991.

43. Gatewood Galbraith, *The Last Free Man in America*, 150.

44. "1991 Primary and General Election Results," Commonwealth of Kentucky, State Board of Elections, https://elect.ky.gov/results/1990-1999/Pages/1991.aspx.

5. The War on Drugs, the Militia, and the Fourth of July

1. Paula Parrish, "Officials Destroyed 823,088 Pot Plants in '91," *Lexington Herald-Leader*, November 27, 1991.

2. Parrish, "Officials Destroyed 823,088 Pot Plants in '91."

3. Bob Geiger, "Galbraith Raising Funds for Governor's Race," *Lexington Herald-Leader*, April 21, 1992.

4. Dottie Bean, "GatewoodStock II Opens '95 Race: Galbraith Says He'll Change Focus to Value of Hemp," *Lexington Herald-Leader*, May 17, 1992.

5. Gatewood Galbraith, *The Last Free Man in America*, 128.

6. Gatewood Galbraith, *The Last Free Man in America*, 175.

7. Bill Estep, "Doctors to Debate Legalizing Marijuana for Medical Use," *Lexington Herald-Leader*, January 17, 1993.

8. Ben Westhoff, *Fentanyl, Inc.* (New York: Atlantic Monthly Press, 2019), 28–29.

9. Bill Estep, "Science and Truth Witnesses Say Marijuana Relieves Many Ills," *Lexington Herald-Leader*, January 19, 1993.

10. Gatewood Galbraith, *The Last Free Man in America*, 175.

11. "Galbraith Seeks Bankruptcy Protection," *Lexington Herald-Leader*, April 16, 1993.

12. Jacob Jones, interview by Matthew Strandmark, December 5, 2020, GGOHP, Nunn Center. All recounting of events from the viewpoint of Jacob Jones is from that interview.

13. Kentucky State Police Marijuana Annual Report, 1988 and 1989 calendar years, https://www.ojp.gov/pdffiles1/Digitization/125700NCJRS.pdf.

14. "State Police Wage High Tech War against Marijuana," *Lexington Herald-Leader*, July 5, 1992.

15. Karen Samples and Eric Gregory, "Family Questions Pot-Patch Slaying," *Lexington Herald-Leader*, August 10, 1993.

16. Kentucky State Police report on Gary Shepherd investigation, 1991–1992, in response to a Freedom of Information Act request by the author, November 30, 2020.

17. Unnamed KSP officer, personal interview by Matthew Strandmark, November 16, 2020.

18. Jacalyn Carfagno, "Shepherd Memorial Draws Protestors to Rockcastle," *Lexington Herald-Leader*, September 19, 1993.

19. "Galbraith Criticizes Pot Eradication," *Lexington Herald-Leader*, August 25, 1993.

20. Carfagno, "Shepherd Memorial Draws Protestors to Rockcastle."

21. Kim Eisner, interview by Josh Burczyk, July 13, 2016, GGOHP, Nunn Center.

22. Susan Sears, interview by Josh Burczyk, July 13, 2016, GGOHP, Nunn Center.

23. This and the two previous quotes are from the Kim Eisner interview.

24. For the Record, *Lexington Herald-Leader*, February 10, 1993.

25. This and the previous three quotes are from Jack Brammer and Bill Estep, "Galbraith Got Out of Heavy Debt through Bankruptcy Proceedings," *Lexington Herald-Leader*, July 16, 1994.

26. Eric Gregory, "Chilly Weather Limits UK Turnout: Students Protest Tuition Increase," *Lexington Herald-Leader*, November 4, 1993.

27. "Galbraith Protesting Law That Bans Marijuana from Conference," *Lexington Herald-Leader*, May 24, 1993.

28. Chad Carlton, "Galbraith Can Display Some Hemp Products," *Lexington Herald-Leader*, May 25, 1993.

29. "Hemp Booth Popular Draw at Environment Conference," *Lexington Herald-Leader*, May 27, 1993.

30. "5 Indicted, Charged with Medicaid Fraud," *Lexington Herald-Leader*, August 27, 1993.

31. Gatewood Galbraith, *The Last Free Man in America*, 205.

32. Gatewood Galbraith, *The Last Free Man in America*, 205–6.

33. Gatewood Galbraith, *The Last Free Man in America*, 207.

34. Jack Brammer, interview by Matthew Strandmark. January 19, 2021, Gatewood Galbraith Oral History Project, Louie B. Nunn Center for Oral History, University of Kentucky Libraries.

35. Jack Brammer, "Labor Leader Hammond, Galbraith Join Forces," *Lexington Herald-Leader*, April 30, 1994.

36. Gatewood Galbraith, *The Last Free Man in America*, 190.

37. "Labor Leaders slam Colleague for Joining Galbraith Ticket," *Lexington Herald-Leader*, May 6, 1994.

38. This and the previous two quotes are from Bill Estep, "Galbraith First to Announce Bid for Governor," *Lexington Herald-Leader*, July 16, 1994.

39. Paul E. Patton, interview by Matthew Strandmark, December 2, 2020, GGOHP, Nunn Center.

40. Gatewood Galbraith, *The Last Free Man in America*, 196.

41. Gatewood Galbraith, *The Last Free Man in America*, 198.

42. "FBI Named Inquiry 'BOPTROT,'" *Lexington Herald-Leader*, May 21, 1992.

43. "Don Blandford Resigns House Seat," *Middlesboro Daily News*, May 4, 1993.

44. Jack Brammer, "Galbraith Won't Accept State Matching Funds: Decision Limits Gubernatorial Slate to $100 Donations," *Lexington Herald-Leader*, August 31, 1994.

45. Brammer, "Galbraith Won't Accept State Matching Funds."

46. Chris Poore, "Galbraith's Speaking Style Is What Hooks Many Admirers: He Has Toned Down His Campaign But Still Expects More Support Than Predicted," *Lexington Herald-Leader*, April 16, 1995.

47. Chad Carlton, "Lt. Governor's Margin Largest in 20 Years," *Lexington Herald-Leader*, May 24, 1995.

48. Gatewood Galbraith, *The Last Free Man in America*, 211.

49. Gatewood Galbraith, *The Last Free Man in America*, 216.

50. Kit Wagar, "Galbraith Arrested after Parade Protest: Two Men Charged in Demonstration Against U.N. Theme," *Lexington Herald-Leader*, July 5, 1995.

51. Gatewood Galbraith, *The Last Free Man in America*, 218.

52. Teresa Isaac, interview by Matthew Strandmark, January 27, 2021, GGOHP, Nunn Center.

53. Jim Gray, interview by Matthew Strandmark, June 3, 2021, GGOHP, Nunn Center.

54. Molly Galbraith, interview by Josh Burczyk, July 22, 2016, GGOHP, Nunn Center.

55. "Patton's Win Margin Certified as 21,560," *Lexington Herald-Leader*, November 28, 1995.

6. "Lean, Mean, Vote-Gettin' Machine"

1. Nick Johnson, *Grass Roots: A History of Cannabis in the American West* (Corvallis: Oregon State University Press, 2017), 147.

2. Johnson, *Grass Roots*, 149.

3. Gatewood Galbraith, *The Last Free Man in America*, 229.

4. Gatewood Galbraith, *The Last Free Man in America*, 230.

5. Gatewood Galbraith, *The Last Free Man in America*, 232.

6. Andy Mead, "Harrelson Holds Hemp Show-and-Tell," *Lexington Herald-Leader*, May 31, 1996.

7. Andy Mead, "Natural Born Tiller," *Lexington Herald-Leader*, June 2, 1996.

8. Andy Mead, "Pro-hemp Teacher Fired," *Lexington Herald-Leader*, July 16, 1997.

9. "Club Buys Marijuana to Help the Dying," *Lexington Herald-Leader*, February 28, 1996.

10. Andy Mead, "High Hopes for Hemp," *Lexington Herald-Leader*, April 7, 1996.

11. Mary Thomas-Spears, interview by Josh Burczyk, June 18, 2016, GGOHP, Nunn Center.

12. Melinda J. Overstreet, "The Politics of Pot," *Bowling Green Daily News*, July 12, 1999.

13. Mary Thomas-Spears interview.

14. Mary Thomas-Spears interview.

15. Overstreet, "The Politics of Pot."

16. Cheryl Powell, "Lexington Woman, 83, Always on the Run with Volunteer Work," *Lexington Herald-Leader*, June 3, 1996.

17. Gatewood Galbraith, *The Last Free Man in America*, 252.

18. Hank Galbraith, interview by Matthew Strandmark, February 25, 2021, GGOHP, Nunn Center.

19. Hank Galbraith, "A Good Deed," 2016, original story in the author's possession, 1–3.

20. Gatewood Galbraith, *The Last Free Man in America*, 233–234.

21. Paul Blanchard, "Paul Edward Patton (1995–2003)," in Harrison, *Kentucky's Governors*, 252–58.

22. This and the previous quote are from Gatewood Galbraith, *The Last Free Man in America*, 254.

23. John Cheves, "Galbraith Asks Judges to OK Pot for Medical Use," *Lexington Herald-Leader*, January 12, 1998.

24. "McCloud Praises Award in HMO Suit," *Lexington Herald-Leader*, October 22, 1998.

25. Bill Estep and Jack Brammer, "No Democrat Steps Forward to Challenge Patton in Primary," *Lexington Herald-Leader*, January 27, 1999.

26. "In Minn., Ex-Wrestler's Opponents Left Dazed," *Philadelphia Inquirer*, November 5, 1998.

27. Lee Mueller, "Patton's Campaign Starts Today—Governor Wary of 'Ventura Effect': Galbraith Will Run, say Forgy, Martin," *Lexington Herald-Leader*, February 10, 1999.

28. Gatewood Galbraith, *The Last Free Man in America*, 255.

29. Gatewood Galbraith, *The Last Free Man in America*, 256.

30. Jack Brammer, "Galbraith Says He's Running, Will Take Tips from Ventura," *Lexington Herald-Leader*, February 24, 1999.

31. Gatewood Galbraith, *The Last Free Man in America*, 258.

32. Brammer, "Galbraith Says He's Running."

33. Paul E. Patton, interview by Matthew Strandmark, December 2, 2020, GGOHP, Nunn Center.

34. Molly Galbraith, interview by Josh Burczyk, July 22, 2016, GGOHP, Nunn Center.

35. Bill Bishop, "Only Half of the Equation," *Lexington Herald-Leader*, May 30, 1999.

36. Mark R. Chellgren, "GOP Could Struggle Just for Second," *Lexington Herald-Leader*, June 28, 1999.

37. Mark R. Chellgren, "Third-Place Finish Could Cost GOP," *Lexington Herald-Leader*, June 25, 1999.

38. Chellgren, "GOP Could Struggle Just for Second."

39. Peter Baniak, "Galbraith Joins Reform Ticket," *Lexington Herald-Leader*, July 2, 1999.

40. Gatewood Galbraith, *The Last Free Man in America*, 257.

41. Gatewood Galbraith, *The Last Free Man in America*, 261.

42. Peter Baniak and Jack Brammer, "Martin Gets Cold Shoulder at Picnic," *Lexington Herald-Leader*, August 8, 1999.

43. Gatewood Galbraith, *The Last Free Man in America*, 260.

44. Peter Baniak, "Wailin' Willie Takes the Stage," *Lexington Herald-Leader*, September 3, 1999.

45. Gatewood Galbraith, *The Last Free Man in America*, 261.

46. Al Cross, interview by Matthew Strandmark, April 6, 2021, GGOHP, Nunn Center.

47. Peter Baniak, "Paul Patton: 61%, Peppy Martin: 23%, Gatewood Galbraith: 15%," *Lexington Herald-Leader*, November 3, 1999.

48. This and the previous two quotes are from Bill Estep, "Galbraith Sends Message," *Lexington Herald-Leader*, November 3, 1999.

49. Blanchard, "Paul Edward Patton (1995–2003)."

50. Jack Brammer, "House-Senate Budget Committee Talks Turn Ugly," *Lexington Herald-Leader*, March 30, 2000.

51. Gatewood Galbraith, *The Last Free Man in America*, 267.

52. This and the previous quote are from Overstreet, "The Politics of Pot."

53. Mary Thomas-Spears interview.

54. Peter Baniak, "Galbraith Gets Reform Nomination for Congress," *Lexington Herald-Leader*, June 30, 2000.

55. Gatewood Galbraith, *The Last Free Man in America*, 269.

56. This and the previous two quotes are from Ernie Fletcher, interview by Matthew Strandmark, December 14, 2020, GGOHP, Nunn Center.

57. "KY District 6," Our Campaigns, www.ourcampaigns.com/RaceDetail.html?RaceID=483.

58. Peter Baniak, "Fletcher Defeats Baesler by Wide Margin," *Lexington Herald-Leader*, November 8, 2000.

7. The Last Free Man

1. Allen J. Beck and Paige M. Harrison, "Prisoners in 2000," *Bureau of Justice Statistics Bulletin* (U.S. Department of Justice), August 2001, https://bjs.ojp.gov/content/pub/pdf/p00.pdf.

2. Mackenzie Buday and Ashley Nellis, "Private Prisons in the United States," Sentencing Project, August 23, 2022, www.sentencingproject.org/publications/private-prisons-united-states.

3. Gatewood Galbraith, *The Last Free Man in America*, 282.

4. "Galbraith Considers Running for Mayor," *Lexington Herald-Leader*, August 9, 2001.

5. Gatewood Galbraith, *The Last Free Man in America*, 297.

6. This and the previous quote are from Teresa Isaac, interview by Matthew Strandmark, January 27, 2021, GGOHP, Nunn Center.

7. Edward T. Breathitt, "City Must Seize Chance to Buy Water Company," *Lexington Herald-Leader*, February 10, 2002.

8. "Mayoral Results," *Lexington Herald-Leader*, May 29, 2002.

9. John Cheves, Laura Yuen, and Nicole Morgan, "Isaac Beats Crosbie to Become Next Mayor of Lexington," *Lexington Herald-Leader*, November 6, 2002.

10. David Fitts, interview by Matthew Strandmark, January 29, 2021, GGOHP, Nunn Center.

11. Gatewood Galbraith, *The Last Free Man in America*, 282.

12. Greg Kocher, "Militia Leader Held on Weapons Charges—Guns, Pipe Bombs, Ammunition Found in Felon's Home Office," *Lexington Herald-Leader*, February 27, 2002.

13. Greg Kocher, "Militia Leader Missing—Puckett Posts 'Last Testament' on Net," *Lexington Herald-Leader*, March 15, 2022.

14. Greg Kocher, "Maybe Militia Chief was Abducted, Lawyer Says," *Lexington Herald-Leader*, March 16, 2022.

15. Louise Taylor and Greg Kocher, "Wanted Militia Leader Surrenders—Puckett Had Fled from House Arrest," *Lexington Herald-Leader*, April 5, 2002.

16. Paul Blanchard, "Paul Edward Patton (1995–2003)," in Harrison, *Kentucky's Governors*, 298.

17. David Fitts interview.

18. Travis Hubbard, "Galbraith to Run Against Fletcher in Sixth District—He's Congressman's Only Opposition," *Lexington Herald-Leader*, August 13, 2002.

19. Gatewood Galbraith, *The Last Free Man in America*, 310.

20. Jennifer Hewlett, "Former Labor Union Executive Jerry Wayne Hammond Dies—Got Toyota to Build Georgetown Plant with Union Workers," *Lexington Herald-Leader*, October 24, 2002.

21. Frank E. Lockwood, "Kentucky Incumbents Return to U.S. House," *Lexington Herald-Leader*, November 6, 2002.

22. Robert Mcg. Thomas Jr., "A.B. (Happy) Chandler Dies: Led Baseball during Integration," *New York Times*, June 19, 1991, www.nytimes.com/1991/06/16/obituaries/ab-happy-chandler-92-dies-led-baseball-during-integration.html.

23. Gatewood Galbraith, *The Last Free Man in America*, 315–316.

24. Albert Benjamin Chandler III, interview by Matthew Strandmark, June 11, 2021, GGOHP, Nunn Center.

25. Gatewood Galbraith, *The Last Free Man in America*, 315–22.

26. "Galbraith Aims for Another Return to Ballot," *Lexington Herald-Leader*, July 2, 2003.

27. Gregory Stumbo, interview by Matthew Strandmark, December 9, 2020, GGOHP, Nunn Center.

28. David Fitts interview.

29. Ryan Alessi, "Galbraith Files for Attorney General—Claims This Race Is His Best Chance to Win Election," *Lexington Herald-Leader*, August 12, 2003.

30. Bill Estep, "Attorney General Hopefuls Defend Their Records: Personal Problems Shouldn't Cost Votes, Candidates Contend," *Lexington Herald-Leader*, September 23, 2003.

31. Bill Estep, "Gatewood Galbraith—He's Behind on Taxes and Still Smoking Pot," *Lexington Herald-Leader*, October 19, 2003.

32. John Cheves, Ryan Alessi, and Jack Brammer, "Tide Turns—Fletcher Is First GOP Governor in 32 Years: Patton Draws Blame from Some Democrats; Republications Win 2 Other State Posts," *Lexington Herald-Leader*, November 5, 2003.

33. "'Cures, Not Wars,' Chant Supporters of Legalizing Marijuana," *Lexington Herald-Leader*, May 2, 2004.

34. Kim Eisner, interview by Josh Burczyk, July 13, 2016, GGOHP, Nunn Center.

35. Mark Perkins, interview by Matthew Strandmark, March 10, 2021, GGOHP, Nunn Center.

36. Steve Flairty, "Gatewood on Gatewood—Galbraith Autobiography Is Just Like Him: Entertaining," *Lexington Herald-Leader*, December 12, 2004.

37. Ryan Alessi and Jack Brammer, "Cabinet Hirings Are Under Investigation: Attorney General Looks at Alleged Transportation Violations," *Lexington Herald-Leader*, May 17, 2005.

38. Ryan Alessi, "Hiring Inquiry Widens—Investigators Search the Offices of Two Top Fletcher Aides; Allegation: Politics Trumped Merit," *Lexington Herald-Leader*, May 18, 2005.

39. Ryan Alessi, "Fletcher Weathers Year of Turmoil," *Lexington Herald-Leader*, September 17, 2006.

40. Bruce Schreiner, "Galbraith to Run for Governor—Henry Postpones His Announcement," *Lexington Herald-Leader*, January 16, 2007.

41. Jack Brammer, "Gatewood Galbraith Files for Governor's Race—State's Perennial Problems Require 'New Blood,' He Says," *Lexington Herald-Leader*, January 24, 2007.

42. Ryan Alessi, "Galbraith Lays Out Platform for Governor's Race—Plan Includes Casinos, College Vouchers, Drug Treatment," *Lexington Herald-Leader*, February 23, 2007.

43. "Gubernatorial Debate," *Lexington Herald-Leader*, April 22, 2007.

44. "Gubernatorial Debate," *Lexington Herald-Leader*, April 8, 2007.

45. "Fletcher Has Raised $3 Million—Galbraith Figure Nearly $18,000," *Lexington Herald-Leader*, April 24, 2007.

46. This and the previous two quotes are from Andy Mead, "He Has Often Run, Seldom Conformed—Gubernatorial Race: Gatewood Galbraith," *Lexington Herald-Leader*, April 27, 2007.

47. Kentucky State Board of Elections, "Report of 'Official' Election Night Tally Results," June 13, 2007, https://elect.ky.gov/SiteCollectionDocuments/Election%20Results/2000-2009/2007/Primary%20Election/STATEwidebyoffice.txt.

48. Kentucky State Board of Elections, "Report of 'Official' Election Night Tally Results," November 27, 2007, https://elect.ky.gov/SiteCollectionDocuments/Election%20Results/2000-2009/2007/General%20Election/STATEwidebyoffice.txt.

49. David Stout and Solomon Moore, "U.S. Won't Prosecute in States That Allow Medical Marijuana," *New York Times*, October 19, 2009.

50. Gatewood Galbraith, "State Should Be among First to Legalize, Tax Marijuana, Hemp," *Lexington Herald-Leader*, May 10, 2009.

51. Jack Brammer, "Galbraith Launches Fifth Gubernatorial Run—Lexington Lawyer Wants to 'Combat Ky.'s Electile Dysfunction,'" *Lexington Herald-Leader*, July 8, 2009.

52. "Galbraith Gets Signatures for His 5th Run: Independent Says Effort Has Energized Campaign for Governor," *Lexington Herald-Leader*, May 28, 2011.

53. "Running Mate Gives Galbraith an Energy Boost but Riley also Brings Baggage to Race," *Lexington Herald-Leader*, October 13, 2011.

54. "Hard to Miss Gatewood Galbraith in Any Crowd; Audacious Independent Ignores Polls, Says He'll at Least Beat Williams," *Lexington Herald-Leader*, October 16, 2011.

55. "Beshear Sees Win as Vote Against 'Rank Partisanship'; Promises 'Lean and Efficient' Government in Second Term," *Lexington Herald-Leader*, November 9, 2011.

56. Susan Sears, interview by Josh Burczyk, July 13, 2016, GGOHP, Nunn Center.

57. Susan Sears interview.

58. Molly Galbraith, interview by Josh Burczyk, July 22, 2016, GGOHP, Nunn Center.

8. A Splendid Torch

1. This and the previous three quotes are from Linda Blackford, "Character Commonwealth—Colorful Kentuckian Who Ran for Governor Five Times Always Spoke His Mind," *Lexington Herald-Leader*, January 5, 2012.

2. Susan Sears, interview by Josh Burczyk, July 13, 2016, GGOHP, Nunn Center.

3. Andy Barr, interview by Matthew Strandmark, June 11, 2021, GGOHP, Nunn Center.

4. Jim Gray, interview by Matthew Strandmark, June 3, 2021, GGOHP, Nunn Center.

5. Jack Brammer, interview by Matthew Strandmark, January 19, 2021, GGOHP, Nunn Center.

6. Mike Galbraith, interview by Matthew Strandmark, February 3, 2021, GGOHP, Nunn Center.

7. Liz Whitehorn, interview by Matthew Strandmark, February 5, 2021, GGOHP, Nunn Center.

8. Edna Galbraith Hancock, interview by Matthew Strandmark, April 22, 2021, GGOHP, Nunn Center.

9. Gatewood Galbraith, *The Last Free Man in America*, 253.

10. Summer Sears, interview by Josh Burczyk, July 1, 2016, GGOHP, Nunn Center.

11. Abigail Sears, interview by Josh Burczyk, August 5, 2016, GGOHP, Nunn Center.

12. Molly Galbraith, interview by Josh Burczyk, July 22, 2016, GGOHP, Nunn Center.

13. Kim Eisner, interview by Josh Burczyk, July 13, 2016, GGOHP, Nunn Center.

14. James Comer, interview by Matthew Strandmark, April 2021, transcript in the possession of the author.

15. John Hudak, "The Farm Bill, Hemp Legalization, and the Status of CBD: An Explainer," Brookings Institution, December 14, 2018, www.brookings.edu/blog/fixgov/2018/12/14/the-farm-bill-hemp-and-cbd-explainer/.

16. "Judge OKs $77 Million Sale of GenCanna Global Assets out of Bankruptcy," Hemp Industry Daily, May 20, 2020, https://hempindustrydaily.com/bankruptcy-judge-approves-77-million-sale-of-gencanna-global-assets-out-of-bankruptcy/.

17. Jonathan Shepherd and Tyler Mark, "Continued Declines in Hemp Profitability Mixed with Marginal Profit Potential for 2021," Agricultural Economics, University of Kentucky College of Agriculture, Food and Environment, January 28, 2021, https://agecon.ca.uky.edu/continued-declines-hemp-profitability-mixed-marginal-profit-potential-2021.

18. "Kentucky Department of Agriculture Licenses 2021 Hemp Growers, Processors," Kentucky Proud Hemp, Kentucky Department of Agriculture, April 29, 2021, www.kyagr.com/ky-agnews/press-releases/2021/Kentucky-Department-of-Agriculture-licenses-2021-hemp-growers-processors.html.

19. James Comer interview.

20. Niels Lesniewski, "Mitch McConnell Touting Victory with Hemp Legalization on Farm Bill," Politics, Roll Call, December 11, 2018, https://rollcall.com/2018/12/11/mitch-mcconnell-touting-victory-with-hemp-legalization-on-farm-bill/.

21. Molly Galbraith interview.

22. Al Cross, interview by Matthew Strandmark, April 6, 2021, GGOHP, Nunn Center.

23. "2019 Kentucky General Election Results," *New York Times*, November 14, 2019, www.nytimes.com/interactive/2019/11/05/us/elections/results-kentucky-general-elections.html.

24. Jack Brammer, "GOP Wins Dominant Control of Kentucky Legislature," *Lexington Herald-Leader*, November 9, 2020.

25. Gregory Stumbo, interview by Matthew Strandmark, December 9, 2020, GGOHP, Nunn Center.

26. Al Cross interview.

27. This and the previous quote are from Ryan Van Velzer, "Beshear Won't 'Bow to Terror' After Protesters Hang Him Effigy," WKYU Public Radio, May 27, 2020, www.wkyufm.org/politics/2020-05-27/beshear-wont-bow-to-terror-after-protesters-hang-him-effigy.

28. "Hard to Miss Gatewood Galbraith in Any Crowd, Audacious Independent Ignores Polls, Says He'll at Least Beat Williams," *Lexington Herald-Leader*, October 16, 2011.

29. Al Cross interview.

30. "What Is the U.S. Opioid Epidemic?," U.S. Department of Health and Human Services, October 27, 2021, www.hhs.gov/opioids/about-the-epidemic/index.html.

31. Kayla Moody, "'A Game of Russian Roulette': Record Number of Deadly Overdoses Attributed to Fentanyl, Pandemic," Spectrum News 1, September 2, 2021, https://spectrumnews1.com/ky/louisville/news/2021/09/02/2020-overdose-fatality-report.

32. Joshua Cohen, "Diseases of Despair Contribute to Declining U.S. Life Expectancy," *Forbes*, July 19, 2018, www.forbes.com/sites/joshuacohen/2018/07/19/diseases-of-despair-contribute-to-declining-u-s-life-expectancy/.

33. Ernie Fletcher, interview by Matthew Strandmark, December 14, 2020, GGOHP, Nunn Center.

34. "Recovery Kentucky," Fletcher Group, April 9, 2019, www.fletchergroup.org/2019/04/09/recovery-kentucky/.

35. Gregory Stumbo interview.

36. "The Overton Window," Mackinac Center for Public Policy, www.mackinac.org/OvertonWindow.

37. Foundation for a Healthy Kentucky, "KHIP: New Poll Shows Most Kentucky Adults Favor Legalizing Marijuana for Medical Purposes," *Northern Kentucky Tribune*, February 6, 2020, www.nkytribune.com/2020/02/khip-new-poll-shows-most-kentucky-adults-favor-legalizing-marijuana-for-medical-purposes/.

38. Adam Barnes, "Legalizing Marijuana Lowers Demand for Prescription Drugs, Study Finds," Changing America, *The Hill*, April 18, 2022, https://thehill.com/changing-america/well-being/3271896-legalizing-marijuana-lowers-demand-for-prescription-drugs-study-finds/.

39. Jason Nemes, interview by Matthew Strandmark, November 20, 2021, GGOHP, Nunn Center.

40. Phil Pendleton, "Ky. House Passes Medical Marijuana Bill," WKYT, March 17, 2022, www.wkyt.com/2022/03/17/ky-house-passes-medical-marijuana-bill/.

41. https://www.kysenatorbourbon.com/.

42. "Discussing Legislative Goals for the 2022 General Assembly," Kentucky Educational Television, January 3, 2022, https://ket.org/program/kentucky-tonight/kentucky-general-assembly-session-preview/.

43. "Report: Black Kentuckians Nearly 10x More Likely to Be Arrested for Marijuana Possession Than White Kentuckians," ACLU of Kentucky, April 20, 2022, www.aclu-ky.org/en/2020marijuanadata.

44. Rachel Roberts, interview by Matthew Strandmark, June 24, 2021, GGOHP, Nunn Center.

45. James Comer interview.

46. Albert Benjamin Chandler III, interview by Matthew Strandmark, June 11, 2021, GGOHP, Nunn Center.

47. Jason Nemes interview.

48. Bruce Schreiner, "Kentucky Senate Passes Bill to Legalize Medical Marijuana," Associated Press, March 16, 2023, https://apnews.com/article/medical-marijuana-kentucky-legislature-9bce9777195f8c2aa07d52524abd7117.

49. Bruce Schreiner, "Medical Marijuana Proposal Gains Momentum in Kentucky," Associated Press, March 14, 2023, https://apnews.com/article/medical-marijuana-kentucky-legislature-e854b35f1a782b61bfe78e8589722f6c.

50. This and the previous quote are from Joe Sonka, "Kentucky Bill Legalizing Medical Marijuana Signed into Law," *Louisville Courier-Journal*, March 30, 2023, https://www.courier-journal.com/story/news/politics/2023/03/30/medical-marijuana-bill-passes-in-kentucky-heads-to-beshears-desk/70062316007/.

Index

Page numbers in italics refer to illustrations.

Kentucky Remembered: An Oral History Series

James C. Klotter, Terry L. Birdwhistell, and Douglas A. Boyd, *Series Editors*

Books in the Series

Conversations with Kentucky Writers
edited by L. Elisabeth Beattie
Conversations with Kentucky Writers II
edited by L. Elisabeth Beattie
Barry Bingham: A Man of His Word
Barry Bingham
Crawfish Bottom: Recovering a Lost Kentucky Community
Douglas A. Boyd
This Is Home Now: Kentucky's Holocaust Survivors Speak
Arwen Donahue and Rebecca Gayle Howell
Burley: Kentucky Tobacco in a New Century
Ann K. Ferrell
Freedom on the Border: An Oral History of the Civil Rights Movement in Kentucky
Catherine Fosl and Tracy E. K'Meyer
Arab and Jewish Women in Kentucky: Stories of Accommodation and Audacity
Nora Rose Moosnick
Voices of African Immigrants in Kentucky: Migration, Identity, and Transnationality
Francis Musoni, Iddah Otieno, Angene Wilson, and Jack Wilson
The Coal Miner Who Became Governor
Paul E. Patton with Jeffrey S. Suchanek
Washington's Iron Butterfly: Bess Clements Abell, an Oral History
Donald A. Ritchie and Terry L. Birdwhistell
Bert Combs the Politician: An Oral History
edited by George W. Robinson
Gatewood: Kentucky's Uncommon Man
Matthew Strandmark
Tobacco Culture: Farming Kentucky's Burley Belt
John van Willigen and Susan C. Eastwood
Food and Everyday Life on Kentucky Family Farms, 1920–1950
John van Willigen and Anne van Willigen
Voices from the Peace Corps: Fifty Years of Kentucky Volunteers
Angene Wilson and Jack Wilson